Fiction and Folklore:
The Novels of Toni Morrison

Fiction and Folklore: The Novels of Toni Morrison

Trudier Harris

The University of Tennessee Press

KNOXVILLE

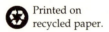
Library of Congress Cataloging in Publication Data

Harris, Trudier.
    Fiction and folklore: the novels of Toni Morrison/
Trudier Harris.
        p.   cm.
    Includes bibliographical references and index.
    ISBN 0-87049-708-1 (cloth: alk. paper)
    ISBN 0-87049-791-X (pbk.: alk. paper)
        1. Morrison, Toni—Knowledge, folklore, mythology.
2. Afro-Americans in literature. 3. Afro-Americans—
Folklore. 4. Folklore in literature. I. Title.
PS3563.08749Z67   1991   90–32019
813'.54—dc20   CIP

For Eva Harris Owens
and
Anna Harris McCarthy—

Thanks for 1984

Contents

Acknowledgments

I began thinking about a book on Toni Morrison's novels while I was a fellow at the Mary Ingraham Bunting Institute at Radcliffe College and a fellow at the W. E. B. Du Bois Institute for Afro-American Research at Harvard University during the 1982–83 academic year. My appreciation for bringing the work to fruition begins naturally with those institutes and with the National Research Council/Ford Foundation for providing financial support during that year. I began drafting ideas for the project in 1983 and continued through a series of lectures and papers I was invited to present at universities around the United States as well as at the University of the West Indies (Mona, Kingston) in 1984.

I am grateful to Lemuel Johnson of the English Department at the University of Michigan for inviting me to present a series of lectures on Toni Morrison in March of 1985; those discussions provided yet another forum for the development of ideas presented here. During the summer of 1985, I was invited to be a resident fellow at the Djerassi Foundation's SMIP Ranch for artists and scholars in Woodside, California, where I was able to begin shaping chapters for the book. I am most appreciative of the productively quiet times the retreat ensured.

Thanks as well to other colleagues who have invited me to discuss my work on Toni Morrison on their campuses. These include: Dr. Cordell Wynn, president of Stillman College (1983); Lynn Bolles, formerly of Bowdoin College (1985); Robert Paul of Emory University (1985); Patsy B. Perry of North Carolina Central University (1985); Father Thomas Savage of Fairfield University (1986); John

Schell, formerly of the University of Arkansas at Little Rock (1987); Elizabeth Schultz of the University of Kansas at Lawrence (1987); Mary Lynn Broe of Grinnell College (1987); Morris Beja of The Ohio State University (1988); Suzanne Ferguson, formerly of Wayne State University (1989); Lt. Colonel John Calabro of the United States Military Academy, West Point (1989); Wanda Macon and Carol Quin of Lane College (1989); Lynda Dickson of the University of Colorado at Colorado Springs (1989); David Ray Norsworthy of Whitman College (1990); and Suzanne Marrs and Charles Sallis of Millsaps College (1990).

A fellowship from the National Endowment for the Humanities in 1989 provided the freedom from teaching responsibilities that enabled me to complete the drafting of the manuscript. Residence at the Center for Advanced Study in the Behavioral Sciences in Stanford, California, provided the final period I needed to prepare the manuscript for circulation to publishers. I am grateful to the endowment, as well as to the Center for Advanced Study for inviting me to become one of the members of its class of 1990. The unmatched resources and personnel at the Center, and the office facilities there, provided the final inspiration for bringing this project to a conclusion. I am especially grateful for the sources of financial support at the Center for Advanced Study, which, in addition to coming from the Center, were provided by the National Endowment for the Humanities, Grant #RA-20037-88, and the Andrew W. Mellon Foundation.

For the generosity of reading this manuscript in a late stage of its development, I thank John W. Roberts of the Department of Folklore and Folklife at the University of Pennsylvania.

As usual, I express my appreciation to the University of North Carolina at Chapel Hill, which granted the leave time necessary for me to complete this project and which provided a Pogue Research Leave in the spring of 1990 to assist in its completion. To my colleagues there who encouraged me in this project, and to my friends and supporters in other places who discussed the work with me, encouraged others to do so, and were generally warm and enthusiastic about my project, I say thank you.

Fiction and Folklore:
The Novels of Toni Morrison

1

Literary History and Literary Folklore

In a 1984 interview, Toni Morrison commented that she tries to incorporate into her fiction "one of the major characteristics of Black art," that is,

> the ability to be both print and oral literature: to combine those two aspects so that the stories can be read in silence, of course, but one should be able to hear them as well. It should try deliberately to make you stand up and make you feel something profoundly in the same way that a Black preacher requires his congregation to speak, to join him in the sermon, to behave in a certain way, to stand up and to weep and to cry and to accede or to change and to modify— to expand on the sermon that is being delivered. In the same way that a musician's music is enhanced when there is a response from the audience. . . . Because it is the affective and participatory relationship between the artist or the speaker and the audience that is of primary importance. . . . To make the story appear oral, meandering, effortless, spoken— . . . to have the reader work *with* the author in the construction of the book—is what's important.[1]

Morrison's culturally sensitive, democratic process in the creation of fiction provides a natural point of departure to begin a study of the influence of oral traditions upon the characters and worlds she creates, as well as upon the very shape of her novels. Her awareness of the inseparability of oral forms and effects from written media in African-American culture is a late twentieth-century statement of a practice that has its rudimentary genesis in the earliest written expressions, for the link to orality is one of the keys to unlocking African-American literary history.

African-American folklore is arguably the basis for most African-American literature. In a country where, as late as the 1830s, there were laws prohibiting the teaching of slaves, it was necessary for the oral tradition to carry the values the group considered significant. Transmission by word of mouth took the place of broadsides, pamphlets, poems, and novels. Themes that were the undergirding of folk rhymes, narratives, jokes, and riddles—such as the quest for freedom, the nature of evil, and the powerful versus the powerless—became the themes of African-American literature. Slaves were certainly aware of their place in the economic system and verbally expressed the disparity in riches long before William Wells Brown's slaves in *Clotel* (1853) verbalized their similar lack of power:

> The big bee flies high,
> The little bee make the honey;
> The black folks makes the cotton
> And the white folks gets the money.[2]

This folk rhyme perhaps capsulizes the history of black/white interactions in the United States and is the epitome of sentiments expressed in protest literature.

Folk beliefs common to slaves not only entered the early literature, such as in Frederick Douglass's account of slaves carrying roots for protection against beatings and for general good luck, but were transposed in the twentieth century in such works as Arna Bontemps's *God Sends Sunday*, where L'il Augie believes his success as a jockey depends upon a good-luck charm.[3] Indeed, early folk beliefs were so powerful a force in the lives of slaves that their masters sought to co-opt that power. Slave masters used such beliefs in an attempt to control the behavior of their slaves, as Gladys-Marie Fry documents in *Nightriders in Black Folk History*. Masters would place little black coffins outside the cabins of slaves in an effort to restrain their movements at night; they perpetuated ghost lore and created tales of horrible "supernatural animals," "marauding night creatures" residing near the plantations, in order to frighten slaves away from escape or trans-plantation visits.[4]

Thematic folk expressions and folk beliefs had their parallels in the structural patterns that later shaped the literature. Tales of slaves running away to the North or Canada and becoming legendary in their escapades led to the creation of the myth of the North as a freer place for black people. Inherent in the myth is the initiation/journey, the archetypal movement from south to north that has pervaded African-American literature throughout its tenure on this continent. Another structure, that of the framed tale, also became prominent. The black folk imagination coincided with universal patterns in that many of the structures frequently showed parallels to the narratives Vladimir Propp analyzes in his *Morphology of the Folktale*, as well as to the mythical journey depicted in *The Odyssey*. Writers adopted these patterns into their works from the earliest days of literary creativity among African-Americans, and they have continued those trends into contemporary times.

Of the writers who fit into this structural tradition, Charles Waddell Chesnutt comes immediately to mind. *The Conjure Woman* (1899) takes its structure from the framed, tale-telling sessions popularized by Joel Chandler Harris's Uncle Remus: an elderly black man tells tales to entertain white audiences; this structure expands upon the framed tales of Mark Twain, in which an educated narrator creates an opportunity for a less-educated person to relate a (usually humorous) tale. Chesnutt drew upon superstitions and other folk practices easily documented in sources such as the seven-volume *Frank C. Brown Collection of North Carolina Folklore*, although he maintained that he had cut many of them from "whole cloth." His incorporation of recognizably historical items of folklore established a pattern for folklore in literature traceable through most African-American writings.

When James Weldon Johnson observed black church rituals and listened to black folk sermons in the second decade of the twentieth century, he was intent upon capturing the authentic flavor of metaphor, rhythm, and structure. The formulas he incorporated into the prayer prologue of *God's Trombones* (1927), for example, can still be heard in traditional black churches:

O Lord, we come this morning
Knee-bowed and body-bent
Before thy throne of grace.
O Lord—this morning—

Bow our hearts beneath our knees,
And our knees in some lonesome valley.
We come this morning—
Like empty pitchers to a full fountain,
With no merits of our own.[5]

Johnson used literature with the specific intention of documenting cultural forms, a hedge against his fear that the "old-time Negro preacher" was "rapidly passing" (11). In his recognition of the "poetry," "rhythm," and repetition in such performances, Johnson captured the ties between oral and written forms.

Contemporary with Johnson, and in keeping with the spirit of the Harlem Renaissance, Jean Toomer traveled to Georgia to immerse himself in African-American folk culture. There he taught school and interacted with sharecroppers and the sons of slaves who kept a vibrant oral tradition alive. In *Cane* (1923), he incorporated "supper-getting-ready songs," the process of legend making, the interactions of heroic figures with their communities, and such traditional folk beliefs as furious activity in the animal world portending human tragedy.[6] Toomer, who believed that there was more "color" in the black part of his mixed family, drew upon black folk sources for literary inspiration in his most celebrated works.

Perhaps the dean of early folk influence upon literary creation was Langston Hughes. His first volume of poetry, *The Weary Blues* (1926), literally imitated the structure and sentiments of the blues, a practice he would follow in his poems and stories from the 1920s to the 1960s. In *Not Without Laughter*, his 1930 novel, a traveling blues musician takes center stage. He lives out the heroic myth of black men who strung their "boxes" over their shoulders, hopped freight trains, and left places like Mississippi for the bright lights of Chicago and other northern cities. Although characters in the story might see the limitations of Jimboy's life-style, they are nonetheless mesmerized by his singing, and his young sister-in-law follows his calling by becoming a blues singer. Hughes continued his concentration on the folk (whom he wanted to "dig" and by whom he wanted to be "dug" in return) through his treatment of black folk religion in his novel *Tambourines to Glory* (1958) as well as in several plays. Without the inspiration of the folk and of black folk traditions, we might not have experienced the phenomenon called Langston Hughes.

Even Richard Wright, who was not particularly enamored of the folk, and who criticized the seeming lack of political or racial consciousness represented by such a focus, could not escape the influence of the traditions in which he had grown up. He portrayed characters from the black masses, including preachers and other church folks who people the fictive imaginations of Johnson and Hughes, and he paused on occasion to allow the playful bantering that takes place between adolescents. Specifically, he incorporated folk rhymes such as the dozens into his short fiction of the 1930s, particularly "Big Boy Leaves Home."[7] As four boys are on their way to a swimming hole, they engage in a verbal contest by shouting at each other: "Yo mama don wear no drawers . . . Ah seena when she pulled em off . . . N she washed 'em in alcohol . . . N she hung 'em out in the hall." That the politically conscious Wright, who had little use for writers with apolitical consciousnesses, could be influenced by African-American folk traditions is further testament to the pervasive power that tradition has held historically for black writers.

Zora Neale Hurston has long been identified with black folk traditions, from her anthropological training to her creation of fiction. In *Jonah's Gourd Vine* (1934), one of her folk novels, she focuses on a black preacher, thereby enabling her to incorporate sermons and prayers reminiscent of oral ones. She also exhibits a fascination with patterns of black folk speech. In fact, she uses folk metaphors so authentically engaging that they fairly compete with theme and character and raise questions about the context in which they appear. For example, expressions such as "Don't you lak it, don't you take it, heah mah collar come and you shake it," which is a folk dare frequently used by adolescents, becomes in the novel the retort of a wife to her husband.[8] On another occasion, a young man named John, who as the preacher will later provide the central focus for the novel, "acts out" a confrontation with his oppressive stepfather, in the black narrative tradition of slaves down at the big gate cussing out the old master sitting on the porch of the big house:

> And you, you ole battle-hammed, slew-foot, box-ankled
> nubbin, you! You ain't nothin' and ain't got nothin' but whut God

give uh billy-goat, and then round tryin' tuh hell-hack folks! Tryin'
tuh kill somebody wid talk, but if you wants tuh fight,—dat's de
very corn Ah wants tuh grind. You come grab me now and Ah bet
yuh Ah'll stop *you* from suckin' eggs. Hit me now! G'wan hit me!
Bet Ah'll break uh egg in yuh! Youse all parts of uh pig! You done
got me jus' ez hot ez July jam, and Ah ain't got no mo' use fuh yuh
than Ah is for mah baby shirt. Youse mah race but you sho ain't
mah taste. Jus' you break uh breath wid me, and Ahm goin' tuh be
jus' too chastisin'. (85)

Unquestionably the speech patterns are in the black folk tradition,
but just as unquestionably, the very compilation of expressions calls
attention to the language *as language* rather than as a medium of expression of anger.

   Hurston's novel thus illustrates one of the potential problems in
the use of folklore in fiction, that is, the extent to which historical
folkloristic items can sometimes overwhelm literary creation. As a
folklorist, Hurston had spent years collecting folklore and immers-
ing herself in African-American folk traditions prior to the publication of her novel. Perhaps in the excitement of a first literary effort,
she wanted to include as much historical folklore as possible. She
therefore packs in folk expressions and beliefs to the extent that the
excessively metaphorical folk language becomes an added character,
plugging up the cracks between theme and plot, not a smoothly
woven, integral part of the whole; language and story seem to have
mutually exclusive functions. Although Hurston would be more se-
lective in the use of folk materials in *Their Eyes Were Watching God*
(1937), in which she more clearly integrated such items into the
theme and plot, the later novel still evinces almost a pause, a conscious signal, when the folklore appears.

   Ralph Ellison's *Invisible Man* (1952) is the transitional work between the traditional incorporation of folklore into black texts and a
broadening of the conceptualization of folklore in fiction. Ellison
includes seemingly isolated historical items of folklore in the novel
that initially hark back to Wright and Hurston. For example, there
are blues lyrics, dozens rhymes, and verses from spirituals. Even the
Invisible Man's encounter with Peter Wheatstraw, a blues man of
words, is a contained unit in the novel, not one that permeates the
whole. Yet we could connect that episode, along with the blues and

spirituals that the narrator hears intermittently, to the theme of knowing one's identity. While isolated folkloric items might seem to add the frills and not contribute to the substance of the plot, we could argue that the entire novel is a composition in the blues tradition. Indeed, the recurring blues song, "What Did I Do to Be so Black and Blue?" aptly describes the Invisible Man's existential condition throughout the novel. Thus Ellison achieves a thematic folkloristic unity in the novel and prepares us well for Morrison's extensive adaptations of a variety of folkloristic genres.

Toni Morrison published her first novel almost twenty years after Ellison published *Invisible Man*. She consciously follows in the Chesnutt, Hurston, and Ellison tradition by adapting folkloristic materials into her novels, but if we expect exact or consistent parallels between her usages and folklore as it exists in historical black communities, we will be continually surprised. Against this familiar literary history of tales, legends, beliefs, trickery, and structure of folk traditions being incorporated into fiction, Morrison simultaneously exhibits a kindred spirit and provides an interesting bas-relief. She may initially use recognizable, traditional items of folklore—perhaps most conspicuously in her first novel, *The Bluest Eye* (New York: Holt, Rinehart, and Winston, 1970)—but more often than not, she transforms historical folk materials. In the process, she creates what I refer to as literary folklore. By "literary" I do not mean to pursue the argument developed by some folklorists that folklore is no longer folklore by the mere fact of its appearance in literature, that it ceases to be folklore because it has been lifted from the oral culture and is now in a static, objectified, nondynamic form. Since folklore can be recorded and collected, "written down," so to speak, without violating its authenticity, I maintain that it can also be incorporated into literary texts without compromising its original quality. Blues lyrics in *Invisible Man* are no less folkloric because Ellison included them in his novel.

When I refer to Morrison's "literary" folklore, I mean that she has gone beyond the mere grafting of traditional items onto her fiction. She takes the use of folkloristic materials and concepts beyond the point where Ellison leaves off. She allows no dichotomy between form and substance, theme and character. In her literary uses of folklore, she has solved the problem of warring genres that plagued her predecessors. She may begin with a joke or superstition in its recognizable, traditional form, but she then takes fictional license in making the lore into something that has never circulated in any folk community. Or she takes the *forms* of traditions within African-American folk communities and gives them fictional substance, so that we recognize the outline of a story, or a joke, or a belief, but we cannot document it in any collected sources we may consult. We recognize folkloric patterns in her work, but she consistently surprises us in the reconceptualization and restructuring of these patterns.

These intersections between folklore and literature raise several questions relevant to a study of Morrison's novels. Can a literary author "create" folklore within a text? Are there folk communities within Morrison's works, or are places like "the Bottom" in *Sula* and "Not Doctor Street" in *Song of Solomon* simply to be viewed as "literary"? If traditional folk forms are deliberately inverted, changed, or parodied, what critical responses do they require? Where is the line to be drawn—if one is or should be drawn—between the incorporation of folk materials and the creation of them? Can a literary text "create" materials that will subsequently enter the oral tradition and be passed down by word of mouth as original folk creations? (Some people have read Morrison's novels and thought they were reading historical folklore.) Does that reversal of influence from literary culture to folk culture invalidate the forms as "folklore"?

As early as the 1950s, scholars wrestled with the problems inherent in the intersections of folklore and literature. Initial approaches emphasized the isolation of items of folklore within literary texts and the location of parallels for them in collections of previously published folklore.[9] This identification-and-interpretation approach was predicated upon the assumption that an author merely *lifts* items of folklore from oral cultures and places them in a text. The job of the scholar was to identify the items *as folklore*, discover collections in which they had previously appeared in order to validate their historical authenticity, and proceed to explain (provide the context for) how the author had used, or changed, such items in the text. This approach would obviously create problems in the study of a literary work like William Wells Brown's *Clotel*, which contains rhymes that were not documented in collections until decades after its publication. Indeed, Brown's novel becomes a collection as well as a created work.

A few scholars offered emendations to these approaches,[10] but the basic pattern of dichotomizing literature and folklore held not only in the writers' conscious incorporation of such materials but in the critics' analysis and evaluations of them. In the 1970s, several folklore scholars made determined efforts to raise the level of the discussion of folklore in literature and to theorize about the requirements for studying these two distinctly different genres.[11] Neil R. Grobman offers a critical overview of previous approaches to folklore in literature, outlining a schema for further study based on an author's exposure to folklore: that learned from his or her community, that acquired from contact with another community, or that assimilated from readings; Grobman then lists literary works in which various simulations appear. Sandra K. D. Stahl enumerates seven counterbalancing features of oral and written media to illustrate intersecting points. While all of these discussions are provocative, and although Grobman touches briefly on this phenomenon, they fall short of illuminating procedures for focusing on the incorporation of folklore into literatures where the oral and written forms are so intimately intertwined historically, as in African-American culture.

A review of relevant criticism, therefore, makes clear that the study of folklore *in* literature inherently perpetuates a dichotomous approach to the topic, a superimposition of the literary process of creation on the folk tendency toward oral forms. The folkloristic material is always treated as a wart on the face of the literature. A few scholars specifically discussing African-American literature have recently tried to expand this pattern. In provocatively argued reversals of influence, from the folk to belles lettres, Houston A. Baker, Jr., and Henry Louis Gates, Jr., posit that traditional oral forms—specifically the blues and the trickster (the Signifying Monkey)—provide the basis for theorizing about African-American literature in its construction and its intertextuality.[12] Both arguments allow for broadly expansive interpretations of folk concepts in the literature. For example, Gates asserts that Hurston's patterns of speech in *Their Eyes Were Watching God* transform the novel into a "speakerly text" that imitates oral narration and indeed becomes a "talking book"; he thereby accounts for not only the recognizable folk forms but the entire composition. Baker offers the "blues matrix" as a method of understanding the narrative voices that writers such as Douglass and Hurston create. He also asserts the merging of "folklore and literary art" in the Trueblood episode of *Invisible Man*. Neither scholar claims that his approach accounts for all possible connections between oral and written forms, but their intriguing discussions will undoubtedly influence how future scholars think about these issues.

Baker and Gates are writing against a tradition where a general tenet has held: we seldom seem able fully to integrate our discussions of folklore in/and literature.[13] Morrison's novels make such clear-cut divisions impossible. What she does may be compared to the concept of "saturation" that Stephen Henderson espouses in *Understanding the New Black Poetry* (1973).[14] There are certain forms, conditions, and ideas, Henderson proposes, so thoroughly enmeshed in the African-American psyche and culture that they are instinctively, intuitively recognizable when they appear in literary form; their appearance evokes in readers a *"depth"* and *"quality"* of experience. "In such cases, where style and subject matter are obviously Black, one may feel, for example, that a word, a phrase, a rhythm, is so *right*, so *Black*, that its employment illuminates the entire composition" (65). Such perception, continues Henderson, whether of images or characters, "comes as a kind of gestalt in which the whole is more than the sum of the parts" (65). An individual can be so "immersed" "in the totality of the Black Experience" (66) that he or she cannot readily draw the line between literary creation, communal psyche, and racial history as far as these saturated concepts are concerned.

I would suggest that Toni Morrison approximates such a saturation in her use of traditional folkloristic forms and in her creation of other forms that resemble the original ones so closely that we often cannot tell where her imagination leaves off and communal memory begins. There is surface (the traditional item approach) as well as depth (the literary folklore) and texturing of all the layers in between for the folklore she incorporates into her works. Instead of seeing her use of folklore as separating or isolating bits of a text, we recognize the saturated effect of her use of folk traditions for the *whole* of a given novel.

Frequently in her works, Morrison replicates the dynamic of folk communities by showing how people interact with each other to shape tales, legends, rumors, and folk beliefs. Instead of simply including isolated items of folklore, she manages to simulate the ethos of folk communities, to saturate her novels with a folk aura intrinsic to the texturing of the whole. A single belief or superstitious practice, therefore, can reflect an entire community's attitude toward a character or involvement in a particular event. National Suicide Day in *Sula* (1974), for example, is not an isolated imposition of a ritual upon a novel; it is a dynamic event that reveals the whole community's attitude toward Shadrack, his attitude toward death, and the place of death in war and in the demise of one's community—all of which are central to the texturing of the novel as a whole. Through such careful attention to the nuances of folk traditions, Morrison is able to show folklore in *process* rather than as the static force many other works picture it as being. Her choices encourage us, therefore, to expand our approaches to her work.

Though Morrison draws upon and replicates folk traditions in numerous ways, her primary folkloristic technique is reversal, where outcomes consistently fall short of expectations. *The Bluest Eye* (1970) is an inversion of fairy tales—the ugly duckling does not become the beautiful swan.[15] Seasons do not presage growth; indeed, summer is winter, and an infertility comparable to that in T. S. Eliot's *The Waste Land* reigns in the novel. Through a process of reversal, Morrison undercuts the belief in the North as a freer place for black people, thereby debunking the myth that informed folktales and blues lyrics about successful journeys to the North. She also refutes the belief that the image of middle-class respectability, reflected in the primer story of Dick and Jane and their family, is applicable to blacks; this refutation in turn undermines the myth of Horatio Alger success stories in the American legends of pulling oneself up by the bootstraps. And she suggests that isolation and insanity may be effective balms for individual ills, thereby depicting a world view antithetical to American notions of integration, "the melting pot," and the possibility for the pursuit of happiness.

Of all Morrison's novels, *The Bluest Eye* is the one in which she incorporates more *specific* items of traditional lore. Such comparative phrases as "as a cat has with side pockets" (17), "cold as a witch's tit" (30), and "as bare-legged as a yard dog" (39) do have lives independent of the novel, as does the phrase "Black e mo" (50). These, however, are but the smaller details of Morrison's overall approach to folklore in literature. More important, she focuses on the cultural beliefs that shape the historical items of folklore, the thought processes or pre-word conditions that give rise to specific beliefs. Folk traditions, after all, are as much concept as they are examples. And their revelation in stories is as tradition-shaping as the substance they contain. *The Bluest Eye* is such a story, and its communal telling involves narrators, characters, and readers.

The pattern of reversal continues in *Sula* (1974), where fairy tale structure, ballad formulas, and African-American jokes and music show Morrison in and out of the tradition against which I am viewing her. Here Morrison also replicates the process by which incidents evolve into folklore (as in *The Bluest Eye* when the children provide their own explanations for various occurrences, such as how one counteracts the possibility of being "ruined"). The community is suspicious of Sula's difference, but they have no concrete evidence to support their uneasiness. When she returns after a ten-year absence, looking surprisingly younger than most of the women, their suspicions join hands with rumor to make her into a witch. The evolutionary process in folklore, in which rumor—through repetition—becomes solidified as legend, usually takes several generations to complete; in Morrison's novel, it is accomplished in a space of weeks. The structure of the novel itself replicates the historical process and thus shows again how Morrison expands upon literary historical notions of the incorporation of folklore into fiction.

In *Song of Solomon* (1977), Morrison again uses folklore to buttress the structure of her novel. She subverts the pattern of the Odyssean journey (antiheroes becomes heroes, and witchlike characters turn into nurturing mothers) and inverts the myth of the traditional journey toward freedom for black people (instead of moving south to north, her characters move north to south). The novel's basis in the African and African-American dualistic world view, in which good and bad merge instead of being mutually exclusive absolutes, gives new meaning to that notion of the secular/sacred clash/blend in African-American culture. Morrison reverses the myth of the flying African by making Milkman one of the few *American*-born blacks who learns to fly. His potential for extranatural activity is matched in other folklorically based material by Pilate's witchlike qualities, by legends of the Seven Days, by the tradition of naming, by initiations, and by the snipe hunt on which Milkman is taken. There is also the creation of folk traditions in Not Doctor Street and the family lore surrounding it.

Jadine, in *Tar Baby* (1981), is in the tradition of Snow White and Sleeping Beauty, but, in this clash of fairy tales with black life, the price of the kingdom is the price of identity, where coats made of the hides of ninety baby seals are preferable to those "ancient properties" that would link Jadine to black people both in her own family and globally. The novel rewrites the story of the tar baby, or, perhaps more properly, it reclaims the tale from its distortions of the past few centuries and relocates it in its Indian and African bases with the female trickster/tempter who has the potential to bring about the downfall of the males she encounters. It thereby examines masculine and feminine conceptions of heroism and suggests acceptable patterns for men and unacceptable ones for women. It also creates myths and legends—from the mythical island to the sentient trees and butterflies to the stories of the blind horsemen.

Beloved (1987) reverses/undermines our expectations of what ghost stories should be, as well as any conceptions we may have about succubi, shapeshifters, and demons. In that undermining, Morrison also blurs the lines of demarcation between history and fiction, folktale and legend, and makes it difficult for us to distinguish clearly what is art and what is life. *Beloved* also extends Morrison's use of folkloristic techniques in the shaping of her tale. By using multiple voices of creation in the novel, as in *The Bluest Eye*, Morrison illustrates how characters can be the *subject* as well as the *transmitter/author* of tales about themselves. Morrison also suggests here, as earlier, that a communal storytelling session is in process, one in which the reader is as intimately involved as are the characters and the author. By breaking down the barriers between fiction and folkloristic process, Morrison again makes clear how saturated the folk materials are within her texts.

Throughout her novels, but especially in *Beloved*, Morrison is concerned with the effect of the past upon the present, with the individual's place in the larger community, and with questions of good and evil, right and wrong, that transcend traditional morality. All of these concerns have as one of their bases the African-American folk tradition, especially that reflected in tales of slavery and in other tales passed on during slavery. In saturating her novels in/ with African-American folk culture, Morrison offers prime territory for provocative discussions of folklore in/and literature.

2

The Bluest Eye

Storytelling in the African-American Folk Tradition

The Bluest Eye (New York: Holt, Rinehart, and Winston, 1970) is not only the story of the destructive effects of inter- and intraracial preju- dice upon impressionable black girls in the Midwest; it is also the story of African-American folk culture in process.[1] Toni Morrison as- cribes to <u>Claudia MacTeer</u> the role of active tradition bearer in the novel, that is, an individual who can shape and tell the community's stories. Like a griot learning her craft, she orders the events of a people's past, assigns values to them, and offers the possibility for future transformation. In her presentation of the educational and psychological functions of folklore, Claudia shows the detrimental effects of certain cultural beliefs upon unsuspecting individuals. In her creation of a tale that, by negative example, offers corrective possibilities for the horrible circumstances inherent in the novel, Claudia is a narrator who makes clear the implications and potential positive consequences of storytelling. The tale of Pecola Breedlove and Lorain, Ohio, then, is a narrative in the best tradition of an African-American interactive, communal event.

By making the novel a storytelling event, with communal audi- ence and correctors in place, Morrison effects the saturation of cul- tural forms that anticipates *Tar Baby*, with its rewriting of trans- cultural versions of that famous tale, and *Song of Solomon*, with its structuring device of the flying Africans. The dynamic process of storytelling finds its raison d'être in the lives and future of the people of Lorain, thus giving it the serious implications that

Morrison explores in greater depth in *Beloved*. Beginning with *The Bluest Eye*, she suggests that narratives can shape lives, whether it is the story of Pauline Breedlove being described as the perfect servant and fulfilling that role, or Pecola Breedlove being shaped by her exclusion from the American story of success and acceptance, or the ultimate transformative potential of Claudia's narration, that is, the novel itself.

As storyteller, it is Claudia's job to shape the past so that it provides coherent meaning for the present audience. When she assumes that role, she identifies herself as an active tradition bearer, who, in her younger as well as her more mature manifestations, has the responsibility of putting a horrible tale into perspective. The tale is one in which the culture has been threatened from without as well as from within; it therefore takes on the form of myth. How can a people survive such assaults upon them? And if they do, who will give voice to their heroic or failed efforts?

Claudia's role as active tradition bearer, the singer of the tale, depends upon her interaction with the people of Lorain, Ohio, as well as with the reader. The story is shaped from the beginning with the expectation of reader involvement and with the presumption of audience. The brief preface that begins, *"Quiet as it's kept, there were no marigolds in the fall of 1941,"* serves to establish Claudia's role as griot, the communal rehearser of tragedy. It is the counterpart to a black preacher's significant pauses in seeking the attention of the congregation on a Sunday morning, or to a guitarist strumming the first few bars to prepare the audience for the songs he or she is about to sing. The desire for explanation (*"There is really nothing more to say—except why"*—3; italics in original) presupposes a communal imperative to know what has happened to the town and to its people, thus exemplifying the storyteller's role in providing perspective on difficult periods in communal history.

The informality of Claudia's narration is further testament to her recognition that there are people listening and that they expect coherence and logic in the tale. Her first-person narration establishes a close relationship with the audience and follows Morrison's written-in invitations to readers to participate in the drama unfolding before them. Morrison has commented: "My writing expects, demands participatory reading, and that I think is what literature is

supposed to do. It's not just about telling the story; it's about involv- *achup reader*
ing the reader. The reader supplies the emotions. The reader sup-
plies even some of the color, some of the sound. My language has to
have holes and spaces so the reader can come into it. He or she can
feel something visceral, see something striking. Then we [you, the
reader, and I, the author] come together to make this book, to feel
this experience."[2] These authorial "holes" and Claudia's informality
reinforce the notion that there is a group toward whom Claudia is
directing her narrative and from whom she gets her cues for what it
needs. When she recounts the seemingly harsh memories of her
mother, she can pause to ask, "But was it really like that? As painful
as I remember?" (7) with the knowledge that some of her audience,
the passive tradition bearers (those who know the stories but do not
actively engage in telling them), may question the accuracy of what
she recalls. After all, they would recognize the group experience, the
forms of caring to which she alludes, even if they were not privy to
its specific manifestation in her household.

This audience would know that older black women frequently
wear asafetida bags around their necks to ensure health (103) and *105*
wrap "their breasts in flannel" (108), that funeral rituals are essential
to African-American culture, that signs of death merit credibility,
that healers/conjurers like M'Dear are "infallible," that the dozens
are a popular African-American game, and that the blues underscore
love and life. As black people who share a common heritage, the
majority of Claudia's audience would be insiders to the culture,
though certainly there are other members of the audience as well.
Morrison said that she felt it necessary, amidst all the "Black Is Beautiful" rhetoric of the 1960s, to develop a story in which all the problems confronting black people were not solved. The tragic story
Claudia relates, then, is partly about stagnation, about the refusal of
the upwardly mobile in the community, or even of the stable poor, to
recognize that black is not beautiful to at least one little girl whose
mind dissolves under the sordid reality of her existence.

The story is about cultural beliefs, which are the essence of folkloristic transmission. Just as early narratives transmitted the discrepancies in wealth and social position between blacks and whites, this
narrative similarly transmits patterns and problems that have a
negative impact upon black people. The belief that black was *not*

valuable or beautiful was one of the cultural hindrances to black people throughout their history in America. That *belief* informs Pecola's tragedy and Cholly Breedlove's rape of his daughter. Morrison emphasizes that the entire Breedlove family *believes* that they are ugly. Without any visible markers to show that belief, they nonetheless act and react as if it were so. Having inherited the myth of unworthiness, the Breedloves can only live the outlined saga to its expected conclusion.

The peculiar form of the cultural distortion for Pecola centers upon blue eyes. Her belief in what blue eyes will accomplish for her is just as strong as the belief in M'Dear's infallibility or the belief that Aunt Jimmy died from eating peach cobbler. Belief is the single most important factor in conjuration as well as in Christianity, the two systems to which Pecola is most frequently exposed. Her prayers to God to make her disappear are predicated upon the belief that such a feat is possible. Her giving of the poisoned meat to the old dog is similarly predicated upon the belief that, if a reaction occurs, her blue eyes will be granted. Hope for a magical transformation under-lies both desires, and Pecola's belief in the possible transformation ties her to all believers in sympathetic magic. Her conviction that the blue eyes have been granted may be viewed as insanity, but it simul-taneously fits the logic that has led to that final reward. It is no stranger than the community women's belief that Jimmy has died from eating a peach cobbler. Belief is the single most important ele-ment in both outcomes.

Pecola's basic wish for blue eyes ties her to all believers in fairy tales and other magical realms. It is Cinderella wanting to be trans-formed from a char girl to belle of the ball, or Sleeping Beauty wait-ing a hundred years for the prince to awaken her. It is the classic tale of the ugly duckling turned beautiful swan, of the beast transformed through love and caring into the beautiful prince, of Sir Gawain's pig lady turned into a dazzling woman. While Pecola seems doomed whatever she does—if she resorts to fantasy, she is considered crazy, and if she tries to live in the real world, there is no place for her—her desire for blue eyes ties her to many heroines of fairy tales, and to many young girls who have wished for features other than the ones they have. While many of the latter wishes are no more than passing fancies, Pecola's is more intense because she is never given the opportunity, in any realm (home, school, playground), to see anything positive in herself as she is. The patterns of caring and incorporation hinted at in some of the occurrences in the novel never reach her strongly enough to reshape her opinion of herself.

Claudia not only tells the story but tries to effect Pecola's fate through her own belief in the power of magic to transform present conditions. Claudia and Frieda attempt to influence Pecola's future by planting the marigolds correctly. They hope, as Pecola does with the offering to the dog, to bring about a kind of sympathetic magic (*"our own magic"*—3), to create a space and circumstances in which Pecola will have a healthier future. When they fail, they blame themselves for not performing the rites correctly, for not having the right amount of belief. Destined to live in the realistic world, which promises a sane future for them, Claudia and Frieda are encouraged to put aside their childish beliefs. Diverging into a different world, Pecola makes the transition into fantasy, into a world from which Claudia and Frieda's destinies have effectively and happily shut them out.

The scene in which Cholly Breedlove fumbles through his first sexual encounter and the white hunters appear is similarly grounded in cultural, stereotypical responses between blacks and whites that have as their basis a manipulation or hatred of blackness. The belief that blacks are inferior leads the white men to treat Cholly as an object, as if he were a mere brute, conjured up before their eyes for their pleasure. This basic cultural pattern of denying black human worth motivates whites just as strongly as a desire for freedom motivated blacks in the earlier expressions of their lore. Cholly has been designated "nigger," defined by whites into a reality that stunts his imagination as well as his moral growth.

Claudia is well aware of the power to name, especially when that power hinders the group or individuals within it. Just as her narrative has the potential to shape an alternative reality for future generations of little Pecolas, so the power of nicknaming and name-calling shapes the realities of those who allow themselves to be defined by factors antithetical to their culture. Pauline is pained that she does not have a nickname; she blames it on the "slight deformity" (86) left from a nail puncture in her foot when she was two years old. To have been assigned a nickname, in the tradition that is old and venerated in the black community, would have given Pauline a much more definite personality as a child. Without that special favor bestowed upon her, and without being teased or having anecdotes told about her, Pauline "never felt at home anywhere, or that she belonged anyplace" (86). Scholars have focused on the tremendous value of nicknames in black communities, the special recognition they bestow upon an individual for a feat accomplished, a trait emphasized, or a characteristic noticed.[3] Without any of these, Pauline never seems to be claimed by her family in any special way, although they do seem to value the quiet place she holds as cleaning person and babysitter. This familial lack serves in part to explain Pauline's attachment to the rich white family for which she works in Ohio when they assign her a nickname—Polly. By so doing, "they even gave her what she had never had" (99), and they thereby claim her attention and loyalty more than Cholly, Sammy, and Pecola are ever able to do. The white family tells anecdotes about her, of how they could "never find anybody like Polly," of how "she will *not* leave the kitchen until everything is in order," and of how she is ultimately the "ideal servant" (99). Guided by a perversion of the functions nicknames serve in black communities, Pauline, as Polly, illustrates the potential identity-shaping purpose such nicknaming provides. She desperately clings to her relationship with the Fishers, but fails to see in her daughter a similar need to be claimed in a special way. Pecola's formal name, reminiscent of movies and books, suggests distance rather than claiming.

To be called "out of one's name," as Bernice Reagon has asserted in some of her research on naming, can be just as negatively powerful as a nickname can be positive.[4] The person so defamed is denied a confirming identity, and thereby suffers a lack comparable to what Pauline feels for not being singled out. Sometimes cruel beyond endurance, the schoolchildren who shout names at Pecola shame her and use her features as a way of denying her admission into their society. When the boys circle her in a ritual of insult and shout "Black e mo Black e mo Ya daddy sleeps nekked" (50), Pecola becomes the victim who invites further abuse because she suffers visibly.[5] Unfortunately, it is a game in which all the children have accepted the externally imposed belief that to be black is to be unworthy. The game is tantamount to a rite of separation. In the process, Pecola is given yet another opportunity to view her status as an outsider. Her rescue by Maureen Peal, Claudia, and Frieda is only temporary, because Maureen indulges Pecola only in an effort to discover if the insult the boys have shouted about her father is really true. Unsatisfied, the light-skinned Maureen draws a circle of acceptance around herself that excludes the other three girls: "I *am* cute! And you ugly! Black and ugly black e mos. I *am* cute!" (56). Conscious of her unattractiveness and her color, Pecola seems to disappear where she stands, unable to join Claudia and Frieda in returning insults to Maureen, or to appreciate that they are fighting for her. She senses too strongly rejection at an irredeemable level. Children, teachers, neighbors, and other adults have mirrored back to her what her mother had concluded upon her birth: that Pecola will never be an insider in the black community and cannot possibly hope for acceptance beyond that community. All age groups, then, combine to reinforce Pecola's belief that the only escape for her is to become beautiful through obtaining the bluest eyes of all, ones that will dazzle everyone into loving her—or at least into tolerating her presence. In the scene with the schoolchildren, the very folk culture that could embrace Pecola plays a part in her ultimate rejection.

The novel, therefore, becomes a myth that defines human worth, that explores the potential greatness of a people who are waylaid by the beliefs they have adopted from outsiders. Not only is Pecola's specific case a tragedy, but the larger story is a tragedy because the people *could* save themselves through the communal orientation of their folk traditions. For example, in the ritual of initiation where Mrs. MacTeer joins Pecola, Frieda, and Claudia after the onset of Pecola's menstrual cycle, there is a demonstrating of nurturing that does not extend consistently throughout the novel. The orientation toward help is there, just as Blue Jack, the old man who befriends Cholly after he quits school, reaches out to share his stories with Cholly, but the bonds get broken again and again. Not only is Blue a nurturer, but he reinforces the communal folk process by being an active tradition bearer of various kinds of tales:

Blue used to tell him old-timey stories about how it was when the Emancipation Proclamation came. How the black people hollered, cried, and sang. And ghost stories about how a white man

cut off his wife's head and buried her in the swamp, and the
headless body came out at night and went stumbling around the
yard, knocking over stuff because it couldn't see, and crying all the
time for a comb. They talked about the women Blue had had, and
the fights he'd been in when he was younger, about how he talked
his way out of getting lynched once, and how others hadn't. (104)

The story about the headless woman ties into many tales of decapi-
tation that circulate in oral tradition, those that are legendary in
form, that is, told for true, and those that are etiological in form,
explaining, for example, how the jack-o-lantern came into existence.[6]

Blue becomes a folk hero to Cholly, and, long into adulthood,
after he has killed three white men and become his own legend,
Cholly remembers the good times he has had with Blue. That ven-
eration comes as much from the stories Blue has told as from the life
he has led—carefree and without responsibilities to anyone. It also
comes from the fact that Blue has been one of the few people, be-
sides Aunt Jimmy, who responded to Cholly as a human being,
rather than as a Presence, a phallic symbol, a "nigger," or a burden.
No such model exists for Pecola; even the prostitutes who befriend
her are alienated from the community, and Blue Jack soon disappears from Cholly's life. The society thus continues to hang in jeop-
ardy because it responds improperly to internal as well as external
threats. Internally, Maureen Peal and Geraldine reject their own
communities because they have accepted the belief that blackness is
ugly, and the community has been assaulted from without by the
images of Mary Jane and Shirley Temple.

As multivoiced narrator, Claudia must make sense of what has
ravaged the community. She is both a participant and the observer
who must ultimately find the transcendent voice in clarifying the
moral imperatives of the tale. In her dual role, Claudia is in the
tradition of the sophisticated, or at least analytical, narrators who
simultaneously identify with and distance themselves from the activities of members of their culture. She remains tied to the other
characters by heritage, family, and color, but she must work out the
complexities of storytelling and of the story in her own imagination.
The other characters, such as Pecola, Cholly, and Soaphead Church,
remain participants, with knowledge of but not the sophistication to
recount the story.

The story is nonetheless a communal event. The voice of Claudia's experience and the voice of her maturity provide two dimensions of that community. In the places where Claudia needs further commentary or must rely solely upon imagination to shape the story, she occasionally gets help from some of the members of her community. In the tale-telling process, Morrison assigns to older and elderly black women, the first in her series of "ancestor figures," the responsibility of filling in the gaps. Age, experience, and event are the motivations for their voices, but small-group tale-telling sessions are the medium.

Like Zora Neale Hurston in her short stories, novels, and essays, Morrison places significant value on the role of gossip in the novel.[7] Although there may be little in gossip itself that would make it traditional, the important thing for Hurston and Morrison is the setting in which it occurs and the stylized interactions of the participants. The holders of information initiate others into awareness of it, thus providing a ritual of exchange of information, one incorporating folk speech, the first-person accounts called memorates, and the repetition necessary for successful transmission of legend. We as readers join the uninitiated Claudia in learning these important details of the novel.

In kitchens or living rooms, or on porches, gossip sessions in *The Bluest Eye* become storytelling devices, rites of participation, that allow characters to comment upon situations and provide exposition for crucial events in the novel. This practical structural consideration gives the gossip sessions an added value and emphasizes as well the integral place storytelling at all levels has in black communities. After Jimmy's death, two of her friends discuss her financial situation. In less than two pages, we learn things that are essential for our understanding of the community's reaction to the death and about how the funeral will proceed (110–11). We learn, first of all, of the widespread belief that Jimmy has died from the peach cobbler. We also learn that Jimmy's insurance is inadequate for burying her; knowing that how one is "laid out" is essential to African-American communities, we witness the potential making of a tragedy in the fact that Jimmy has paid dutifully into an insurance that will yield only eighty-five dollars to bury her.[8] Our conjured images of rip-off artists posing as insurance agents dim somewhat in the face of the women and men who form the community of which Jimmy is a part, for we know that their own desires for impressive burials will ensure that they will bury Jimmy properly (and the loving stitching of the white dress has already started that process). We also get information in the conversation that Jimmy's brother will take Cholly "back to his place," "a nice place. Inside toilet and everything" (111). And we learn the time of the funeral as well as where the funeral banquet will be held.

In a very short space, Morrison has been able, through two unnamed characters, to provide several pieces of information. What the women say gives us a *feel* for the events and adds an emotional tone that the young Cholly, in his first experience with death and in his initiation into the tradition, cannot provide. While the women may seem to be talking *about* people, they are also talking *for* them, in that their concerns for the community and for what will happen to Cholly are genuine. They are not merely chewing up and spitting out people's lives, as some of Hurston's gossips do. Morrison is thus able to illustrate how effective the oral tradition is even in the seemingly small details of exchanging information.

Two other gossip sessions provide the "grown-up" commentary in the parts of the novel Claudia narrates; one introduces Claudia and Frieda to some of the adult things that they do not understand, and the other fills in the gaps about what has happened to Pecola. Initially, early in the novel, Mrs. MacTeer engages in a conversation with one of her neighbors about Mr. Henry. The conversation introduces those adult voices that talk at Claudia and Frieda more than to them while it functionally explains how Mr. Henry came to live in the MacTeer home. As the two girls wash canning jars, they overhear how Della Jones's husband left her because she "was just too clean for him"; the "old dog" "wanted a woman to smell like a woman" (8) rather than using so much lilac water. Now, Mr. Henry, who has lived in Della's house for fifteen years, is leaving because of her onset of senility. And speculation about them goes on, from why he has not married her to comments on differences in their ages. At this stage, the girls must infer meaning from tone and whatever else they can sense in their mother's and the neighbor's words. They get glimpses into a world from which they are separated in age, responsibility, sexual maturity, and insight. Occurring near the beginning of the novel, the conversation emphasizes what the girls will have to confront throughout—trying to understand an adult world that is seldom intent upon making things clear to them. It also introduces a contrasting image to the Mr. Henry who will sexually abuse Frieda a few months after his arrival at the MacTeer home. The women's gathering, like Paule Marshall's "wordshop" of the kitchen where Bajan women fascinated her when she was growing up, is as traditional for them as barbershops are for men. They can dissect character, gauge the temper of the community, and educate their children in the process.

A few months later, in the summer section of the novel, Claudia and Frieda can more easily decipher the conversations they overhear, for they have become more sexually knowledgeable by sharing in the onset of Pecola's menstrual cycle, by looking at Mr. Henry's "girlie magazines;" and by having to confront Mr. Henry's fondling of Frieda. They know more about what it takes to make babies and are able to bring that knowledge to bear when they hear the tales about Cholly Breedlove and Pecola. When they overhear "pregnant," "her daddy," and "that dirty nigger" (148), their imaginations can supply the details fairly accurately, and they can "piece a story together, a secret, terrible, awful story." Through selling their seeds and going into the homes of women like their mother, the two girls learn what the omniscient section of the novel has already provided. The gossip session here, then, serves the functional purpose of bringing the omniscient and first-person narrations to the same level of knowledge. With that convergence, the sections of the novel become one, and Claudia's nonjustified margins merge with Morrison's justified ones as the girl-turned-adult takes over the reminiscence for the final few pages of the novel.

The mostly unnamed voices of the women providing the gossip sessions thus play central roles in providing information necessary to understanding character and events in the novel, and at least two of them are measures of Claudia's and Frieda's growth. By offering essential information in a traditional gossip setting, Morrison is able to show value in such gatherings and to retrieve them, partially, from the negative associations usually connected to them. More important, the sessions illustrate the communal nature of the revelation that takes place in the novel. Not only are the characters a part of the audience to whom Claudia narrates the tale, but they offer the corrective, additional information essential to the perpetuation of a negative story that could change lives in a positive way.

Claudia's recounting of Pecola's tragedy is in the tradition of blues narrative. In many ways, *The Bluest Eye* is similar to Ralph Ellison's *Invisible Man* (1952) in its very theme and structure: "What Did I Do to Be so Black and Blue?" Conscious of it or not, that question must reverberate in Pecola's mind throughout her adventures in the novel. Again and again, she is confronted with people who emphasize to her that she must "stay back" because of her blackness. Again and again, she is "boomeranged" over the head with the knowledge that little black boys do not want to "haul no coal" or be identified with a "stovepipe blonde" and that most of her friends, family, and neighbors believe that "white is right." She lives the blues twenty-four hours a day, through each of the long minutes drawn out in each of those hours. Mrs. MacTeer can sing about "hard times, bad times, and somebody-done-gone-and-left-me times," not having "a thin di-i-ime to my name," hating "to see that evening sun go down" (18) and about "trains and Arkansas" (75); and Poland can sing about "blues in [her] mealbarrel/Blues up on the shelf" (38) and about "a boy who is sky-soft brown" (44), but Pecola can give both of them lessons in living the blues. The ugliness that she believes is hers is just as blues-inducing as those levees breaking to release floodwaters in the Mississippi Delta. At least there was release from floods, and perhaps the pantry can be replenished, but Pecola's ugliness is there to stay. The potential for release from her state of the blues will never be fulfilled because the world around her does not believe that relief is her just due; it will always convey to her that the blues is her permanent condition, not a temporary one from which she can reasonably anticipate escape.

Her adventures, like those of her father, would "become coherent only in the head of a musician" (125), or in Claudia's imagination as the architect of the structural composition of a novel that resembles a blues creation. Yet the blues are a way for people to touch their pain and that of others, to sing of what, in any given instance, is but an individualized account of collective suffering. But Pecola is unable to articulate the pain she feels or channel it through the form of the blues. Like her belief in fantasies derived from outside the black community, her state of the blues is familiar, but she has no model for it to serve as a way of connecting her to the community rather than cutting her off from it. As singer/narrator of the tale, however, Claudia holds out the possibility for the exorcising function of the blues that Langston Hughes depicts so vividly in "The Weary Blues." If the tale of tragedy is told/sung, rehearsed and replayed, perhaps, just perhaps, the listener/reader will be touched enough to move beyond the cathartic effect into a transformation of current conditions.

Through subtle and not-so-subtle ways, therefore, Toni Morrison suggests that the vibrancy of the folk culture persists through the fortunes and misfortunes of the characters, and it serves to baptize them into kinship with each other (whether or not they claim such kinship). From folk wisdom to the blues, from folk speech to myths and other beliefs, Lorain, Ohio, shares with historical black folk communities patterns of survival and coping, traditions that comfort in times of loss, and beliefs that point to an enduring creativity. Though the characters may not fully recognize or take advantage of these connections, the fragments of strong cultural traditions appear sufficiently frequently to signal what the possibilities for growth and renewal would be if the characters were more sensitive to their heritage. Claudia's narration of Lorain's horrible past is functionally designed to heighten that sensitivity.

A Wasteland in Lorain, Ohio

The cultural beliefs that inform the storytelling in *The Bluest Eye* are manifested in a reversal of cultural health for black people, an acquiescence to destructive myths. Morrison creates an environment and a landscape in which infertility is the norm, where values with the potential to sustain have been reversed or perverted, and where few individuals have the key for transcending their inertia. Her depiction of the cycle of seasons without growth, from autumn to summer, evoke, in their mythological implications, comparisons to the legend of the Fisher King and to the world T. S. Eliot creates in *The Waste Land*. The novel is a ritualized exploration of the dissolution of culture and the need for an attendant rite of affirmation. How can the society be saved from itself? What hero, heroine, or heroic change of mind will effect its repair? But Morrison also accomplishes more than these surface comparisons; by setting her novel in a black community, and showing the superimposition of external values upon it, she emphasizes even more the need for rites of renewal, for rebirth from within the community as well as outside of it. The strands of tradition that she fuses in the novel enable Morrison to enrich her story line, to show the peculiarities of her characters, and to connect them to the larger human community.

In Eliot's wasteland, people engage in sex without sharing, indeed without even a minimal concern for their partners; money is valued above all else; there is a meaninglessness in human interactions; and a general malaise exists in which abortions are preferable to delivery, infidelity is common, and culture has collapsed into bar hopping. In Morrison's world, marriage becomes, for most of the characters, an escape from their humdrum previous existences; sex is economic (for the prostitutes), pristine (for the likes of Geraldine and Soaphead Church), or degenerative (for Pauline); change, though constant, does not bring improvement in people's lives; and potentially sustaining values (love, morality, belief in God) have been destroyed by the very institutions that should perpetuate them (church and family). Though Claudia's family provides an oasis in the desert of mythological infertility in the novel, Morrison's world is primarily one in which stagnation is the norm, and where the pursuit of values alien to one's culture ultimately leads to destruction. The seasons of infertility become a metaphor for a larger condition that wears away at the very foundation of the society.[9]

Morrison's choice of the story of Dick and Jane, their mother, father, dog, and cat as the comparative connection for a tale of a little black girl who desperately wants blue eyes makes clear, initially, the listlessness so characteristic of middle-class existence. The outer shell of that myth of perfection might be enviable—a house, a nuclear family, no economic worries, pets, a smiling response to life—but there is a patterned sameness to it that eliminates spontaneity and guarantees a duplication millions of times over. The absence of individuality in the pattern becomes its own kind of inertia and infertility; the mold resists reshaping; those who would aspire to it must reshape themselves to fit the already established pattern. It is unfortunate when people who do not have the economic means aspire to the pattern, but it is more unfortunate when that straitjacketing pattern has been presented to them as normal and desirable. For black people to attain such status, to escape the colorfulness, as Jean Toomer would say, as well as the spontaneity of black life-styles, reflects a self-hatred that manifests itself in Pecola Breedlove's desire for the bluest eyes of all.

The middle-class status itself becomes a monster for what it represents, not for what it offers, for certainly there is nothing intrinsically negative in a desire for self-improvement. On the path to this kind of self-improvement, however, individuals must give up too much of themselves in order to view the world from a particular—usually condescending—perspective, as Morrison so vividly depicts in the character of Geraldine. Middle-classness makes her untouchable, closeted, disdainful of the very roots she has used to grow her new status. The individual components of the image are subsumed under the total representation, the "I am better than you because I have it made" attitude that Geraldine conveys to Pecola and that we can imagine her many twin sisters conveying to other unattractive little black girls who mistakenly intrude upon their sacred grounds.

Cleanliness to the point of blandness, houses made into artifacts rather than comfortable abodes, and children who become possessions to be pointed out are just a few of the pitfalls of the middle-class status Morrison depicts; if there are any virtues in being middle class, she does not emphasize them. She is consistently intolerant of those who allow themselves to fit the mold, who allow individuality to be consumed by their notions of progress. Their status becomes another of the wedges splintering the community into almost unsalvageable pieces. As Pecola finds her way through the splinters, she can only reap cuts and bruises, not a pattern for healthy growth.

In Morrison's world, the working-class family has failed in its ability to nurture just as surely as the middle-class family has failed because of its insipidity. A contrasting look at the Breedloves and Geraldine and her family will illustrate the point. Cholly and Pauline probably started out with the usual high hopes and prospects of any newly married couple—having children, acquiring property, becoming respectable citizens. But there are problems stemming from what each spouse brings to the marriage. Cholly marries Pauline on a whim, perhaps because she conveys to him that he matters in ways that he had mattered to no one since his Aunt Jimmy's death. After becoming "free," as Morrison describes him— free to kill, to nurture, or to contribute to someone else's happiness—Cholly probably sees no great commitment in responding to Pauline's desire for a special presence in her life, so he proposes.

By the time Sammy and Pecola are born, however, the marriage has deteriorated into a round of fights, moviegoing, and isolation from people who could possibly give them release from their own hatred of each other. Certainly Pauline goes to church, but she has twisted that institution to serve the purposes of her hateful marriage. Thus the home life that should provide the basis of growth turns out to be a prison in which Sammy and Pecola are trapped along with their parents. Family to them is an abstraction, not something that has a tangible, healthy counterpart in the world. Indeed, it is ironic that the Breedlove family is a nuclear one, for they are no more sustaining in their seeming wholeness than a less unified family would be, and perhaps a family of lesser "completeness" would be much more nurturing.

The very notion of family is predicated upon the assumption that the members in the unit accept its raison d'être. And, presumably, if parents set out to have children, there would be a modicum of acceptance for those children. The breakdown of the structure begins with Pauline's rejection of her children because they are, to her mind, ugly. She says of Pecola when she is born: "*Eyes all soft and wet. A cross between a puppy and a dying man. But I knowed she was ugly. Head full of pretty hair, but Lord she was ugly*" (97–98; italics in original). In this undermining of one of the basic foundations of the family institution, there can be no happy outcome for the Breedloves, for, in rejecting her children, Pauline not only denies them love, but she denies to them the opportunity to see love exhibited; therefore, if they should grow into marriage and children of their own, they will have no basis upon which to show love or nurturing.

Throughout the novel, we see the consequences of the failure to show love in Pecola's reaction to the world. Since she has received only harsh treatment at home, she expects only harsh treatment from the world outside. She is forever crushed into herself in anticipation of rejection, and her belief that she is ugly, combined with the physical fact, ensures that rejection. Her belief provides for a way of acting and reacting that evokes venom in many of the small children she encounters; when they, in their innocent cruelty, see a target willing to be abused, they willingly oblige. And Pecola, believing that they will abuse her, is unconsciously, eternally the victim. The cycle, vicious in its repetitiveness, is one that is too ingrained to be broken. No change can occur because of the failure in the marriage and family structure, and because of society's faulty way of viewing its members.

Failure to instill a healthy self-conception, the negative examples of parenting, and the absence of role models worthy of emulation all ensure that Sammy and Pecola cannot depend upon their own family unit as a way out of this stagnated wasteland. No values are passed on to them that would sustain them, and they are too outside the community—Pecola in her hypersensitivity and Sammy in his running away—to have the leisurely occasions on which to draw sustenance from sources beyond their home.

The problems inherent in the Breedlove family structure are duplicated in Geraldine, who, for all her security, is no more loving, or sustaining, or worthy of emulation than the Breedloves. She prefers the *form* of family to the substance. Geraldine plans her marriage and family as if they are a million-dollar painting to be admired from afar. She gets just the right education to catch the right man, the hard worker who will do her bidding and respect her idea of what the home should be; of her type, Morrison comments that "this plain brown girl will build her nest stick by stick, make it her own inviolable world, and stand guard over its every plant, weed, and doily, even against him" (65). She will become more attached to a pet than to her own offspring, but for that child (only one, Morrison emphasizes), she will be perfect in caring for its needs and in keeping it out of her affections. "Geraldine did not allow her baby, Junior, to cry. As long as his needs were physical, she could meet them—comfort and satiety. He was always brushed, bathed, oiled, and shod. Geraldine did not talk to him, coo to him, or indulge him in kissing bouts, but she saw that every other desire was fulfilled" (67). Incapable of giving genuine affection to another human being, Geraldine serves as the model for her Junior's insensitive treatment of Pecola. There is a perversion in her very damming up of emotions usually destined for family members. Although she wants the family structure, she also recognizes it as having the potential to violate the sanctity she desires, and she refuses to allow that violation.

Consequently, her husband Louis becomes an "intruder" and Junior a hateful youngster who heaps his abuse upon those who cannot fight back, namely the cat and Pecola. Here, there is no family relationship to break down, for Geraldine has built the holes into it. She does not wish for more than the picture of happiness, for the substance is perhaps too "funky" for her, just as body odors, disorder, and sex are. Because this is the house that Geraldine built and the family that she failed to build, and because her husband is more an appendage than a personality in the home, she becomes the center of control and activity. There is thus more responsibility on her shoulders for the failure passed on to Junior; indeed, her family ironically resembles a negligent single-parent home rather than a nuclear family structure.

Morrison attacks the hollowness surrounding women like Geraldine, their blind, unquestioning pursuit of a vapid existence that, though outwardly secure, can last for only one generation. It would be hard to imagine Junior repeating his father's role in relation to a woman like his mother, for he understands too well the consequences of the arrangement. He could reject his mother's lifestyle by becoming the epitome of those representative of "loud and dirty niggers," or he could follow her path more intensely by becoming one of the persecutors of those despicable "niggers" (certainly his behavior with Pecola would portend the latter pattern). Geraldine gives more thought to her own comfort than to the future; she seems to have no desire, no need to contemplate what happens to the house that she has built once she is no longer there.

From such an insensitive, uncaring woman, Pecola can expect no mercy when Junior claims that she has killed the cat Geraldine loves. In the time between accusation and reaction, Geraldine sees Pecola as the ghost of all that she has escaped—poverty, disorder, "funkiness," "niggerishness." Pecola potently reminds Geraldine of the necessity of building nests against intruders, even those within the home itself. She can therefore only call Pecola a "nasty little black bitch" (72) and demand that she get out. Pecola's encounter with what she does not have—a pretty mother and a lovely home—leaves her unsettled, for there is an obvious contrast between the exterior beauty and the ugliness the "pretty lady" had hurled at her. The society has many faces, but it mostly mirrors back to Pecola the same ugliness she sees in her own family. The exceptional MacTeer family, in whose home Pecola spends a short while, cannot counteract the numerous insults heaped upon her by so many of the other members of her community.

Geraldine and Pauline also illustrate, in their relationships with their husbands, the unhealthy, unregenerative nature of conjugal sexual relationships in this wasteland. From beautiful sexual encounters with Cholly, in which she is reminded of berry picking, her mother's lemonade, and other good times "down home," which all come together in a rainbow image, Pauline moves through two pregnancies and fisticuffs with her husband to the point where sex is a chore, an unregenerative exercise that she tolerates because, from her Christian perspective, it fits into bearing her husband "like a crown of thorns" (98). She trades the absence of sexual pleasure late in the marriage for church and God; she recognizes the change in her relationship with Cholly, but asserts that it does not matter:

> *Most times he's thrashing away inside me before I'm woke, and through when I am. The rest of the time I can't even be next to his stinking drunk self. But I don't care 'bout it no more. My Maker will take care of me. I know He will. I know He will. Besides, it don't make no difference about this old earth. There is sure to be a glory. Only thing I miss sometimes is that rainbow. But like I say, I don't recollect it much anymore.* (102; italics in original)

Sharing and giving have degenerated into detachment and burden-bearing. Bodies come together, but there is no pleasure or procreation, and barely any release; husband and wife use sex for ulterior motives, Cholly to retain some control over his wife and Pauline to show how much she suffers as the wife of Cholly Breedlove. Neither perspective is healthy, and neither perspective has a future in it.

Pauline and Cholly execute a fascinating reversal in the novel; one views sex as a burden and the other as a weapon, and they derive their sexual pleasure from their ritualistic physical battles. Wife- and husband-beating become as pleasurable to them as the

height of orgiastic release; they get complete satisfaction and fulfillment from each other only by inflicting pain upon each other, the
pain associated with kicking, biting, slapping, and hitting each other
with objects such as sticks of wood and frying pans. "Cholly and
Mrs. Breedlove fought each other," Morrison writes, "with a darkly
brutal formalism that was paralleled only by their lovemaking. . . .
They did not talk, groan, or curse during these beatings. There was
only the muted sound of falling things, and flesh on unsurprised
flesh" (32). The fight precipitated by Cholly's negligence in bringing
in coal for the stove ends in Pauline picking up the stove lid and
"knocking him right back into the senselessness out of which she
had provoked him" (33). She is "surprised," after having tossed a
quilt over the unconscious Cholly, when Sammy demands that she
"kill him." The fight that agitates her son and makes her daughter
want to disappear only brings a quiet calm to her, one following a
tremendous release. The peculiar sickness she and Cholly have is
theirs alone, their pleasure, a part of the perversity of their existence,
and the pleasure would be terminated if she did indeed kill Cholly.
She wants him alive to repeat the pleasure, for fighting is the only
sexual rite they have; this pleasure might be a long way from where
they began, but it is no less fulfilling to both of them.

The memories of a rainbow during the times Pauline and Cholly
enjoyed their sexual encounters have no parallel in Geraldine's relationship to her husband. From the beginning, Geraldine is close to
where Pauline and Cholly end up. For her, there is no pleasure in
sex; it is the price she must pay for the control she needs over the
"intruder" and for begetting the one child. Women like Geraldine
spend their lives getting rid of "the dreadful funkiness of passion,
the funkiness of nature, the funkiness of the wide range of human
emotions" (64). Sex must therefore be limited, controlled, as ordered
as the other features of her life; the man in her life will not know in
advance that "she will give him her body sparingly and partially. He
must enter her surreptitiously, lifting the hem of her nightgown only
to her navel. He must rest his weight on his elbows when they make
love, ostensibly to avoid hurting her breasts but actually to keep her
from having to touch or feel too much of him" (65). Such responses
make Geraldine's relationship unnatural, and they make sex perverted and misdirected. Eliot's typist, who has a succession of lov-

ers, is no more mechanical, no more methodical in sex than is Geraldine, and perhaps the typist at least derives a momentary pleasure from the encounters.

In substituting sin for sanctity by rejecting her home life for the church, and in viewing herself as a "martyr" (29), Pauline does not turn from being lost to being saved; the movement pushes her into another set of stagnant values, another perversion reflecting the ills of the society. Church is not an institution in which Pauline Breedlove expects to find a formula, in the tradition of Jesus and the Beatitudes, for living in this world. She uses it instead as a basis for rejecting this world while she anticipates the next. Her brand of morality becomes a fortress to keep her inviolate against the criticisms of her neighbors, the needs of her children, and the drunkenness of her husband. She claims Jesus as a traditional solace as well as a traditional lover; He welcomes her when others would reject her, and He accepts her even without teeth or the ability to pronounce "children" correctly. Irony is again at work in that what Pauline expects Jesus to forgive in terms of her own faults is precisely what she cannot forgive in others—their shortcomings, their failures to measure up to a standard of behavior or beauty. The church becomes a hiding place from reality as well as a whip Pauline uses to lash out at others by emphasizing her own piety.

Soaphead Church represents another dimension in the dissolution of traditional church values, for his background certainly influences his reaction to Pecola. Initially a minister, he turned from that profession to one fairly close to it; he became a healer, an urban hoodoo doctor, ministering to physical and spiritual ills. In an extension of what Pauline has done by staying in the church and using it to her own ends, Soaphead Church has taken the functions of the church into the little room he rents from Bertha Reese. There he can be preacher, father confessor, and god, an individual whose powers are limited only by the imaginations of his supplicants. In the breakdown of traditional bonds of caring, Soaphead ministers to people not because of altruistic love, but because he is able to extend his detachment from them by doing so. "His hours were his own, the competition was slight, the clientele was already persuaded and therefore manageable, and he had numerous opportunities to witness human stupidity without sharing it or being compromised by it, and to nurture his fastidiousness by viewing physical decay" (131). In short, he is able to nurture his misanthropic tendencies.

In one of the final ironies of the book, then, it is uniquely appropriate that Pecola, in her perverted desire, would seek out someone whose attitude toward God and humanity, especially little girls, suits him particularly well to "grant" her request. He is able to do something that neither God nor man has done thus far; he therefore believes himself superior to them. His lack of altruism in helping Pecola ties up the web of circumstances in solidifying her pariah status. Or perhaps his helping Pecola is the one time he transcends his rejection of humankind to feel something for the plight of one of his clients. He certainly tries to convince himself that he has been touched by her request, in spite of the fact that Pecola will rid him of the loathsome dog in exchange for her gift.

Soaphead shares kinship with other characters in the book as far as a perversion of sexuality is concerned, which ties in with his capitalizing on the beliefs of his neighbors in making a religion of spiritual healing. Soaphead's notions of sexuality are just as pristine as Geraldine's and just as unhealthy as Cholly Breedlove's turn out to be. His "keen sexual cravings" do not lead to acceptable release because he "never relished physical contact. He abhorred flesh on flesh. Body odor, breath odor, overwhelmed him" (131–32). And, having no desire to beget children, he does not tolerate such inconvenience even to the extent that Geraldine does; rather, he turns his attention to caressing little girls, "those humans whose bodies were least offensive" (132). He convinces himself that his fondling of them is "clean," more innocent than lewd; with them, there is no "nastiness," "filth," "groaning," or "any long funny . . . look that makes you feel dirty afterward" (144), as his wife Velma had. Soaphead tells himself that he is not hurting the little girls, that they like what he is doing because they come back not only for the ice cream and mints he gives them, but for his touch; they had "parties." His assumed tenderness for them, and the moment of pity he feels for Pecola, place him in the same category with Cholly Breedlove, who views himself as a missionary sent to save his ugly daughter when he pictures himself "fucking her tenderly" (128) in his violent rape of her.

These images of sexuality combine with those of the sterile

middle class to point out again the wretchedness of the wasteland where physical human contact follows in paths antithetical to the perpetuation of the society, except in the most unhealthy of ways. Soaphead will never make contributions to the society in a direct, less than clandestine way, and Cholly, through his drinking, wife beating, and negligence of his children, will never form the role model for parenting essential to the continuation of the family. Though he may claim tenderness, even love, as the motive for his incestuous act, his conclusion in the stupor of liquor will never win approval from the society of which he is a part.

The absence of healthy models for sexual behavior in this wasteland is also apparent in the happy prostitutes who are so generous in their attention to Pecola. China, Poland, and Miss Marie, like Pecola, are outsiders in their community. Their kindnesses to Pecola might make them acceptable, to an extent, to us, but they do not win approval from the characters in the novel whose viewpoint will probably win the day, such as Mrs. MacTeer. Indeed, when we see Mr. Henry caressing the prostitutes in the MacTeer home, we sense in Claudia and Frieda's evaluation of their mother's possible reaction what the majority opinion would be; these are "the fancy women of the maroon nail polish that Mama and Big Mama hated" (59–60) and who have violated decency by coming into their home. They also make Claudia's "flesh crawl" and the back of her neck "itch." Claudia remembers that Marie is "the one church women never allowed their eyes to rest on. That was the one who had killed people, set them on fire, poisoned them, cooked them in lye" (60). The community uses the church and legend to instill in the girls its notions of which role models are acceptable and which not. As haters of "all men," scorners of most women, "whores in whores' clothing," China, Poland, and Marie are too hardened as human beings and too committed to prostitution to provide anything more than a temporary respite from the ugliness of the community they share with Pecola. Unbridled sexual activity as a model for behavior would be as detrimental to Pecola's development as are the rape by Cholly and the child abuse by Soaphead.

The number of ways in which sex is used degradingly in this wasteland is almost commensurate with the number of characters. For the prostitutes, the money it brings enables them to flaunt their hatred of men. For Cholly, it is connected to the embarrassment he recalls when the white men forced him to continue his first sexual encounter. He in turn uses it as a weapon against his wife, to wage war against the piety she claims under the guise of Christianity. He then rapes his daughter in an extension of the confused feelings he has for his wife. Sex for Geraldine is a form of selfish procreation as well as an inconvenience she uses to maintain her hard-won house and status. For Mr. Henry and Soaphead Church, sex takes the form of child abuse, although Mr. Henry also probably engages in sex with the prostitutes. In none of these instances is the coming together of human bodies in sexual embrace a positive or caring experience for either partner involved.

For none of these characters is fertility and sharing the primary goal of their encounters. Growth cannot occur even when actual procreation is effected, as in the case with Geraldine and Pecola, for Junior is as stunted as his mother, and Pecola's pregnancy leads to a miscarriage. In the absence of giving and sympathetic interaction with other human beings, sex is destined to be ugly, "nasty," "filthy," and "dirty." It offers no outlet for Pecola, who is already wallowing in the bed of physical ugliness. If the actions of human beings are equally as ugly as she believes herself to be, then there is little left for her to be or to do.

The breakdown of the bonds of human caring in the novel reflect the general absence of ethics and morality. Those who are in the church have no clearly defined set of rules by which they treat others in an altruistic manner, and those outside the church have no concept of living by ethics as basic as the golden rule. People abuse each other and take advantage of each other in many of the significant relationships in the novel; so many of the major characters are victimized by such lacks that they, in turn, cannot form a basis for identifying with others. For example, Cholly's brief and emotionally violent interaction with his father serves to wipe away everything he has remembered of good treatment by his Aunt Jimmy, and it sets him on a path of destruction and death. His father's failure to treat him as a human being is comparable to the white men denying his humanity by shining the flashlight on him during his first sexual encounter (with Darlene). His rules for dealing with people, then, are informed by rejection, violence, denial, and negligence. A man who tests his own humanity by taking the lives of others—as Cholly has probably done for the three white men he killed in retaliation for the peculiar "humiliations" and "emasculations" (32) he had felt with Darlene and his father—cannot possibly be expected to form an ethical base for living in the world. Instead, like Bigger Thomas, he has accepted in part the animal status to which he has been assigned. When he tries to burn his home, his neighbors conclude that "he had joined the animals; was, indeed, an old dog, a snake, a ratty nigger" (12). His drinking and further deterioration have already been set in motion by his early experiences.

Pauline, Geraldine, Soaphead Church, and the prostitutes similarly make clear the absence of a moral base in this degenerative environment. They all share in believing that human beings can and should be exploited at some level. Pauline exploits Cholly for his sins and her white employers for their acceptance of her; she is comparable to Ellie and Vi in Douglas Turner Ward's *Happy Ending* (1964) in that she is getting as much from her white employers, especially emotionally, as they are getting from her in physical labor and devotion to their child. Geraldine exploits her husband for his labor and her child for his place in the world she has created, and she is willing to step on all other black people in order to keep that little world intact. Soaphead Church obviously exploits Pecola by using her to get rid of the dog he hates, but he also exploits the little girls who find their way into his "clean" sexual embraces; further, he hides behind the role of healer and exploits the community for a living when he has no respect for any of its inhabitants. And the prostitutes are committed to blatant exploitation of all men of all races and ages.

Morality in the novel comes from two sources, one of which Pecola never encounters and the other of which she encounters only too briefly; neither is strong enough to bring about the widespread renewal needed in this blighted land. Aunt Jimmy and her friends are keepers of a way of life, unwritten rules for living that have enabled them to survive abuse by white men, white women, and black men, that have enabled them to raise their children in spite of obstacles, and that have brought them contentedly into old age. Keepers of tradition and a morality flexible enough to ensure their survival, these women are identified by their hands and arms, the connectors for them to reach out and bind themselves to the generations following them:

> They beat their children with one hand and stole for them with the other. The hands that felled trees also cut umbilical cords; the hands that wrung the necks of chickens and butchered hogs also nudged African violets into bloom; the arms that loaded sheaves, bales, and sacks rocked babies into sleep. They patted biscuits into flaky ovals of innocence—and shrouded the dead. They plowed all day and came home to nestle like plums under the limbs of their men. (108)

Morrison describes these culture bearers as "free," but the freedom they experience is one wrought in nurturing their children and grandchildren, not in defiance and destruction of them. His aunt's rescue of Cholly from the junk heap by the railroad is perhaps too unromantic for him, for "when he watched Aunt Jimmy eating collards with her fingers, sucking her four gold teeth, or smelled her when she wore the asafetida bag around her neck, or when she made him sleep with her for warmth in winter and he could see her old, wrinkled breasts sagging in her nightgown—then he wondered whether it would have been just as well to have died there" (103). Too young or too steeped in unregenerative genes to appreciate fully his aunt's nurturing, Cholly rejects the tradition that prefers life to death, the morality that draws all homeless waifs into those hands of caring.

Cholly neutralizes the potentially healthy effects represented by the women of Aunt Jimmy's generation; he effectively buries all they have taught him and is only too eager to look for their opposite: his father. Therefore, he severs the ties that could bind him to his own children in passing on to them acceptable values for living; Pecola is thereby denied a strength and an ethical system that could save her. She is also denied the elementary parenting that Cholly should have been able to offer, but, "having no idea of how to raise children; and having never watched any parent raise himself, he could not even comprehend what such a relationship should be" (126).

The hands that could have saved Cholly, but which he rejects, have their counterpart in the hands of Mrs. MacTeer, similarly gruff and unromantic, but which carry in them the bonds of love. They

stroke fevers out of Claudia and encourage her back to health. Although Claudia may have objected to her mother's rough hands
rubbing salve on her chest, she rightfully recognizes the act as "a
productive and fructifying pain" representative of love "thick and
dark as Alaga syrup" (7). She remembers feet padding into her room
and hands that "repinned the flannel, readjusted the quilt, and
rested a moment" on her forehead. When she remembers autumn,
she thinks "of somebody with hands who does not want me to die"
(7).

The hands that tend Claudia so well also guide Pecola into the
bathroom for care at the onset of her menstrual cycle. Mrs. MacTeer
has been more successful in passing on rules for living to Claudia
and Frieda than the women in Aunt Jimmy's group have to Cholly,
for we see the effects of her teaching in their concern for Pecola. Her
teachings about sexuality are clear in her response to the assumption
that the girls have been "playing nasty" and in her response, along
with her husband's, to Mr. Henry fondling Frieda. To this traditional
mother, little girls must be protected against their own potentially
unsavory desires as well as against the unscrupulous individuals
who would pervert their growth. As a woman who works hard to
raise her children, Mrs. MacTeer is the model for parenting and
caring in Morrison's wasteland. Though her brief encounter with
Pecola cannot save the young girl, Mrs. MacTeer still has a very solid
place in the novel as the spark of healthy fertility in the world of
stagnation and a light in so much spiritual darkness.

Although Mr. MacTeer has a less conspicuous place in the novel
than his wife, his concern for his daughters equals hers, and he
works equally hard to ensure their moral development. He accepts
the responsibility as family man that Cholly never could: "Wolf
killer turned hawk fighter, he worked night and day to keep one
from the door and the other from under the windowsills" (47). Pro-
vider, loving parent, protector, Mr. MacTeer is justifiably angry when
Mr. Henry fondles Frieda. He throws a tricycle at Mr. Henry's head
and knocks him "off the porch" (77); he curses and grabs a gun from
a neighbor with the intention of shooting Mr. Henry. Related by
Frieda rather than dramatized, the events are still effective in showing a father who understands his parenting role and who has a clear
sense of the moral values that should guide his actions. Though he is

not as prominent a figure as his wife, his values are no less worthy of emulation.

Through Mrs. MacTeer and the women of Aunt Jimmy's generation, Morrison illustrates that the values that can sustain and provide the guidelines for growth are not alien to the community; they have been there, quietly pervasive, in those women who had "carried a world on their heads" (108). Cholly and others too restless to see their potential contributions are destined to lose their way, and Pecola and others too unaccepting of the basic blackness inherent in the very existence of these women are similarly destined to lose their claims on reality and on the self.

A Modern Quest for a Holy Grail

In explaining the peculiar neuroses to which little black girls like Pecola are heir, critics have pointed to the place of black girls and women in America in relation to the larger white society, especially as far as criteria for beauty are concerned. Pecola is representative of young black girls who have not had their own features mirrored back to them as acceptable, and in her acute need for acceptance she is more than representative; she becomes a particular intensified reflection of the type. Pecola's society has taught her not merely to want to be beautiful but to be the most beautiful of all, for only in such supremacy can she erase the lack of affection, the constant lack of approval.

Morrison has long been recognized as creating new myths as well as drawing upon those already in existence. One way in which we can read *The Bluest Eye* is for its focus upon the journey motif central to many myths. In this reading, Pecola Breedlove becomes a "victimized-heroine," to use Vladimir Propp's terminology in *Morphology of the Folktale*.[10] She tries to battle her way through the "dragons" of abuse to reap the reward for her trials: the bluest eyes of all. In this journeying, Morrison paints Pecola's encounters with various "monsters" as a series of potentially educational experiences. Because Pecola cannot absorb healthy lessons from these experiences, her journey backfires, and her quest leads to insanity. Instead of conquering, she becomes the conquered in a scapegoating ritual as old as society. This inversion, typical of Morrison's work, shows that blighted, unexpected outcomes frequently result from hopeful expectations.[11]

The mythology Morrison explores in the novel centers upon the standard of beauty by which white women are judged in this country. They are taught that their blonde hair, blue eyes, and creamy skins are not only wonderful, but they are the surface manifestations of the very best character God and nature ever molded. Oral traditions bolstered by literature and other media have solidified their pedestalization, a place of honor light years away from Pecola Breedlove. The Shirley Temple cup and the Mary Jane candies allow Pecola to carry the image through her very being, to become one with it for short periods of time. However, she believes that seeking after and obtaining the bluest eyes, the most irreproachable feature in the world, will allow permanent union with those currently transitory features. The bluest eyes become the metonymical representation of the myth. Having blue eyes means having everything—love, acceptance, friends, family—in short, a truly enviable place in the society.[12]

Pecola's quest for blue eyes, her magical talisman, is as consuming and as permeated with mythological implication as the quest for the holy grail, the quest for the silver fleece, or the pursuit of the three golden apples. All entail tremendous trials and sacrifices to prove oneself worthy of recognition so that the sought-after object might be revealed or granted to the quester. If Pecola endures long enough, seeks hard enough, and prays fervently enough, then perhaps—just perhaps—she will receive her reward.

To illustrate the depth of Pecola's motivation for the quest, Morrison uses several characters, incidents, and images to depict the kind of world into which Pecola has been born and the effect of the myth upon her. By comparative analysis, we see how Pauline Breedlove, consciously and unconsciously, passes on certain attitudes toward color to her daughter. And we see how Claudia and Frieda are able to resist being absorbed into a mythology of self-denial, but the pressure upon them, considering their stronger background, shows what a difficult time the weaker Pecola has resisting the indoctrination—even if she were inclined to do so. Movie images, white baby dolls, little white girls, and little "white" black girls are constant reminders that blackness is of lesser value to the majority of the inhabitants of Lorain, Ohio.

The dolls so antithetical to negroid features were presented to little black girls like Claudia and judged to be their most sought-after wish come true. Claudia muses: "Adults, older girls, shops, magazines, newspapers, window signs—all the world had agreed that a blue-eyed, yellow-haired, pink-skinned doll was what every girl child treasured" (14). To the parents, the dolls are unfulfilled longings of their own childhoods, and Mrs. MacTeer and other adults cannot understand Claudia's destruction of them; she tears them apart in an attempt to find the source of their loveliness, what makes the world treasure them. She would similarly like to tear little white girls apart to uncover "the secret of the magic they weaved on others" (15).

Little white dolls—and the inherently implied superiority toward which blacks should strive or by which they should see their shortcomings—were a way of life that few people questioned until the 1960s, when the demand for black dolls became general and when manufacturers noticed that there was a substantial market for a different kind of product. In 1941, that was not the case, and Frieda and Claudia are just as susceptible as Pecola to being indoctrinated into the cult of believers in the myth. For the sisters, however, there are stronger ties to family and black tradition; for example, Claudia treasures spending time with her Big Mama and Big Papa more than playing with little white dolls. The good times she remembers spending in her grandparents' kitchen, and the music her grand–father played just for her, have instilled in Claudia the possibility of another world, a black one, in which she has "security and warmth" (15) that will never be available to Pecola. Playing with dolls, then, becomes for Claudia merely an interlude, a stage through which she will pass, and not a quest; it is therefore not the representation of what her future will be.

Grown-ups might be disgusted and puzzled by Claudia's destruction of the dolls ("You-don't-know-how-to-take-care-of-nothing. I-never-had-a-baby-doll-in-my-whole-life-and-used-to-cry-my-eyes-out-for-them. Now-you-got-one-a-beautiful-one-and-you-tear-it-up-what's-the-matter-with-you?"—14), but they do not reject her because of that action. By contrast, the household into which Pecola is born is one in which the mother, Pauline, has long ago rejected images of blackness for ones of whiteness. Pecola is doomed, then, to see the dolls and other images of little white girls as reflecting her lacks. As a seeker, though a victimized-heroine, therefore, she must journey to obtain the lack, a trait that Propp notes in many of the tales he examined.

The first stage of Pecola's journey naturally begins with her mother, and that is also where her problems begin, for Pauline only highlights what Pecola lacks. Possessor of a tenuous identity from her days in Alabama and Kentucky, when she was a part of a family but did not receive any special attention, Pauline has early in her move to Ohio turned her attention to the movies for the glamorous identity she experiences vicariously. In those darkened theaters so conducive to a dreamlike state, she can transport herself from the fights with Cholly about money and alcohol, from the cramped apartment they share, to the world of Hollywood, where hairstylists live in abundance and where mansions are the size of football fields. In that world, money is never a problem. The people, in their beautiful whiteness, allow Pauline to look in upon them, absorb their concepts of beauty, share in their world, and thereby judge hers for its failure to begin to approximate their standard. Pauline quickly discovers that she is *"happy"* only when she is watching movies because she is able to *"move right on in them pictures"* (95; italics in original). Her appreciation of the ways white men care for their women gives her *"a lot of pleasure, but it made coming home hard, and looking at Cholly hard"* (95–96; italics in original). As she watches movies, then, Pauline inculcates the values by which she harshly judges her husband and rejects her children. A daughter born of a mother who has spent her pregnancy watching movies that oppose the child's very being cannot possibly find a welcome from that parent.

In her imitation of the movies, Pauline initially seeks to transform herself by fixing her hair like Jean Harlow. When the loss of a tooth mars the image and makes her realize that exact imitation will not accomplish her purpose, she lets her physical appearance deteriorate, but she retains the criteria for passing judgment upon her own family. Sammy and Pecola are born looking like the black children they are, not like blonde-haired, blue-eyed dolls, or the cuddly images of the movies. In gesture, attitude, and attention, Pauline succeeds over the years in showing her children that she does not approve of their looks. It is no accident that Sammy runs away from home twenty-seven times by the time he is fourteen or that Pecola's only prayer is the never-ending one for blue eyes. At the moment Pauline gives birth to Pecola, she sends her on a journey for self-acceptance; with no models to the contrary, Pecola can only accept the journey doomed to failure. Yet the novel's depiction of her attempt, of the quest that leads to insanity, is painfully revealing in its exploration of such a quietly pervasive and insidious psychology.

By the time we get our first glimpse of Pecola, the damage has been done; she is already on her way to worshipping those blue eyes and all they represent. A "case" brought to the MacTeer home, a clearly unfortunate child whose father has put the family *"outdoors,"* Pecola is further neglected by the mother who has chosen to live through this period of exigency with the white family for whom she works. Pecola's drinking of milk from "a blue-and-white Shirley Temple cup" and lingeringly gazing "fondly at the silhouette of Shirley Temple's dimpled face" (12–13) alerts us to a child with an underdeveloped self image—or none at all. Frieda and Pecola's conversation on how "cu-ute Shirley Temple" is might seem innocuous, until we learn that Pecola has drunk three quarts of milk in a very short time solely for the pleasure of gazing at Shirley's image. The whiteness she does not have can be claimed vicariously for each of the few minutes she holds the cup, and she renews the loving caress as frequently as she can.

Shirley Temple, herself a "dream child," serves as do the Mary Janes in providing Pecola with the opportunity to savor what she is not. She takes her three pennies to buy the nine pieces of candy that will allow her fantasy to blossom:

> Each pale yellow wrapper has a picture on it. A picture of little Mary Jane, for whom the candy is named. Smiling white face. Blond hair in gentle disarray, blue eyes looking at her out of a world of clean comfort. The eyes are petulant, mischievous. To Pecola they are simply pretty. She eats the candy, and its sweetness is good. To eat the candy is somehow to eat the eyes, eat Mary Jane. Love Mary Jane. Be Mary Jane.
>
> Three pennies had bought her nine lovely orgasms with Mary Jane. Lovely Mary Jane, for whom a candy is named. (38)

Responding instinctively to images that have been presented to her, and perhaps not yet able to articulate clearly what acceptance and rejection mean, Pecola is nevertheless able to exhibit at a primitive level the basis of the psychology that will destroy her. She gets a pleasurable feeling when she sees particular images; somewhere in her life, those connotative connections have been made positive to her. Pauline obviously has never said directly to her children that they are ugly, that she does not love them, and that they should try to be white, but she has undoubtedly conveyed those feelings in any number of ways. Pecola, then, has absorbed the insinuations and is seeking after the formula for understanding them.

Her education on the doomed journey to self-acceptance continues with the arrival of Maureen Peal, another little "dream child." Having all the advantages that light skin and excessive confidence have given her, Maureen is only a slightly lesser version of the demon come to life to torment those who worship its image. Shirley Temple and Mary Jane are representations; Pecola now sees in her own neighborhood a little girl who is revered purely for the external features she has admired in those images—long hair, pale skin, and good clothes. Maureen is a bit of the silver screen brought to life in blackface, but her closeness to the ideal makes it clear to Pecola how far she has to journey in trying to transcend her own blackness. Stable-minded Claudia is ironic, bitter, and accurate in her description of Maureen: "A high-yellow dream child with long brown hair braided into two lynch ropes that hung down her back. She was rich, at least by our standards, as rich as the richest of the white girls, swaddled in comfort and care" (47). The dream child is picture perfect in wardrobe and behavior, wearing clothes that none of the average parents can afford and eliciting responses from teachers and other students that black girls like Claudia, Frieda, and Pecola cannot. With her "sloe green eyes, something summery in her complexion, and a rich autumn ripeness in her walk" (48), Maureen weaves a magical spell over the community:

> She enchanted the entire school. When teachers called on her, they smiled encouragingly. Black boys didn't trip her in the halls; white boys didn't stone her, white girls didn't suck their teeth

> when she was assigned to be their work partners; black girls
> stepped aside when she wanted to use the sink in the girls' toilet,
> and their eyes genuflected under sliding lids. She never had to
> search for anybody to eat with in the cafeteria—they flocked to the
> table of her choice, where she opened fastidious lunches, shaming
> our jelly-stained bread with egg-salad sandwiches cut into four
> dainty squares, pink-frosted cupcakes, sticks of celery and carrots,
> proud, dark apples. She even bought and liked white milk. (48)

"Bemused, irritated, and fascinated," Frieda and Claudia are understandably overwhelmed by this beauty who seems to have no flaws.
The entire community shows them that it is bewitched by a phenomenon that they and Pecola will forever be outside of. Neither teachers nor students pause to contemplate the image created before
them, the perfect exterior that they have been taught to accept
through movies and other media, folk tradition, and history. Indeed,
in 1941, Maureen would have been viewed as a black person worthy
of imitation precisely because of her considerably toned-down black
features.

Few stop to consider that this awe-inspiring little princess is also
vicious and cruel, the side of her that Morrison uses to convey that
reconsideration of the myth needs to begin somewhere. Maureen's
responses to the world have been shaped by a power and freedom
she attaches to color as well as by the compliments she has undoubtedly received over the years for her silver-screen features. Given a
closer look at her, we see that Maureen is scornful of black people,
insensitive toward them, and so egotistical that she is a walking
insult to all black people. City-bred and thereby more sophisticated
in some ways than the other girls, Maureen easily discusses legal
suits, movies, sex, menstruation, and the preferences of black people
for little girls like herself. Her "good" hair gives her license to deride
those who do not have such: "My mother told me that a girl named
Audrey, she went to the beauty parlor where we lived before, and
asked the lady to fix her hair like Hedy Lamarr's, and the lady said,
'Yeah, when you grow some hair like Hedy Lamarr's,'" and she
laughs "long and sweet" (53–54). A child to whom few things have
been denied, Maureen provides in her physical features and wealth
one side of the image to which Pecola aspires. In her vicious insults
to Pecola about her father, and in calling her black, she reverts to the

power those so gifted have in rejecting those who seek identification with them. Maureen could easily be visualized as the keeper of the castle into which a knight seeks entry for years, but then, upon finally entering, is told to start the journey over again. And Pecola, a feeble form of that knight, is ever willing to forgive the cruelty and try again. As long as she believes the fault lies within herself, she will be susceptible to whatever trials are placed in her path.

Pecola has blindly, destructively internalized what Claudia is able to see about Maureen in a more analytical light:

> If she was cute—and if anything could be believed, she *was*—then we were not. And what did that mean? We were lesser. Nicer, brighter, but still lesser. Dolls we could destroy, but we could not destroy the honey voices of parents and aunts, the obedience in the eyes of our peers, the slippery light in the eyes of our teachers when they encountered the Maureen Peals of the world. What was the secret? What did we lack? Why was it important? And so what? . . . envy was a strange, new feeling for us. And all the time we knew that Maureen Peal was not the Enemy and not worthy of such intense hatred. The *Thing* to fear was the *Thing* that made *her* beautiful, and not us. (57-58)

What they lack is a verbal tradition of acceptance; they have been kept out of the mythology of beliefs that has shaped cultural norms for beauty in America.[13]

The dream child within the black community can at least be touched and communicated with. The one in the white world into which Pecola, Claudia, and Frieda go is untouchable. The doll come to life is one that only Pauline can touch, and it is Pauline who "protects" her against Pecola and the other girls when they come to the kitchen of the white home where she works to pick up wash. The dream vision appears to the three black girls while Pauline is briefly out of the room:

> Another door opened, and in walked a little girl, smaller and younger than all of us. She wore a pink sunback dress and pink fluffy bedroom slippers with two bunny ears pointed up from the tips. Her hair was corn yellow and bound in a thick ribbon. When she saw us, fear danced across her face for a second. She looked anxiously around the kitchen. (84)

The little girl's fear and Pecola's nervousness lead to the spilling of the berry cobbler and to Pauline's mean and unnatural treatment of her own daughter. In the face of the little white child's cries and Pecola's awkwardness, Pauline spits out words "like rotten pieces of apple" at the black girls and turns to "hushing and soothing the tears of the little pink-and-yellow girl" (85). To the little girl's repeated question, "Who were they, Polly?" the faithful servant responds, "Hush. Don't worry none," "and the honey in her words complemented the sundown spilling on the lake" (85). The mother who has not come to inquire about her daughter while she was at the MacTeers' is shown in her true colors of having rejected her black offspring for the white child. Pecola is made to feel ugly and stupid, generally "wrong," beside the little white girl, who represents everything that is "right."

A negative example of what blue eyes represent, the incident nevertheless serves to spur Pecola on her quest for the bluest of them all. Perhaps her mother will coddle her as she does the little white girl if Pecola only has the bluest eyes. Perhaps little black boys will not shout insults at her, and perhaps pretty ladies in green houses will not accuse her of killing their cats. Transformation, love, acceptance, and understanding are all to be had if only those blue eyes are granted. With models like Pauline illustrating to Pecola how the magic works, what the change can effect, it is no wonder that she prays even more fervently for those revered blue eyes.

Pecola's quest is her religion, for she believes in it just that fervently. And by believing, she has unwittingly made herself a victim, to be sacrificed on the altars of various public opinions. Because she *believes* she is ugly and *believes* that her quest for blue eyes will lead to beauty and acceptance, she cannot escape lapsing into insanity when the achievement of her quest only causes further rejection. Too innocent to transcend the negative influence of her neighbors, Pecola acquiesces in her own sacrifice. The irony is that her scapegoating does not purge the community of its reliance on alien standards of beauty; it merely solidifies those images. To be ugly and outcast leads to destruction; to be beautiful and in the community provides one of the strongest possibilities for salvation.[14]

The many characters and attitudes she encounters serve as negative impetuses for Pecola in her quest. They continue to push her along toward the insane accomplishment of her goal. While Pauline and others probably would not consciously admit their complicity in Pecola's insanity, Claudia, in retrospect, is able to see the responsibility of the entire community. "All of us—all who knew her—felt so wholesome after we cleaned ourselves on her. We were so beautiful when we stood astride her ugliness. . . . We honed our egos on her, padded our characters with her frailty, and yawned in the fantasy of our strength" (163). Perhaps a bit too harsh on herself—though certainly not on some members of the community— Claudia and her family have at least tried to care. The damage to Pecola, however, had been done long before she came into the MacTeer home as a "case"; she had already, like Rufus Scott in James Baldwin's *Another Country* (1962), received "the blow from which she could not recover." Insanity and death are the only releases from such torture, and Pecola's insanity might just as well be a death.

3

Sula

Within and beyond the African-American Folk Tradition

The Bluest Eye (1970), with its grounding in Lorain, Ohio, provides at least geographical identification with events in the world as we know it. What the people do to each other there might be cruel and insensitive, but those characters approximate many we have seen. There is a verisimilitude in the cruelty of the children who reject Pecola, and we can easily visualize the likes of Pauline Breedlove in her adherence to a loyalty and love for the white family in preference for her own. With the creation of the Bottom in *Sula* (New York: Knopf, 1974), Toni Morrison removes that grounding in a known place and locates her characters in a territory that invites the fantastic and the mythical as easily as the realistic. In the political-racial-economic confrontation surrounding its creation, the Bottom differs from other fictional communities; it was concocted out of hope, belief, and the power of dreams to transcend the harshness of the real world. It lends itself, therefore, much more readily to occurrences that are strange or fantastic and to characters who are at times more nether creatures than flesh and blood.

Toni Morrison has asserted that she writes the kind of books she wants to read.[1] We might conclude, therefore, that in her use of folklore she is fascinated by the magic of fairy tales and intrigued with

Although Morrison copyrighted the novel in 1973, it was actually published on 7 January 1974. I am therefore using the 1974 date for consistency with other *publication* dates used throughout the manuscript.

the horrors to be found in monsters, or at least in monstrous behavior. In *Sula,* Morrison continues her creation of literary folklore by drawing upon and expanding historical patterns.

Morrison may begin with structural components of tales or peculiar traits of characters with which we may be superficially familiar, but she quickly embroiders upon these patterns. Her familiarity with African-American folk communities and with other oral traditions enables her to touch base with them in the outline of her materials, but to differ in the details. What Morrison does might be compared with what Charles Waddell Chesnutt did in *The Conjure Woman* (1899); beginning with the outlines of tales he had heard in North Carolina, he expanded details to shape political statements disguised as seemingly innocuous stories. Chesnutt's tales seem so true to black folk tradition that many students of his work have searched for exact parallels in published collections of folklore. Although Morrison surrounds her novel with an aura of unreality that discourages seeking exact parallels, her lore is further fictionalized beyond the mere germ of a traditional idea. Though we can see those basic inspirations in the ideas that shape the structure of the novel, delineate the characters, and develop the themes, it is also clear where Morrison has created something else.

Three oral sources are helpful in illuminating the structure of *Sula.* First of all, the structure evokes the formulaic opening of fairy tales from European cultures; secondly, it evokes a pattern of joking in African-American communities; and, thirdly, it evokes the form of the ballad, which, in its incremental development, in turn reminds us of jazz composition. In the first paragraph of the novel, Morrison establishes an almost mythical status for the Bottom, claiming kinship for it with the many places in which strange, almost supernatural, incidents have occurred. "In that place, where they tore the nightshade and blackberry patches from their roots to make room for the Medallion City Golf Course, there was once a neighborhood" (3) deviates little from the "Once upon a time" formula for fairy tales; the fictional reality of the Bottom is thus juxtaposed with the lack of reality of some of those never-never lands.[2] The formula establishes distance, a perspective from which to view the incidents about to be related. It is a signal that we can sit back and read of marvelous events, or at least that is what the formula usually conveys.

As we begin our journey into that other world Morrison has created, we quickly discover a series of reversals: the fantastic events are disturbingly real, and the formula promising wondrous occurrences moves them from the realm of imagination to commonplaces such as war, poverty, and murder. The expected distance collapses, but it does not collapse thoroughly enough for us, without reservations, to accept Shadrack as the guy next door or Sula as the girl next door. Expected dragonslayers become frightened young soldiers afraid of their own hands, afraid that war has taught them not only to kill others but to kill themselves. Ogres are alcohol and drugs, and those strong enough to kill, such as Eva, cannot separate evil from the innocent victims it inhabits. Fires that save Hansel and Gretel or the three little pigs become scars upon the soul of a mother who kills her only son and upon a daughter who quietly watches her mother burn to death.

In another classic Morrison reversal, *Sula* is antithetical to the basic premise of the fairy tale—that the heroine is a helpless, passive creature who must depend upon some man, preferably a stranger, to save her from whatever "fate worse than death" she has innocently or stupidly managed to get herself into.[3] There is little passivity in *Sula*, and innocence is not treasured; indeed, as is typical of Morrison's girl/women, Sula and Nel seem to blossom into adolescence with more knowledge than is comfortable for either of them. In fact, as the experimenter with life, the Ethan Brand type who explores the limits of sin, Sula is an active, destructive artist who, in the absence of "paints, or clay" or a knowledge of "dance, or strings" (121) makes human beings her adventure in life. She is as active as Jack the giant killer and as amoral as Brer Rabbit the trickster.

In this literary folklore, therefore, there is a marked gap between expectation and outcome, between what the familiar leads us to anticipate and what Morrison's changing of the familiar actually provides. She undercuts any potential fairy tale outcomes by making Sula, her princess, a despicable user who needs rescue from no one; by making Eva, her fairy godmother, impotent at the most crucial moment of her life (Hannah's burning); and by making Shadrack, her potential prince, an outcast from the world where his services are most needed. None of these characters portends the "happily ever after" dimension of the formula. By novel's end, the princess is dead, the prince has unwittingly led many of her adversaries to their deaths, the twin sister is almost crazy with grief, and the kingdom is slowly being destroyed.

Its destruction has been foreshadowed in the second structural pattern underlying the novel, the "nigger joke" about the origin of the Bottom. The story fits a classic tale cycle of the black man being duped by the white man:

> A good white farmer promised freedom and a piece of bottom land to his slave if he would perform some very difficult chores. When the slave completed the work, he asked the farmer to keep his end of the bargain. Freedom was easy—the farmer had no objection to that. But he didn't want to give up any land. So he told the slave that he was very sorry that he had to give him valley land. He had hoped to give him a piece of the Bottom. The slave blinked and said he thought valley land was bottom land. The master said, "Oh, no! See those hills? That's bottom land, rich and fertile."
>
> "But it's high up in the hills," said the slave.
>
> "High up from us," said the master, "but when God looks down, it's the bottom. That's why we call it so. It's the bottom of heaven—best land there is."
>
> So the slave pressed his master to try to get him some. He preferred it to the valley. And it was done. The nigger got the hilly land, where planting was backbreaking, where the soil slid down and washed away the seeds, and where the wind lingered all through the winter.
>
> Which accounted for the fact that white people lived on the rich valley floor in that little river town in Ohio, and the blacks populated the hills above it, taking small consolation in the fact that every day they could literally look down on the white folks. (5)

The tale presents two archetypes of African-American folklore: the white man of means and the "blinking," almost minstrel black man who learns too late the true nature of the bargain he has made. The basic discrepancy inherent in such interactions is also apparent: power (including the language skills to control or create reality) versus the absence of power. The twist in the tale is that the white farmer is the trickster, the figure who dupes instead of being duped.

The story is an etiological one, in that it serves to explain how the current state of affairs came to be. In a world in which the black man is destined to lose, because of or in spite of his labor, the slave here fares no better. The rules of the games will always be changed, as Daryl C. Dance astutely observes in her discussion of etiological tales in *Shuckin' and Jivin'* (1978) and elsewhere; the black man will always receive the reward of lesser value.[4] But Morrison turns the joke around; it is difficult to grow things there, but it is "lovely up in the Bottom" (5), and the trees are so "wonderful to see" (6) that whites speculate on the Bottom indeed being "the bottom of heaven" (6). In spite of their ancestors having been shortchanged, the black folks create reasonably happy lives for themselves in a place almost animate in its influence upon them.

Reminiscent of the storefront, communal, interactive culture that Zora Neale Hurston describes in *Mules and Men* (1935) and other works,[5] the Bottom is a joke where the tables are turned, for a time, back on the joker. For that portion of the novel where the Bottom is vibrant—despite its occasional strangenesses—the last laugh is really on the whites, because they have not been able to destroy the will to survive of those blacks up in the Bottom. Indeed, the philosophy exemplified in the Bottom is one of survival at all costs, of making all mountains, built by whites or blacks, into mole hills. The black folks in the Bottom place white folks like the man in the tale in the large category of evil that will later contain Sula, and they resolve to withstand all of it. "The purpose of evil was to survive it and they determined (without ever knowing they had made up their minds to do it) to survive floods, white people, tuber-culosis, famine and ignorance" (90).

Morrison allows them to invert the stereotype of their existence (that they deserve and should be resigned to content themselves with less) for almost a hundred years. Ultimately, the structure im-posed by the "nigger joke"—that outcomes will always fall short of expectations—reigns in the novel. Blacks who moved to the Bottom and expected to be left in peace are not. Eventually, the whites de-cide that the Bottom is ideal for suburbs and a golf course, so the blacks who have not voluntarily moved away are displaced once again. Although slight variations have occurred over the years, the basic structure is retained: whites get what they consider the best, and blacks must settle for what is left.

This structure also provides a backdrop against which to view the actions of the characters, especially those of Sula. In a world in which expectations are invariably short-circuited, it is not surprising to find Sula's actions a series of expectations that she measures against some invisible yardstick and finds wanting. Life is in many ways the "nigger joke" that has been played on her. From her twelve-year-old discovery that her mother "loved" rather than "liked" her, to her twenty-seven-year-old Weltschmerz, Sula learns that life holds few genuine adventures for her and even fewer pleasures. The cards dealt out to her are all marked with the notation that she is black and female; therefore, winning hands must be kept from her. Paralleling the structure that defines the fate of the Bottom, the fate of Sula's existence is similarly determined.

Sula's personality, along with the snake-like birthmark that so intrigues those who encounter her, makes her the closest thing to a witch that the Bottom will ever have. Yet, in its ability to contain contradictions, the community provides for her, as Morrison has noted on several occasions, the only place that will accept her and the only home she will ever know.[6] Her wanderings away from the Bottom can only bring her full circle, like Eva, back to it, for it is able to absorb if not to condone her "otherness," and it gives her the identity that locks her both inside and outside the community's folk traditions. People in the community grant to her the power she has, and she accommodates them by living out their fantasies of otherness.

The third structural pattern in *Sula* evokes the ballad tradition, in which a "leaping and lingering" method of storytelling pauses on significant events in each character's life. In the ballad "Lord Rendal," for example, we are not told of Lord Rendal's birthplace or his growing up; we meet him as a young man who has gone into the woods and been poisoned by his "true love"—for some inexplicable reason.[7] The murder, the encounter with his mother asking what has happened, and his request that his mother make his deathbed "soon" are the three significant points in his life. The whys and wherefores are less important than the consequences of the bloody confrontation. Thus Rendal's life is reduced to the three incidents that lead to his death; perhaps the ballad, over years of telling, has lost some of its detail, but probably not much. The form of the genre

demands brevity and heightened scenes, the tableau scenes, as Axel
Olrik calls them in reference to the major incidents recorded in
folktales.[8]

We can see a similar sparse depiction in the ballad of Barbara
Allan, in which Sir John Graeme's failure to toast her is less central
than the consequences of that action.[9] As a result, he pines and dies;
then Barbara, sensing that he has indeed cherished her, anticipates
her own death. The deaths here, like the murder and anticipated
death in "Lord Rendal," keep the listener's attention. The same is
true of traditional African-American ballads, such as "Stagolee." The
"central event" is the gun battle between Stagolee and the other
man, who has various names, the most common of which is Billy
Lyons. Background on the two men is not particularly important;
indeed, Billy Lyons exists only to allow Stagolee to act out his fate as
a bad man. Some versions of the ballad include Stagolee's early
encounters with his father or law officers (individual will versus
authority in any form), but the ballad is basically stripped to its
essential details.[10]

In an oral tradition, where memory could be subject to error,
such standout scenes insured the singer a better chance of recalling
what the audience was most interested in—the criminal activity surrounding rape, death, murder, hanging, and infanticide, and the pa-
thos surrounding unrequited love. If there are valleys and peaks in
an individual's life, then the peaks consistently receive attention
("peak" is used here to refer to emotional intensity, either good or
bad, and not exclusively to pleasure or happiness). In relating her
tale of passions, burnings, drownings, and witchery, Morrison, too,
is interested in the highlights, the peaks, rather than the ordinariness
represented by the valleys.

Morrison does not purport to be realistic to the minutiae of
following characters on a day-to-day, year-by-year basis; her very
labeling of the years she does dwell on (1919, 1920, 1921, 1922, 1923,
1927, 1937, 1939, 1940, 1941, 1965) indicates the leaping and lingering
tradition. She selects the most impressive events and concentrates
upon them for each of her most impressionable characters. The effects of the war upon Shadrack are finally more important than
physically depicting him in battle, although the one scene he does
recall is a striking one in which a soldier whose head has been blown

off continues to run in spite of that catastrophe. The bloody images of the war lead to Shadrack's perennial celebration of National Suicide Day, and the visit from Sula, the other tableau scene in his life, serves as his last untainted tie to humanity.

Eva's life is crystallized in several scenes: pushing lard up Plum's rectum in the midst of unbearable poverty, knowing that hating BoyBoy after his return will give her peace, trying to save Hannah from a burning death, and being carted off to the old folks' home. The loss of her leg is certainly important, but we are left to speculate about the circumstances under which that occurred; what that loss enabled her to do is more significant. Nel and Sula's friendship solidifies on the day Sula hears Hannah's frank, but destructive, comment on her motherly feelings—which is also the day Sula accidentally kills Chicken Little. Nel's marriage collapses into the few minutes she finds Jude and Sula together, and her grief careens off the tombstones on the day, after her visit to Eva in the old folks' home, that she realizes the extent of her love for Sula. Perhaps the bits and pieces of these lives, as Morrison said about Cholly Breedlove, would make more sense in a musician's head, but they also make sense in the tradition that does not expect fairy tale completeness. Leaping and lingering, frequently with the bloody, or at least the violent, consequences of the ballad tradition, Morrison tells her story in sketches, in vignettes that encourage us to feel that we know her characters, but that really point out the facility with which their complexity is kept before us—and sometimes just beyond our reach.

The leaping and lingering of the ballad tradition suggests the jazz structuring of the novel, where the theme of death has many variations and improvisations upon it as Morrison manifests its meaning for various of the characters. Death is the stable point of this jazz composition, the center to which each year returns in spite of its individual departure. This allowance for individuality within an overall structure contrasts sharply with what is possible for Sula in the Bottom; the community would prefer that she play the straight refrain of the blues rather than the creative deviation allowable with the jazz comparison.[11]

While these structural patterns are illuminating, they do not explain all that happens in the organization of the novel (we could also talk about the structure of a journey, in which Shadrack moves from innocence to experience to innocence, or where Nel moves from innocence to an almost unbearable knowledge); nor do they in any way confine Morrison to identification with these forms. Instead, they show how Morrison has used folk traditions to expand our expectations of what a novel should be and do. That expansion adds a richness and complexity to her work that is frequently absent in the works of other authors who draw upon oral traditions.

Within the structures Morrison devises for her novel, she creates many characters who echo either specific or general concepts from folk tradition. Local characters, such as Sula, and anecdotes about them, are particularly inspiring for Morrison. From Shadrack, who acts as a chorus to open and close this human drama, to the three deweys, Morrison's characters elicit comparison to those from other folk communities and various wonderlands. Communities that designate some of their inhabitants "weirdos," "crazies," and "loonies" have usually observed several traits in them. They are unusual in appearance and/or mannerisms, and frequently in terms of habitat. Youngsters are taught to fear boogie men and women, whose otherness may be defined by something as tangible as alcoholism or as intangible as an assumed ability to cast the evil eye. Some merely outsiders and others pariahs, these characters serve psychological as well as educational functions in their communities; they illustrate the dangers of talking with strangers (the possibility of disappearing into some peculiar abode), and their weirdness soothes the community as it measures its normalcy against their unusualness. That is certainly what the community does to Pecola Breedlove in *The Bluest Eye*; they can gauge how normal and beautiful they are by emphasizing Pecola's insanity and ugliness.

Omniscient narration gives readers an understanding of Shadrack's otherness, but the folks in the Bottom are never so privileged. They know that he went off to war normal and came back abnormal; the whys and wherefores of that transformation are mere abstractions and do not prevent them from defining Shadrack as one of the weirdos, however formed, who demands a special psychological and physical space in their worlds. A man who comes down the street ringing a cowbell and dangling a hanging rope every January third is not exactly an untainted representative of rationality, yet the community incorporates Shadrack's ceremony without diminishing itself or sanctioning him. They take note—from a distance when they can—of his cursing fits and drinking spells.

Still, like the local characters from oral tradition, he is able to make unspoken claims upon the community even as an outsider. The people in the Bottom evince a degree of responsibility for Shadrack (as one of the wounded whose injury is more intense than their own) by buying the fish he catches and by enduring his curses and morbid parades. He provides diversion from their normalcy; though they do not wish to emulate him, his antics make them secure in their own identities. Seeing Shadrack expose his private parts could only make the ladies more appreciative of their husbands' clothing and make the husbands appreciate the covering that prevents them from being evaluated so publicly. Shadrack's cabin by the river could hold out to them a possibility for freedom, but it is negated by their knowledge of his mental cages. Tolerated but not loved, a part of the community but not truly in it, Shadrack exemplifies the type of character around whom legends and anecdotes grow, who is a source of entertainment as well as a source of dread, who seems through his life-style to be imminently dispensable, but who is the epitome of the community penchant for survival.[12]

It is appropriate that Shadrack is seen at the beginning and the ending of the novel, for the white man who made the Bottom a "nigger joke" and perpetuated white domination of black lives is representative of the system that has also overwhelmed Shadrack. His experiences in the army have been more costly than the slave's loss of land, and the effects have gone on longer. Not only has Shadrack been blasted mentally and suffered through more than forty years of that disorientation, but he must now watch with Nel as the remnants of the Bottom give way to a golf course and fancy houses.

In his strangeness, Shadrack is comparable to an overly sensitive poet/philosopher who has seen so much of the horror of life that he has been blasted beyond the reaches of mundane influences. He brings a knowledge to his people, but the ironic price of his experiences is that he has lost his ability to communicate in a language they understand. His bell and rope, initially more disturbing than enlightening, are more of a barrier to Shadrack's desire to impart truth than Tiresias's blindness or Diogenes's lamp. Rather than understanding that death can be put in perspective if it is given its recognizable place in human existence, the black folk of the Bottom are only reminded of its power to separate them from the living, of the mysteries it holds. To them, therefore, Shadrack is a loony who disturbs things that are best left alone; instead of reducing the fear of death, he evokes more.

Shadrack's mental blighting clearly sets him apart from the rest of the community. His insanity becomes one of the distinguishing physical characteristics that black folks have long used to recognize "otherness" in their midst. Such characteristics, like M'Dear's height and isolation from the community in *The Bluest Eye*, connect the possessor to powers beyond those of ordinary means. They hail such persons as conjurers, witches, or devil worshippers. Since the power identified with them can be used for evil as well as benign purposes, it ensures respect for them in the communities in which they dwell, respect that comes from fear or from belief. The inhabitants of the Bottom treat Sula's birthmark as such an indication of otherworldliness and use it to turn her into a witch. Who but a witch, the women probably rationalize, could use their husbands so thoroughly and discard them at whim? Who but a witch would progress to putting Eva in an old folks home?

The initial evidence against Sula is circumstantial, but it offers the beginning of the reinforcement of belief so central to the creation of outsiderness. From calling Sula a "roach" for putting Eva in the old folks home and a "bitch" for sleeping with Jude, the people in the Bottom come to recognize her true witchery when they discover she has slept with white men; that is the ultimate sign of deviation from their norm, and it puts Sula in league with all manner of strange beings. Knowing that strangeness does not mean weakness, they guard themselves accordingly: "So they laid broomsticks across their doors at night and sprinkled salt on porch steps" (113). After a couple of attempts to "collect the dust from her footsteps," perhaps with the intention of using it in a potion against her, they content themselves with the power of gossip. They "know" she has power when Teapot trips and falls on her steps. The extent of her power gets verification in what happens to another neighbor: "Mr. Finley sat on his porch sucking chicken bones, as he had done for thirteen

years, looked up, saw Sula, choked on a bone and died on the spot"
(114). They conclude that the birthmark over her eye "was Hannah's
ashes marking her from the very beginning" (114).

The birthmark explains why Sula is not content with the life the
other women in the Bottom lead, why she must travel all over the
country in search of something that they cannot begin to imagine.
Indeed, her ten-year absence from the Bottom serves to highlight a
mysterious, legendary quality about her in the same way that many
figures in traditional narratives have some unexplained or missing
part of their lives. Sula's difference, like Shadrack's, must be labeled
so that the community can go on about its business. Since her neighbors have no words to explain Sula's personality, and no previous
encounters with anyone who could help them explain it, they label
her difference as witchery and thereby justify shunning her. They
can also soothe their ambivalent pride when she casts their husbands aside:

> Among the weighty evidence piling up was the fact that Sula
> did not look her age. She was near thirty and, unlike them, had lost
> no teeth, suffered no bruises, developed no ring of fat at the waist
> or pocket at the back of her neck. It was rumored that she had had
> no childhood diseases, was never known to have chicken pox,
> croup or even a runny nose. She had played rough as a child—
> where were the scars? Except for a funny-shaped finger and that
> evil birthmark, she was free of any normal signs of vulnerability.
> Some of the men, who as boys had dated her, remembered that on
> picnics neither gnats nor mosquitoes would settle on her. Patsy,
> Hannah's one-time friend, agreed and said not only that, but she
> had witnessed the fact that when Sula drank beer she never
> belched. (115)[13]

Imagination gives the community diversity from its own stupored
monotony; it comes together to make a monster out of difference in
the same way that various groups in *Song of Solomon* respond to
Pilate's lack of a navel. Sula's "don't give a damn" attitude makes
her an easy target for the tales, for she lacks an egotistical concern
for reputation. Not interested in fighting back, her very silence gives
truth to the rumors as far as the women are concerned. And indeed,
they do not really need justification for the tales they tell; rumor

exists for its own satisfaction. When Teapot falls down Sula's steps and fractures his skull, it is much more exciting to attribute the incident to witchery than to call it an accident. There is as much pleasure in telling the tales, perhaps more, than in looking into the truth of Sula's life.

The community also judges Sula to be in league with the devil because Shadrack is civil to her. When Dessie sees him tip his hat to Sula, she is convinced that she is witnessing a greeting between two of Satan's disciples. And woe to her that she does so, for a "big sty" (117) is her reward for seeing what she should not have seen. Sula becomes the measure of evil for the community, their catch-all explanation for natural and unnatural occurrences, their chance to triumph, day after day, over the devil in their midst. Sula's place among them is as secure in its deviance as Shadrack's is in its insanity.[14]

While the Bottom may work hard to prove that Sula is a witch, it already has one in its midst. Ajax's mother is reputed to be "an evil conjure woman" (126) who, when Ajax is gone, sits "in her shack with six younger sons working roots." Her knowledge of good and evil is real, whereas the evidence of the knowledge assigned to Sula is "contrived." Perhaps because of her commitment to her sons, and theirs to her, this woman has found a place in the community; Sula is too antithetical to everything they believe in for them to accept her as readily. Ajax's mother would be beautiful, Morrison asserts, if she had any teeth or ever straightened her back, thereby emphasizing that her deviance is not the thing that sets her apart from her feminine self, which is a contrast to Sula. Stephanie A. Demetrakopoulos works through the implications of the masculine/feminine contrast of the two women in her discussion of the novel.[15]

If Shadrack represents the outer realm of the community's obligation and focus, then the deweys represent its center. Shadowy though they may be at times, they are nevertheless firmly entrenched in Eva's house, which provides a center for the Bottom. From a folkloristic perspective, the deweys extend the concept of twins (exemplified in the novel by Sula and Nel) into triplets. As such, they have identical relationships to those around them and serve in identical capacities. It does not matter that Eva asks for *a* dewey to perform a chore, for they are all orphans, dependent, easily intimidated, and as strange as their personalities and Eva's house make them; they are "a trinity with a plural name . . . inseparable, loving nothing and no one but themselves" (38). Made comical by their antics and diminutive size, they remain children into their adult years. In their youth, they provided the comic relief to the mystery surrounding Eva, to the brooding Sula, and to the sexually active Hannah. They are also a part of the joking cycle in the novel, for they illustrate the almost comic perversity with which good intentions are sometimes pervaded. They are wild things in the Bottom, who, as a part of that tables-turned phenomenon, debunk the myth of maternal concern surrounding adoptions. Though Eva provides shelter and food for the deweys, she is about as much a mother to them as Teapot's Mamma is to him before his encounter with Sula.

The townspeople eventually notice that "the deweys would never grow. They had been forty-eight inches tall for years now" (84). Their size, combined with their acquisition of only the basic, functional command of language, gives their mental otherness a physical dimension. Yet they nevertheless figure more frequently as a concept than as separate entities in the novel; the lower-case references to them reinforce this idea. The question to ask, then, is "What is a dewey?" A dewey is a shadowy presence at 7 Carpenter's Road, hard to visualize but always concretely creating problems or running errands. A dewey is an individual who exists on the borderline between tolerable behavior and trying out for reform school. A dewey is contained lawlessness, just as a Shadrack is contained insanity. A dewey is rootless and uncommitted, existing from day to day with no knowledge of past or future. A dewey is an idea manifested in triplets whose very physical appearances defy that appellation. A dewey is the physical manifestation of Eva's power to control the environment around her.

Eva initiates the creation of the deweys as local characters, and Hannah and others perpetuate it when they force the teacher to admit all three youngsters—in spite of their differing ages—into the same grade. The denial of individual dewey reality gives way to one of Eva's pastimes: she creates the concept of the deweys for her own amusement. She names them and thereby determines their fate.[16] Community sanctioning of her joke makes it all the more appealing;

it gives Eva a goddess-like characteristic. In that folk-like community of the Bottom, where legends and superstitions abound, the path by which the deweys come to be local characters allows us to glimpse a clear-cut origin that has few counterparts in oral tradition.

In a less dramatic way, Eva also contributes to the community perception of Tar Baby, the white mountain drifter who finds his way into a small back room at 7 Carpenter's Road. As uprooted as Shadrack and the deweys, Tar Baby is another figure about whom tales can develop—Is he really white? Why does he drink? Why does he live in the Bottom rather than in Medallion? What drives him to sing "In the Sweet By-and-By" so pathetically? Eva directs the course of information about Tar Baby's ethnicity and makes a joke of it: "Most people said he was half white, but Eva said he was all white. That she knew blood when she saw it, and he didn't have none. When he first came to Medallion, the people called him Pretty Johnnie, but Eva looked at his milky skin and cornsilk hair and out of a mixture of fun and meanness called him Tar Baby" (39–40). He provides Eva with another source of amusement. In her confinement to her sprawling house, she brings a world of diversions to fill the space when she does not wish to create her own. Tar Baby and the deweys are perhaps grateful for having the shelter of Eva's home; they desire about as much as she is willing to provide, thereby making her relationship to all of them as informal and as vaguely committed as their otherness and her temperament warrant. She can laugh at them or control them, because she is ultimately disinterested in them; as a part of the landscape she has created in that huge house, they have as much or as little claim to belonging as any of the other inhabitants. Like a perverted artist out of a Hawthorne tale, Eva gives them a place in her home as well as a place in the lore of the Bottom; together, they increase Morrison's population of "grotesques," as Darwin T. Turner labels her characters.[17]

However, to label them grotesques is perhaps to miss a fundamental component of the historical black communities that might have inspired the creation of the Bottom. Such communities have a large capacity for containing those unlike themselves, especially if the issue in question concerns sanity. Morrison writes of Shadrack: "Once the people understood the boundaries and nature of his madness, they could fit him, so to speak, into the scheme of things" (15).

Shadrack and other characters might be conspicuously different from the norm, but there is a space for them within the larger community. If they do no more than provide a yardstick for measuring acceptable group behavior, they nevertheless serve a function. When the Bottom no longer has Sula to establish its limits of morality, there is a noticeable hole, a palpable emptiness in the community. There was a place for her there, even if that place was not in line with the majority of the community's norms.

What Eva does with the deweys and Tar Baby, together with how the community responds to Sula, enhances the notion that the Bottom is a consciously contrived black folk community in which the folk create and venerate their own traditions, much as the people do in Paule Marshall's mythical Bournehills and in Zora Neale Hurston's Eatonville.[18] Legends, superstitions (signs and beliefs), and rituals combine with the local characters to make *Sula* as akin to historic folk communities as any literary creation can be. In their observance of National Suicide Day, their most prominent ritual, the folks in the Bottom can be compared to contemporary communities observing rituals such as the Fourth of July or Groundhog Day, or to the Bournehillers' annual pageant to celebrate Cuffee Ned's rebellion. Cyclical, repetitive ceremonies provide these communities with a way of defining as well as explaining themselves.

The institutionalization of National Suicide Day is a measure of how thoroughly the community has absorbed Shadrack's strangeness as well as of how quietly that process of absorption takes place. The folks in the Bottom may not mark their wall calendars for the January third ritual, but they internalize the date and its events. Women mark labor and birth by that date as much as slaves in Alabama marked such occurrences by the year the stars fell. Even folks who choose to avoid doing things on National Suicide Day are nonetheless responding to its effect upon them. And the grandmother who maintains that "her hens always started a laying of double yolks right after Suicide Day" (16) contributes her share to the ritual by building a superstitious lore around it. Familiarity and repetition enable the inhabitants of the Bottom to contain National Suicide Day. Initially unable and later unwilling to deny it a place, they soon discover that what seemed horrible was more sounding brass and tinkling cymbal than destructive. Unfortunately, their effort to see National Suicide Day more as symbol than substance backfires on that day in 1941 when Shadrack leads his jubilant followers to a muddy death in the tunnel at the end of the New River Road.

Again Morrison executes a reversal by giving true meaning to an initially farfetched and hollow idea. The respect for death that made Shadrack so crazy after participating in the white man's big war is now paralleled by the "murder" of black people by the whites who commissioned and worked on the tunnel. Over a period of fourteen years, the whites have killed black hopes for working on the new road as well as on the tunnel. Some men have died and others have grown up and gone away while waiting for those hopes to be fulfilled. Their hopes have been as inconsiderable as those of the slave who desired good bottom land. It is perversely fitting, therefore, that National Suicide Day be given the tangible reality that silence and neglect have conferred on it for all those years, and it is equally perversely fitting that the song they sing, "Shall We Gather at the River," is one that has traditionally brought comfort to black people and the expectation that life after this world would be much better than that lived here. When the deweys, Tar Baby, and others die in the tunnel, their deaths denote the end of a particular kind of hope, the end of an era of belief that justice would be done through an unprompted, natural course. The tunnel catastrophe will provide tales for years to come about the "crazy" black folk of the Bottom who thought they could halt progress with their bodies. The story of their deaths will overshadow many of the tales that sustained these folk during their lifetime.

Just as it created local characters and instituted rituals, the Bottom also has its share of legends. Told for true, these stories take the shape of memorates, a first stage of legend formation in that the details of the narrative have not yet been fully fleshed out (and frequently the teller of the tale can claim to have been an eyewitness to the occurrence).[19] For example, people surmise various causes for the disappearance of Eva's leg, but a prominent, single-stranded, developed story has not been accepted over others. Still, the one detail believed to be true is generally agreed upon: Eva sacrificed her leg for the money that would ensure her family's survival. How that essential fact was brought about is where the accounts differ:

"Somebody said Eva stuck it under a train and made them pay off. Another said she sold it to a hospital for $10,000—at which Mr. Reed opened his eyes and asked, 'Nigger gal legs goin' for $10,000 a *piece*?' as though he could understand $10,000 a *pair*—but for *one*?" (31). Sula absorbs the tale about Eva's leg, and, as an adult, uses it to try to equalize the distance between Eva and herself. When Eva claims that nobody can talk to her with disrespect, Sula maintains:

> "This body does. Just 'cause you was bad enough to cut off your own leg you think you got a right to kick everybody with the stump."
> "Who said I cut off my leg?"
> "Well, you stuck it under a train to collect insurance." (92-93)

Sula turns perhaps the most significant occurrence in Eva's life against her by suggesting that the circumstances surrounding the loss of the leg place Eva in a category similar to Shadrack. The irony is that Eva has contributed to the growth of the lore about her missing leg. When she mentions it, usually "in some mood of fancy, she began some fearful story about it—generally to entertain children. How the leg got up by itself one day and walked on off. How she hobbled after it but it ran too fast. Or how she had a corn on her toe and it just grew and grew and grew until her whole foot was a corn and then it traveled on up her leg and wouldn't stop growing until she put a red rag at the top but by that time it was already at her knee" (30–31). An active tradition bearer in much of the lore of the Bottom, Eva is no less stinting with tales about herself.

By contrast, Sula's derisive recounting of the tales about Eva's missing leg shows how she breaks with tradition and perhaps even alters the lore in an effort to undercut her biological relationship to Eva. By negatively reinforcing the stories, Sula shows a disrespect not only for Eva but for the tradition itself. This small exchange illustrates well her severing of ties with the community. The lore is not entertaining for her; she uses it to control Eva's behavior and finally to threaten her. She redefines the function of folklore by telling her stories as a leveling device to gain power over Eva and to diminish her self-concept in the process. She therefore simultaneously devalues the vibrancy and purpose of the oral tradition while strengthening her reputation as a *ba-ad* woman.

Morrison's community has its superstitions and folk beliefs in addition to its folk characters. Traditionally, the natural world has been the logical place for people in folk communities to look for signs and meanings to be revealed to them. The unnatural and peculiar things that happen before Hannah's burning are a sign to Eva that some significant occurrence is about to take place. She cannot find her comb, which is out of its "natural" place; there is an unusually strong wind that does not bring the release of rain; and Hannah dreams of a wedding in which the bride wears a red dress, the color of which Eva will later interpret to mean that it portended Hannah's burning death. Her knowledge that dreams go by opposites strengthens her interpretation of the death; the wedding, a happy occasion, really portends some impending misfortune. The plague of birds before Sula's return to the Bottom is looked upon as a portent of evil, for, like Eva, the folks have learned, from their closeness to nature, to read its signs and prepare themselves for whatever is coming.

Signs and beliefs such as the wind without rain, the bride in the red dress, the plague of birds, and Eva burning the hair she combs from her head (so that enemies cannot get it and use it to direct spells toward her—91) might be realistic enough to have their counterparts in *The Frank C. Brown Collection of North Carolina Folklore*, or some other collection, in that there is a demonstrated present occurrence linked to some future disastrous possibility.[20] However, the responses to Sula's birthmark form another kind of belief in the novel, one for which few historical parallels exist. Many characters believe that Sula is evil; when they view the birthmark, they project onto it features reminiscent of those assigned to boogie men. To Nel's impressionable children, Sula's birthmark is a "scary black thing" (97–98); Jude views it as a copperhead (103) and as a rattlesnake (104) when he sees Sula as a potentially dangerous element introduced into his home; and the people in the Bottom view it as "Hannah's ashes" (114).[21] Such reactions contribute to making Sula into a legend in the community. The mark becomes as distinguishing as any of those, such as blue or red eyes, limps, or warts, that Newbell Niles Puckett identified in his discussions of distinctive features of conjurers.

Through her creation of characters like Eva, Sula, Shadrack, and the deweys, and the legends and tales surrounding them, Morrison shows that folklore can be used for purposes of enhancing characterization, advancing plot, and putting forth themes. Such functions have been recognized by folklore scholars Alan Dundes and Hennig Cohen in their early studies of folklore and literature.[22] Yet Morrison goes further in attempting to recreate the very atmosphere in which folk cultures, with all their layers and characters, blossom and grow. Like Ernest Gaines in many of his works,[23] she makes her characters and her community the substance of a pervasive aura of folk tradition, a saturation frequently recognized more by suggestion than specifics, but that succeeds very well in showing Morrison's ties to black folk culture.

How to Become a Legend in Your Own Time

In its logic that defies syllogistic equations and in its morality that approximates amorality, if not immorality, the world Morrison has created in *Sula* shares similarities, in its interpersonal relationships, to some of the realms inhabited by the likes of Brer Rabbit and other creatures who do not adhere to the fundamentalist teachings of Protestant churches. Brer Rabbit is independent in a world where community cooperation is the norm; he frequently acts against the wishes of the community or takes advantage of their work. For example, in the tale where he steals milk or butter from the other animals during a joint farming venture, he either denies his guilt or blames Brer Possum for the offense and personally leads the act of revenge against Brer Possum.[24] He is without compunction for shirking work as well as for leading the assault against Brer Possum. He does as he pleases, guided by what suits him rather than by any communally accepted ethical system.

The trinity of women who share the spotlight in *Sula*—Eva, Hannah, and Sula—have much in common with this world view. Their breaks from expected codes of behavior also enable them to transcend the usual depictions of black women in African-American literature, thereby debunking numerous stereotypes and myths. Eva is a slap in the face to all traditional matriarchs, for there is no God-centered morality informing her actions; yet she is paradoxically matriarchal in the power she wields as she sits "in a wagon on the third floor directing the lives of her children, friends, strays, and a constant stream of boarders" (30). Hannah defies expectations of matronly morality by randomly sleeping with her neighbors' husbands. She also defies expectations of how a mother should feel by asserting that she loves but does not *like* her daughter. Sula, though, is the epitome of independence; she throws the community's morality back in its face by redefining behavior. She, therefore, most closely approximates the world in which Brer Rabbit lives. In her disrespect for traditional mores, in her casual use of people around her, in her refusal to feel guilty for any of her actions, Sula exhibits the folk logic and the folk amorality of the trickster.

The peculiarly moral world view of African-Americans, especially as it relates to women, has perhaps prevented the appearance of many female trickster figures. Since women essentially held the group together during difficult periods of black history in America, to depict a female who stole, robbed, or killed would have had the effect of undermining the basic survival of the group. Instead, the focus was on male tricksters, and the violence associated with Brer Rabbit became the violence traditionally identified with the male world of competition and war. Still, a few female tricksters, such as Aunt Dicy, survived, and a few women clearly adopted the survival strategies of Brer Rabbit.[25] Black women historically could, if forced to, steal for their children—though their motives were certainly more altruistic than Brer Rabbit's; he sometimes used his children (or imaginary ones) as the excuse for amoral actions.[26] And we know that a few women did poison their masters and that a few killed their children to prevent them from becoming slaves. Many workers in white homes wore the mask of acquiescence to cover clandestine activities designed to aid their families, such as appropriating food and clothing.

In contemporary literature, three such characters are Ellie and Vi in Douglas Turner Ward's *Happy Ending* (1964), and Mrs. Grace Love in Ted Shine's *Contribution* (1969). These women resort to role-playing characteristic of the trickster in order to acquire food and clothing for their families and to bring about the deaths of some of their white employers. Both Ward and Shine show the breakdown of traditional morality, but their characters nonetheless adhere to a logical, more flexible standard of behavior. Morrison's women similarly refuse to be bound by traditional morality or traditional roles. In their new guises, then, they exhibit the freedom, the ability to make or create themselves, that is more closely associated with black folk culture than with historical black communities.

Eva certainly starts out as a traditional mother. She tries desperately to keep her family alive after her husband's departure, but her efforts very shortly become ineffectual. Her redefinition of role begins with her depositing her three children with a neighbor and not returning for eighteen months. She chooses self over sacrifice, borders on immorality, and therefore becomes free. Her separation from people in the community and acting against their norms enable her to develop an ironic posture in relation to them; she can live with them because she is now superior to them. Her freedom, somehow tied to the loss of her leg, gives her the ability to love, hate, create, conquer, and kill, with responsibility and accountability only to herself. She is free to be moral if she wishes, amoral if it pleases her, and immoral if necessary. Her transformation is like Cholly Breedlove's when he becomes free through killing three white men; he has stretched the bonds of humanity and can now accept or discard them at will.

The first test of Eva's newfound transcendence of human bonds comes when her husband BoyBoy visits the year after Eva returns. She watches his cool, big-city ways, and his shallow arrogance in bringing his lover with him, and consciously, deliberately decides to hate him: "Knowing that she would hate him long and well filled her with pleasant anticipation, like when you know you are going to fall in love with someone and you wait for the happy signs. Hating BoyBoy, she could get on with it, and have the safety, the thrill, the consistency of that hatred as long as she wanted or needed it to define and strengthen her or protect her from routine vulnerabilities" (36). Hatred keeps her "alive and happy" (37). In making hate into a positive and sustaining emotion and motivation, much as Claude McKay does in his poetry, Eva inverts notions of right and wrong, thereby standing morality on its head and identifying with the folkways that defy absoluteness in behavior.

Eva has no vengeful God watching over her, ready to cast down fire and brimstone in punishment for her deviation from a traditional path. Rather, she is on her way to becoming a goddess, one whose self-creation has been inspired in part by her hatred of BoyBoy. She therefore forces other men to worship where her husband has not—literally at her feet. Such domination—sometimes subtle and sometimes not—is again one of the traits of the rebel who has destroyed human bonds and reshaped them to suit her. Eva presents the many men who visit her over the years with a tantalizing morsel that they will never have the opportunity to savor. By encouraging their presence and flirting with them, Eva assures herself of the male attention that must unwaveringly atone for BoyBoy's desertion. She manifests her hatred and scorn of men in what they see as her attraction for them, her inability to live without their attention. Her attitude toward them is not unlike that of Erzulie, the Haitian goddess of love, who demands great sacrifices of her devotees.[27]

The provocative dynamic at work is that Eva uses the men while they believe they are bestowing their masculine attention upon her. Only a mind that has transcended mundane evaluations of the need for men in her life could effect the revenge Eva does. The freedom that has made hatred a virtue begins Eva's movement toward separation from other human bonds. Like Cross Damon in Richard Wright's *The Outsider* (1953), Eva can now assume the position of passing judgment upon others; in the process, she has put herself beyond similar judgment. In the ultimate elevation to goddess, however, she appropriates the power over life and death.

In deciding that her son Plum would be better off dead, Eva recognizes no authority, no morality except herself. Plum's drug addiction offends her sense of what a man should be, especially someone she had forced to keep on living when he was a baby and for whom she had probably sacrificed her leg. To see such sacrifices thrown back into her face negates the very existence Eva has carved out for herself. In the mixture of love and revulsion surrounding her burning of Plum, Eva egotistically eliminates what offends her. No matter the motivation, her killing of Plum is just as self-centered as those murders committed by Cross Damon. Eva becomes the vengeful goddess in destroying a creature who has failed to worship in an appropriate manner at her altar. Like Satan in Mark Twain's "The Mysterious Stranger," she "blots out" what would defile her existence.[28] If Plum were to live a healthy and drug-free life, Eva believes that would be a small price to pay in compensation for her loss of a leg and a husband, and for having suffered other indignities during those unmentionable eighteen months.

Plum's death is a blood sacrifice—whether that ritualized conception is clear in Eva's mind or not. She never considers rehabilitation for her son; the effrontery of his misuse of his life is sufficient for her to take it. She rewards those who serve her well; she casts aside those who do not. That is the distinction between her murder of Plum and her risking of her own life to save Hannah's. Hannah, Eva's oldest child, has served her mother well; after her husband's death, she had moved back into Eva's house "prepared to take care of it and her mother forever" (41). She has also accepted the "manlove" bequeathed to her and has carried out, vicariously, the sexual activity to which Eva may allude but from which she has been restrained by infirmity and inclination. Thus shaped in the image of the goddess and responsive to her wishes, Hannah earns Eva's greatest sacrifice.

Also, in killing Plum and trying to save Hannah, Eva exhibits a preference for the woman-centered consciousness that pervades most of the novel. Perhaps Plum, in his addiction, is too sharp a reminder of the ineffectuality of BoyBoy as husband and father. Perhaps Eva sees history about to repeat itself in him. Her contemplation of "no-count" males, then, is further motivation for Eva to end a seemingly useless life. With deliberation, she murders Plum, but her attempt to save Hannah is instinctive, borne of an intuitive identification with her daughter. Since Sula has already established her tendency to otherness, Eva perhaps senses that Hannah is the last opportunity for her to perpetuate something in her own image—or at least some portions of it. She also sees that, through Hannah, more of the vengeance against men is carried out. In her sexual freedom, Hannah parallels Eva in being independent of the community's mores, in finding no code of behavior except that inspired by her own desires.

In any world but the one Morrison has created, Hannah Peace would be considered a slut. However, Morrison does not allow such a moral judgment in the novel. Hannah becomes an acceptable embodiment of a pleasure principle; the women may be "exasperated" with her because she "seemed too unlike them, having no passion attached to her relationships and being wholly incapable of jealousy" (44), but even the whores who resent her "generosity" and the church women who call her "nasty" are not inclined to believe that she is evil. Her reputation for kindness and altruism counterbalances the brief affairs she has with the husbands of her friends and neighbors. Although she has few women friends, she does not appear to be lonely or isolated. She has a secure place in the community in spite of the prevailing disapproval.

Hannah, like Eva, lives by her own set of rules. She does not equate promiscuity with immorality; it is simply a matter of getting "some touching every day" (44), which she had determined to do after her husband's death. Still, no matter the aura of earthiness surrounding Hannah's actions, they are nonetheless antithetical to the tenets of her community. Her sexual independence makes her a disruptive force in a quiet place like the Bottom, where everybody's business is everybody's business. Hannah's disregard of expected codes of behavior makes her a rebel, albeit a tolerable one. In seeking to satisfy only herself, her desire is not far removed in kind from the likes of those trickster figures for whom sexual superiority (if not the act itself) was one of the primary motivating forces; Brer Rabbit's amoral exploits frequently involve winning the hand of a female, and he can be unscrupulous in achieving his goals. Hannah's casual attitude may be sweeter, but it certainly achieves a similar satisfaction for her.

Hannah weakens the structure of the community's morality, but she does not completely topple it. That is evident in the way the women whose husbands she has slept with take care of her body after she is burned to death: "the women who washed the body and dressed it for death wept for her burned hair and wrinkled breasts as though they themselves had been her lovers" (77). Perhaps they are awed in the face of death, but perhaps, too, they unconsciously respect the rebel in Hannah; she has done what their ties to church and community strictures would not allow them to do. She may have thrown their morality in their faces, but she is simultaneously one of them and more than they are; she has become a legend. In taking their men, Hannah had formed an unacknowledged bond with these women in which they showed their appreciation for the same things, slightly comparable to the way in which Sula and Nel share and compare boys when they are teenagers. Hannah's attention to their men, since she is the embodiment of WOMAN, is a way of "complimenting the women" (115) on their good taste. Her deviation from the norm, therefore, no matter how immoral, is still not as personally insulting to the women as are Sula's actions.

Sula begins her separation from the community and follows a different set of rules with the death of Chicken Little. Certainly she feels remorse for the accidental drowning of Chicken, but in her refusal to confess or ask for forgiveness from any source (even herself), the incident becomes a measure of how far an individual can live outside the dictates of a community's morality and still be "safe." Confession and acceptance of responsibility for the death would at least have been recognition of values, of a morality outside of herself, recognition that an individual has voluntary ties to the community in which she lives and must respond to those ties whether or not someone demands that she do so. The absence of "punishment" for Chicken's death signals to Sula that she can do what she wants. Life, death, responsibility, the limits of behavior— all are contained in Chicken Little's death. Once Sula ignores them and moves into a realm of her own unrestrained seeking and exploration, she is forever outside the world view of the Bottom.

When she returns after her sojourn, therefore, it is because she has exhausted the possibility for freshness of experience; she may as well be back in the Bottom if human beings she encounters elsewhere do not deviate substantially from those she has left. She returns content to continue, among the native population, whatever explorations are left. Her indifference and irresponsibility encourage the neighbors to believe that she is a witch. She is so unlike the women in her community—so young where they have aged, so thin where they are large, so complete unto herself where they need husbands and children—that they link her to extranatural forces and can never envision her sleeping with their husbands as a compliment to themselves. Instead, they view her as a sexual experimenter, someone who is picking through the men in the town the way a shopper selects tomatoes. She touches and discards each of them because none measures up to whatever undefined standard she uses for judgment.

In her indifferent and experimental behavior, there is more vengeance in Sula than in Hannah, a vengeance all the more cruel because it does not consciously identify itself as such. Sula does not respect the men enough, is not interested enough in them, to give conscious direction to her vengeance. Its very effectiveness is in its static quality, which serves to deny the manhood and nearly the humanity of the men with whom she sleeps, and it certainly denies any ties she has to the community. More so than Eva, she is the love goddess who perverts that name, who can never find a worthy mate among the puny pickings available to her. In a world in which people are tied to each other as often by their lacks (needing to borrow an egg or a cup of sugar) as by their bountifulness (giving a neighbor a mess of greens or corn), Sula's wholeness amounts to her telling the community to go to hell.

Of the three Peace women, Sula is more clearly immoral, because she sees herself as the center of the universe around which other people can revolve or not—as she needs or uses them. Eva's actions had at least been motivated by love for her children and hatred for her husband, and Hannah fulfilled a physical need in sleeping with so many men. Sula simply is—whatever she decides is convenient or desirable or pleasurable. None of her motivations comes from caring about or hating or fearing anyone. She is simply in the community; what it does or how it responds to her is of no consequence to her. The only reactions she has concerning other people are her slight remorse that Nel has responded so unexpectedly to her sleeping with Jude and feeling that she has become possessive enough of Ajax to drive him away.

If she were separated geographically from the community, as M'Dear is in *The Bluest Eye*, or like Shadrack is, Sula's difference might be more tolerable, but her placement in the center of the community, in Eva's house, makes her conspicuously a little world revolving unto itself. Still, Sula is consistent in living by the philosophy she has evolved for herself; when she becomes ill, she does not turn for assistance to the people she has ignored all along. Instead, she suffers alone. It is only upon Nel's visit that she requests medicine, and she does so with pride, not with the humility of an outsider. What Nel judges to be arrogance even in the face of death is really the logical carrying out of the philosophy Sula has adhered to all along. She has not whined or complained loudly about life, and she refuses to complain about death or the manner in which she is dying. It is all a part of the experiment that has been accountable only to itself, not to anyone or anything beyond her.[29] That spirit, basically antithetical to the tenets of the community and to most human relationships, is what ultimately serves to make Sula a pariah. The greatest measure of her lack of status is the way people respond to her death. They do not come running to wash the body or lay it out; instead, they leave the work to the white people. We need only think of the loving way in which Aunt Jimmy is laid out in *The Bluest Eye* to understand the importance of funeral rituals and mourning to these communities. When the neighbors gather to sing at Sula's funeral, it is not out of respect for her but the continuation of a tradition much larger than their momentary rejection of Sula, for they are determined not to let anything "keep them from their God" (150).

In a world in which logic is sometimes familiar and sometimes not, that which guides the actions of the Peace women and the community's response to them is similarly ambivalent, if not contradictory. In a world in which whim matters as much as premeditation, confusion results. Ultimately, we may understand and be engaged by all of the Peace women, but they are finally unacceptable except as reflections of a community that is dying. Sula carries no values that would sustain a society; Hannah would chip away at any established values; and Eva is too harsh, if not warped, in her judgments to create any but a very narrow world. While we may withhold judgment of their individual trespasses, the accumulations of their world views reflect the license-free, sometimes destructive, interactions characteristic of African-American folk culture, not their realistic counterparts for behavior.

Of Purification and Exorcism:
The Limited Powers of Fire and Water

In almost every one of the years Morrison pauses upon in *Sula*, a death occurs. The end of life becomes awesome because few of the deaths are due to natural causes or reflect a graceful demise; all of them are violent. They are also tied to fire or water, traditional symbols of purification, which become destructive when used to excess. Continuing the pattern of reversal that defines the structure of the novel, Morrison depicts deaths that negate the traditional rites associated with fire and water. Excess becomes the norm—characters are baptized into death rather than life, into stagnation rather than activity.

The fire that Eva sets to kill Plum succeeds in destroying him, but it also becomes a blot upon her soul. Plum may be removed from his misery, but his death has not brought a purification for the Peace household. The burning negates Eva's willingness to endure her son's suffering, and, from Hannah's point of view, it negates motherly affection. It creates a gap in family ties that culminates in Hannah questioning Eva about the death and in Sula accusing Eva of murder and threatening to eliminate her in the same manner. If Eva's crying explanation to Hannah can be believed (71–72), it is clear that the burning has not served as the cleansing release she desired. Rather, it has left her with an unmelting lump of grief, undissolvable and unconfessable to any comforter outside of family members.

As the sacrificial ritual plays itself out, Plum is as willing to die as Eva is to kill him. To his addict-blurred vision, Eva seems to be bestowing a blessing upon him: "He opened his eyes and saw what he imagined was the great wing of an eagle pouring a wet lightness over him. Some kind of baptism, some kind of blessing, he thought. Everything is going to be all right, it said. Knowing that it was so he closed his eyes and sank back into the bright hole of sleep" (47). The kerosene dousing amounts to the giving of last rites before Eva lights the torch in a ritual designed to erase all traces of her son. She could just as easily have killed him with a knife, or with poison, or with an overdose of the heroin he uses. Instead, she chooses fire, with its potential for total obliteration of Plum and his drug paraphernalia. An ancient ceremony for eliminating evil or the diseased from the midst of society, Eva's use of it backfires because Plum's death only makes memory vivid. She cannot destroy what she carries in her mind without destroying herself.

The second death by fire, Hannah's burning, is also a reversal of the expected release that weather and circumstances have portended. The strange events that Eva notices prior to Hannah's burning include a roof-rattling wind: "people waited up half the night for the first crack of lightning. Some had even uncovered barrels to catch the rain water, which they loved to drink and cook in. They waited in vain, for no lightning no thunder no rain came. The wind just swept through, took what dampness there was out of the air, messed up the yards, and went on" (73). The expected rain turns into the fire of Hannah's burning, not the release of cooling water. Formerly consumed by passion, Hannah ironically turns into a self-contained inferno, fueled by the breeze she creates in trying to escape herself.

Eva's inability to save her daughter leads to another reversal—not the diminution of grief over time, but a sharpened focus upon it. The man who saves Eva's life boasts of "an indisputable fact which she herself admitted and for which she cursed him every day for thirty-seven years thereafter and would have cursed him for the rest of her life except by then she was already ninety years old and forgot things" (77). There is no cleansing, no purification here; even the body of the lovely Hannah Peace is changed into a blistery, bubbly thing in respect of which the coffin remains closed at the funeral.

The death by fire also separates Eva and Sula across a chasm that can never be bridged. While Eva fought so desperately to save Hannah, she remembers seeing Sula watch her mother burn, "not because she was paralyzed," as the neighbors tried to explain, "but because she was interested" (78). Hannah's death burns away whatever bonds of kinship Eva and Sula have, except biologically.

Water, traditional symbol of life, is also frequently associated with death in *Sula*. It brings death and baptism into secrecy about Chicken Little's death, and it brings death to the people who make Shadrack's National Suicide Day a reality. These tunnel deaths mirror the death of the townspeople's dream that the Bottom will ever be connected to Medallion in an economically beneficial way. Their dreams of steady jobs go down under the rush of water that takes so many of their lives.

On the occasion that Chicken Little drowns, the peacefulness of the water belies its destructive capabilities—it opens up and quietly closes "over the place where Chicken Little sank" (61). The quiet here certainly contrasts sharply with the rotting, deteriorating corpse of Chicken Little brought home a few days later, but it manifests itself in a tangible way in Sula's and Nel's minds. Repeatedly, the smoothness of the water into which Chicken Little sank is referred to as a "place," as if there is actually a marker there: 61, "she stood looking at the closed place in the water"; 62, "the dark closed place in the water"; 101, "the closed place in the water spread before them"; 118, "on the bank of a river with a closed place in the middle"; 141, "the closed place in the water"; 170, "water closing quickly over the place." But the marker is something that Nel and Sula carry with them in their common guilt, their common enjoyment, of what has happened to Chicken Little.

Chicken becomes a sacrifice to Sula and Nel's friendship, for there has been an accidental/intentional aura surrounding the drowning. On that day, Sula and Nel had been experiencing growing pains and were "looking for mischief" (56). An "unspeakable restlessness and agitation held them" (59) before Chicken arrived at their play site by the river, and they had both joined in mimicking him when he asserted that he would share his tree-climbing venture with his "brovver." Initially separated at Chicken's funeral, the girls then form an inseparable bond, one tied to Chicken's death: "They held hands and knew that only the coffin would lie in the earth; the bubbly laughter and the press of fingers in the palm would stay aboveground forever" (66). They will be reminded of Chicken's enjoyment of Sula's swinging him as well as the responsibility that both she and Nel have for his death. The signal that they will be bonded in secrecy surfaces quickly as they walk home from the funeral; "they relaxed slowly until during the walk back home their fingers were laced in as gentle a clasp as that of any two young girlfriends trotting up the road on a summer day wondering what happened to butterflies in the winter" (66).

The image of secrecy, grief, and sharing is realized as muddy leaves that crystallize for Nel in the little ball of fur after Jude's infidelity with Sula. Rather than a baptism or purification, the water reminds Nel and Sula of their playful killing of Chicken Little. Water that should cleanse and purify instead leads to a clogging of human emotions, a beaver's dam on the souls of the two girls. That initial blockage for Sula takes the form of not caring enough about people to be truly interested in them, an emotional constipation and superficial existence comparable to that of Avey Johnson in Paule Marshall's *Praisesong for the Widow* (1983). For Nel, the blockage is the bond she shares with Sula, which suggests that they will always be faithful to each other because of their secret; it represents a place held sacred for the entrance of only one other. When Sula sleeps with Jude, then, and breaks that bond, thereby creating a disrespect for the secret, the water imagery returns to haunt Nel in the form of muddy leaves trying to stir, which in turn are transformed into the gray ball initially described in similar muddy images: "A gray ball hovering just there. Just there. To the right. Quiet, gray, dirty. A ball of muddy strings, but without weight, fluffy but terrible in its malevolence" (109).

The gray ball follows her for more than twenty years before she realizes that her love for Sula, what they have shared together (especially the killing of Chicken Little), takes precedence over the emotional blockage separating them. With realization comes release and the combining of the two images: "Leaves stirred; mud shifted; there was the smell of overripe green things. A soft ball of fur broke and scattered like dandelion spores in the breeze" (174). It gives way to crying that has "circles and circles of sorrow" that evoke, in their concentric image, the place in the water where Chicken Little has drowned. Chicken Little and Jude are what both women have shared, one in the greenness of their girlhood ("overripe green things") and the other in their adulthood. Only Sula was able to realize that the basic tenet of sharing had not changed; if they could keep a secret as dark as Chicken Little's death and survive, then they should be able to survive the presumed infidelity with Jude. When Nel understands the connection, the blockage can be released—just as Avey Johnson's bowels and bladder give way on the boat to Carriacou—and the cleansing, the purification identified with water and baptism, can be effected. Assuredly, Nel is baptized into grief, but it is a grief that portends a conclusion, not one that will persist in stagnation for another twenty-five years. What began in Chicken Little's death by water eventually leads to Nel's rebirth through cleansing tears, a rebirth that at least brings an understanding of her life and of her best love.

The other deaths by water in the book are surrounded by irony, lost hope, and lost dreams. It is ironic in 1941 that Shadrack is able to get the citizens of the Bottom to follow him in his National Suicide

Day ritual; never before had they been so playful or so tolerant of his obeisance to death. In following him to a wet, smothering grave, they simultaneously give meaning to his ritual and signal the death of their community. The water symbolic of life takes nearly thirty people to a denial of rebirth and regeneration except in an afterlife. Ironically, they who had intended to kill the tunnel that represented so many false promises to the town are themselves killed. Their suicide/death carries the ambivalence characteristic of this elemental force that can be beneficial if controlled or deadly in excess.

It is ironic, too, that the folks who have believed so fervently in God have one of the most potent symbols of their religion turned against them. "Shall We Gather at the River" is indicative of the assumption that they will one day reach and cross the chilly Jordan. It is the song sung at Sula's funeral in an act that is simultaneously ironic and affirming. No one believes that Sula will cross the Jordan, but they appropriately sing a song fundamental to their religion at a funeral characteristic of their beliefs. Sula gets the benefit of something in which she does not believe, and the townspeople are self-righteously able to congratulate themselves for being generous even to one of the devil's disciples.

Ironically, though, it is not the chilly Jordan at which the righteous gather; it is the chilly construction site of a tunnel of unfulfilled promises, and it is a river of their own making. The river is not symbolic of having lived and worked faithfully in God's vineyard, but of the frustration that has attended their lives in this world. The tunnel represents the "leaf-dead" promises of jobs that have been made to them and ignored, which have resulted in "the teeth unrepaired, the coal credit cut off, the chest pains unattended, the school shoes unbought, the rush-stuffed mattresses, the broken toilets, the leaning porches, the slurred remarks and the staggering childish malevolence of their employers. All there in blazing sunlit ice rapidly becoming water" (161). In their effort to kill the tunnel already being overtaken by water, the people of the Bottom create the catastrophe that leaves a huge number of them dead. Their deaths by water bring the end to Shadrack's compartmentalization of death and make destructively immediate and irrevocable a symbolism to which they have adhered.

4

Song of Solomon

Milkman Dead: An Anti-Classical Hero

Many scholars approaching Toni Morrison's *Song of Solomon* (New York: Knopf, 1977) have tried to explain the novel in traditional mythological terms. They place Milkman's birth in the company of those of Moses, King Arthur, Achilles, Prometheus, and other legendary figures treated by Lord Raglan in *The Hero* and by Joseph Campbell in *The Hero With A Thousand Faces*.[1] When parallels to these leave off, they turn to heroic patterns derived from classical Greek and Roman mythology in an effort to identify and incorporate the various allusions Morrison draws upon in the novel.[2]

These approaches lead to focusing upon the dangerous circumstances surrounding Milkman's conception and birth as explanations for his difference. There is magic in Pilate giving Ruth a potion to administer in Macon Dead's food in order to ensure Milkman's conception, and there is the added trauma of Macon trying to force an abortion once he learns that his four-day renewed sexual attraction for his wife has led to her pregnancy. To minimize the danger, Pilate, the witchlike godmother, watches over Milkman's advent into the world with all the care of one of the wise men anticipating the birth of Christ.

The mythical connections continue in Milkman's adult life in the quest he undertakes in search of gold. Comparable to Jason's search for the silver fleece, or to Odysseus's journey home, Milkman's travels eventually lead to his salvation as well. Helpers and hinderers on that journey are also comparable to those peopling the myths of the world. The classical Circe immediately comes to mind in the episode where Milkman meets a woman with the same name, a strange being in an unkempt house full of dogs. And who can fail to think of Icarus throughout the book as Morrison focuses upon Milkman's desire to fly?

Other critical mythology-seekers concentrate on smaller connections in the novel, such as the ghost of Pilate's father and rituals of scapegoating, which indicate Morrison's familiarity with a variety of cultural myths. Such symbol mongers seek in vain for some pattern that will explain the whole of the novel, but they are left with the bits and pieces of the myths and mythological characters Morrison has alluded to in her work. They quickly discover puzzling loose ends. The Icarus myth might be relevant, but that is not what the novel is ultimately about, and it does not serve to account wholly for Milkman's actions. Milkman may be in search of something, but he also carries "something" within himself that he must uncover as he makes his geographical and psychological journey. The pieces of those familiar patterns, therefore, in the final analysis do not add up to a wholeness of approach to the novel. They leave the myth hunters pleased with their recognition of the various myths, but dissatisfied that such myths do not bring them to a single, complete understanding of the novel—not to mention the various multiple strands of understanding.

The problem with such approaches is the refusal by critics to see the classical allusions as additional layers that enhance but are not designed to explain the novel. Morrison recognizes that the use of such stories to explain African-American culture would amount to a grossly ineffective superimposition of an alien world view on a culture that she has consistently shown to be resistant to such externally imposed concepts. Trying to explain Milkman Dead solely in terms of Greek myth is just as erroneous as trying to explain the Breedlove family in *The Bluest Eye* in terms of the tale of Dick and Jane.[3]

There is undoubtedly mythology in *Song of Solomon*, but it does not derive solely from outside the black community. Morrison herself has said of "the flying myth" in *Song of Solomon*: "If it means Icarus to some readers, fine; I want to take credit for that. But my meaning is specific: it is about black people who could fly. That was always part of the folklore of my life; flying was one of our gifts. I don't care how silly it may seem. It is everywhere—people used to talk about it, it's in the spirituals and gospels."[4] Those who insist exclusively upon traditional mythological approaches to the novel, therefore, fail to realize that the African-American world view will not align itself wholly with Greek myth.

The Greek and Roman world views are ones in which the dichotomies between good and evil are usually fairly clearly delineated—Odysseus is good; the Sirens are bad. Jason finally merits our approval; Medusa is expendable. The fickleness in that world belongs more to the gods than to the characters on earth who are acting out or against the wishes of the gods. Characters who earn our sympathy do so in unambiguous ways. We never stop to think that the Harpies may have some legitimate complaints, or that Circe may have her reasons for turning men into swine. We are asked simply to see the world in an either/or relationship to the events, issues, and characters presented.

Such an approach to *Song of Solomon* is impossible. A complex world, the one Morrison has created draws upon a dualism as old as African-American existence in the New World. That world view presupposes an intertwining of the secular and sacred realms of existence. Individuals who worked all week and went to root doctors on Saturday could just as easily shout in ecstasy through calling upon the name of the Lord on Sunday. Such a history sets the stage for a dualistic world view, but it does not inform exactly the world Morrison has created. Few characters in Morrison's novels are religious; in fact, those like Soaphead Church in *The Bluest Eye* are parodies of religious fervor, and Pauline Breedlove, though she clings to the church, worships a god more of her own creation than one reflecting an absolute morality beyond herself. Eva Peace and her daughters loved men, not God; indeed, Eva sets herself up as a goddess. Only Ruth in *Song of Solomon* practices conventional religion; then, she perverts the very notion of Christianity by worshipping her dead father.[5]

Morality, then, or any code of ethics based on how other human beings should be treated in *Song of Solomon*, does not grow from roots of Christianity. Yet we can conclude that certain actions are right and others wrong. The dualism develops when Morrison continues to blur the line between one person's right and another person's wrong. She refuses to allow us to be comfortable in our conclusions because the evidence for such evaluations keeps shifting. The circumstances surrounding the death of Ruth Foster Dead's father are a prime example of this. Did she caress his corpse, as Macon Dead claims? Did Macon kill her father, as Ruth claims? Who is right or wrong? Both and neither. When we consequently try to fit the actions of Milkman Dead into a pattern, we arrive at the same ambiguous conclusions. Should all of his former trespasses be forgiven just because he learns to fly? Was he right in emotionally abusing and neglecting Hagar? Wrong in telling Macon about Corinthians's affair with Porter? As Joseph T. Skerrett, Jr., has pointed out, stories of various kinds are key to the structuring of the novel, and the presentation of everybody's versions of events about themselves and others—frequently contradictory—reflects the essence of the African-American storytelling tradition.[6]

Morrison ultimately intends Milkman as a heroic figure whose heroism can only be defined through dualistic, sometimes ambiguous actions, and whose qualifications for heroism do not depend upon his goodness. As folklorist John W. Roberts has illustrated clearly, definitions for heroism vary with cultures and with circumstances within cultures: "figures (both real and mythic) and actions dubbed heroic in one context or by one group of people may be viewed as ordinary or even criminal in another context or by other groups, or even by the same ones at different times."[7] Milkman's deviation from classical western perceptions of heroism, therefore, do not in themselves preclude his eventual elevation to that status. Milkman's childhood is not shadowed in a mood of anticipation that he will perform some great act for the community, as is Jimmy's in Ernest Gaines's *The Autobiography of Miss Jane Pittman*.[8] Milkman is not chosen; rather, he is roused from his inconsequential state only as long as it takes Ruth to satisfy her desperate mothering urges. During his early years, Milkman does not do or think; he simply *is*— frequently a shadowy figure, sometimes an embarrassment, but never of any real consequence to anyone in his family.

His lack of development under any clear-cut moral strictures begins his erratic bouts with traditional notions of right and wrong. He sees his father disrespect his mother and dispossess tenants, and

Macon early teaches him that material values are preferable to spiritual ones; certainly no dictum such as "love thy neighbor as thyself" guides his actions toward strangers or family. As a teenager, therefore, it is easy for Milkman to disobey Macon and go to Pilate's house because that environment represents a new thrill for him. He can also sense his future value to Macon and thereby gauge the limits to which he can take disobedience. He can dismiss his sisters as inconsequential, dead replicas of his mother, and he can dismiss his mother as a mere shadow of a woman. However, he may use his difference from the women, his maleness, to direct his straying from the straight and narrow path Macon sets down to govern his actions toward Pilate.

Milkman's underdeveloped moral sense also accounts in part for his unkind treatment of Hagar. His rent collecting for Macon has instilled more of a sense of power than one of responsibility toward other human beings. Hagar, just another thrilling convenience, can be dismissed with impunity when Milkman tires of her. Yet it is Milkman's rather than Hagar's perspective that Morrison follows through most of the relationship. She forces us to wait and wait through it, to consider Hagar expendable even if we do not consider Milkman innocent. She urges us to accept the *possibility* that something great is in the making and to tolerate Milkman's destructiveness until he, like Velma Henry in Toni Cade Bambara's *The Salt Eaters* (1980), discovers his mission on earth.

A spoiled brat, Milkman becomes a trial to our sympathies during this waiting process. Why doesn't this thirty-year-old man hurry up and find himself, we ask, and quit being so inexcusably and repulsively childish? Uneasiness notwithstanding, we do sense that Milkman has a special relationship to Pilate, and that is the direction from which the measure of tolerance we feel for him comes. If Milkman can be saved from his spiritual inertia and his human detachment, then Pilate is the course through whom that saving must come.

A helper in the tradition of those recognized by Vladimir Propp in his *Morphology of the Folktale*, Pilate becomes a surrogate mother for Milkman—for he barely has a relationship with Ruth—and she also becomes his spiritual guide into a world where commitment replaces detachment and where materialistic pursuits are dwarfed by inner fulfillment.[9] The dualism in Milkman's life, then, can be measured by his interaction with members of his family as well as by his relationship to Guitar and the Seven Days.

For Milkman, the murderous activities of the Seven Days mean little in comparison to his own seeking after thrills. The eye-for-an-eye rationale for the murders of white people in retaliation for the deaths of blacks is inconsequential to Milkman. We condemn the murders precisely because of the rationale, for it leads to the kind of predicament Bigger Thomas finds himself in with the murder of Bessie Mears: murder of the oppressor eventually leads to murder of the oppressed. Because Milkman has no political consciousness, he does not care that Guitar's actions are psychologically warping—until he becomes the prey in Guitar's predatory hunt. Before this, he neither applauds nor condemns Guitar; the activities of the group are simply not incorporable into his life-style or into his limited moral vision. He is content to exist with any ugliness in the world as long as it does not directly injure him—even when he has had a hand in creating the ugliness, as with Hagar.

Actions contrary to those expected in the traditional hero are apparent in Milkman's conspiring, with Guitar, to steal from Pilate's house what they believe is a bag of gold. The robbery is a violation comparable to rape. Pilate, Reba, and Hagar have welcomed Milkman into their home. They have fed him and given him spiritual sustenance, and Hagar has welcomed him into her bed. Without compunction, Milkman robs them of what he believes is their most valuable possession. Traditional heroes who steal, such as Jack and Prometheus, do so for altruistic purposes—to save a starving family, to find the way home, to rescue a captured princess, to aid humanity in general. A larger moral purpose guides their small infractions of morality. Milkman has no redeeming purpose or qualities during this incident; it is only our hope that he may one day be redeemed that saves him from utter dismissal.

Warped values, inadequate character formation, and self-centeredness all define Milkman's incomplete vision of the world. He treats Pilate's house, which we have come to view as tranquil, invigorating, almost sacred, as a lair of monsters through whom he must negotiate safe passage with his stolen gold. While it may be viewed as a prank, the robbery nonetheless has the overtones of greed and self-aggrandizement that have characterized Milkman in relation to Macon. Instead of condemning or excusing the action at this point, we are encouraged to wait for whatever outcome Morrison has in store for Milkman and for us. That response is taught in part from our experiences with Morrison's earlier novels, but also from the shades of gray that permeate this novel.

And why does Morrison ask us to withhold judgment on Milkman for so long? The answer lies in part in the paradoxical elements of his nickname. The name suggests dependence and immaturity that will eventually lead to strength. It suggests nurturing by the women in his life, and it anticipates the time he will move beyond the need for that nurturing; the dualism in the name is symbolic of the dualistic world view in the novel.[10] Nurtured initially by Ruth, his biological mother, Milkman is nursed far beyond the time during which suckling is appropriate. Seeking through this act to become almost an extranatural influence upon Milkman in order to alleviate her dissatisfaction with her own life, Ruth instead delays Milkman's maturity and leaves him in a state of underdevelopment that she does not have the skills to rectify. Milkman thus hangs in limbo until Pilate enters his life to take over the nurturing function as the true extranatural mother. Ruth is too bound by her father's memory and Macon's oppression to develop the imagination or acquire the freedom that Pilate has. It is this *new* mother, who spiritually attended at Milkman's birth, who must guide him beyond the peacock plumage of materialism that binds him to earth and teach him how to fly.[11]

Ruth and Pilate are contrasting nurturers who reflect the dualistic world view in the novel. Ruth represents the sacred part of the traditional secular/sacred dichotomy in African-American cosmology. She respects tradition, is understandably conventional, and worships at the altar of her father's memory. While these things may be of an un-Christian, untraditional religious nature, in the *forms* they take, they nevertheless tie Ruth to rules carefully observed in religious environments. Such connections show strictures almost as tangible as the house in which the Dead family is trapped, and they ensure that Milkman can never achieve his potential as long as he is in the environment where his mother can influence him. Ruth's brand of obsession, no matter its origins or extenuating circumstances, can only mean closure and heaviness for Milkman, not free-

dom and flight. Unable, however, to push Milkman beyond her influence willingly, Ruth can only watch as he discovers Pilate's
world. She has no ultimate redress against her role being usurped by
Pilate, the surrogate mother, for Milkman must escape the Dead
house, must go into that world, if he is to grow.

Pilate represents the secular side of the traditional dichotomy—
nonconformity, freedom to explore, ties to history that transcend
written records, and the extranatural quality that Ruth's limited
imagination can barely glimpse. Her lack of a navel symbolizes her
extranatural mothering role, as well as the mythical connotations of
an individual who, as Morrison has observed, had to "literally in-
vent herself."[12] Such a distinguishing feature, along with her height,
ties her to M'Dear in *The Bluest Eye* and to Sula in suggesting that
she has more than human power. And indeed others view Pilate as
having the traits of voodoo doctors and conjurers: "Pilate, who
never bothered anybody, was helpful to everybody, but who also
was believed to have the power to step out of her skin, set a bush
afire from fifty yards, and turn a man into a ripe rutabaga—all on
account of the fact that she had no navel" (94). Milkman and Guitar
heighten this perception of her extranatural qualities by being
"spellbound" by the stories she tells (36). Unlike most people, she is
not afraid of death, and she carries on conversations with her "men-
tor," her dead father (147, 151). This breaking down of planes of
existence anticipates *Beloved*, where the living not only talk to the
dead, but the dead dwell with the living.[13] Pilate is also a "natural
healer" (150), perhaps through her receptivity and sensitivity to the
physical world around her. Though her absent navel leads people to
designate her "mermaid" or "witch," she is incapable of holding
malice against anyone.[14] She has a special "way of being in the
world," one that highlights her ability to make contact beyond this
world. Her flat stomach becomes the metaphor for her "otherness,"
as Sula's birthmark and Pecola's ugliness have been in Morrison's
earlier novels, though certainly Pilate's persecution is not as consistently dramatized as theirs.

Absence of that physical bond between mother and child in this
world makes Pilate the only appropriate guide and nurturer for
Milkman to extranatural perception. We must recognize, then, that
Milkman's period of confusion, during which so many of his tradi-

tionally immoral actions occur, is linked to the time in his life when he is essentially "motherless," before he accepts enough of Pilate's influence to arrive at his long-delayed manhood. The period of Pilate's influence is made up of incidents from which Milkman could gather the values necessary to know himself and his family. The lessons Pilate subtly offers, if Milkman is sensitive to them, could provide the solid perch from which he can fly. Her lessons also show, sometimes by negative example, how he can shape responses to the world; those responses will enable him to become Pilate's successor as the keeper of family honor and believer in family traditions.[15]

As one of Milkman's lessons, consider the incident with Reba's lover. Pilate rescues her daughter from a man stupid enough to beat a woman who has been more than generous to him. Milkman watches as Pilate, grasping the man around the neck with one hand and wielding her knife over his heart with the other, placidly lectures him on the limits of motherly tolerance. Milkman is impressed by the showmanship of the incident without realizing its greater value: Pilate shows a commitment to family first of all, and she shows it without a destructive outcome. She controls her temper, and she controls the man who has harmed Reba. Such actions are in contrast to Milkman, who, despite his more than six feet of height, is still immature; when a potentially violent scene develops in the Dead house, Milkman responds to it by threatening more violence to Macon in retaliation for Macon slapping Ruth. Pilate's patient settling of the dispute, her generous response to the stranger, is in marked contrast to Milkman's self-centered attitude. Her actions are also a contrast to Milkman's treatment of Hagar.

Pilate and Reba's caring for Hagar, though sometimes extreme in its tolerance, nevertheless indicates that they are basically self-sacrificing where family is concerned. They are both appalled when Hagar maintains that there have been days when she was hungry, because they are committed to taking care of all of her physical needs. Once they realize that she refers to a different kind of hunger, their anxiety subsides. Their treatment of Hagar, which Milkman witnesses for a time before he becomes her sexual partner, is in direct contrast to his later abuse of Hagar. He has learned nothing from them about human relationships of an altruistic nature; instead, he keeps the women in a corner of his mind marked "other" and continues on his self-destructive, materialistic ways.

Pilate also provides him with the opportunity for reevaluating his relationship to his parents, especially his father. Although Pilate and Macon have been estranged for years, she nevertheless finds her way, finally, to her only other living relative. That means more to her than remembering whatever it was that initially separated them. She and Macon are not completely reconciled, but she has at least made the effort to find him and to move near him. That kind of geographical, spatial support portends a commitment to kin that Milkman cannot begin to fathom. Pilate and Macon may not be on regular speaking terms with each other, but in some ways she is closer to him than Milkman could ever be, and she is similarly closer to Ruth than Milkman is to his mother. Macon and Pilate, and Pilate and Ruth, have shared traumas of existence that make failures to socialize or petty squabbling inaccurate measures of the depth of their relationships. Milkman superficially chooses Pilate's license and freedom over his father's strictures without realizing that the two are complementary, inseparably bound in their meaning for his destiny.

These specific lessons that Milkman fails to learn are but the fractional representations of the philosophy of wholeness that Pilate practices. When Milkman goes into her home, he goes into a peaceful environment, one unmarred by the shadowy figures of his sisters or the blistering hatred his parents have for each other. He finds a soothing place, one in which nothing is required of him, except perhaps that he give himself wholly to its influence. It is an oasis in a world where the sands of materialism promise to smother even the most altruistic soul. Here, the love of money has no meaning. Middle-class dress and fancy whatnots are just as alien as Milkman is initially in Danville, Pennsylvania, and Shalimar, Virginia. Pilate, Reba, and Hagar have allowed the world to pass them by, at least the world in which most people find themselves trapped. In their voluntary retreat, however, they have managed to salvage more valuable things—a leisurely appreciation of life, joy in each other's company, a love of music, and the simple, credulous wonder in things as they are, with which most adults have lost contact. Most important, Pilate has a security in, and a comfort with, herself that

Milkman will perhaps never achieve; contentment with being, and with being without encumbrances, are Pilate's forte. What others judge to be her disrespect for progress can also be viewed as her hold onto sanity in a world content to drive itself mad.

This philosophy is what she offers to Milkman, but he is so intent upon marveling at her difference that he fails to meditate upon its intrinsic healthy qualities. Pilate is herself a living example, a walking metaphor, for Milkman, but his vision, too coated with his father's materialism and the narrowness of the world on Not Doctor Street, cannot penetrate the surface of Pilate's existence to stare upon its life-saving depths.

When Milkman learns to fly, we evaluate his success as a testament to Pilate's piloting. He emerges as a heroic personality precisely because he has been more human than superhuman, more sinning than saved. Like Brer Rabbit, he has experienced the flexibility of morality. Like John the slave, he has been as much manipulator as manipulated. He has survived a life-style comparable to that many black preachers reject in their bids to become representatives of their people.[16] And he has shown that goodness alone is not the major prerequisite for heroism. Through him, Morrison illustrates that a simplistic approach to the evaluation of heroic deeds will not suffice for the complexity so integral to her novel. Her blurring of the lines of absolute values is characteristic of the trends in African-American folk culture that help to define Milkman and that give Morrison's writing such a distinctive flavor.

A Journey That Works

The Bluest Eye and *Sula* depicted characters in search of something they could never achieve, on journeys of seeking that left them insane, complacent, or dead. Pecola's search for blue eyes shows that the archetypal fairy tale pattern of seeking is antithetical to, and ultimately cannot allow fulfillment for, members of black communities. Pauline Breedlove's search for an identity outside of her blackness and her black heritage also ends in disaster, for that reversal is similarly antithetical to her true existence. The journey north for Pauline and the journey inward for Pecola both backfired. Sula's wandering can also be viewed as an aborted attempt to find meaning in her existence; unable to do so on southern or northern soil, she returns to her home in the North, more out of resignation than accomplishment. In her first two novels, therefore, Morrison depicts no pattern of seeking that leads to contentment for her characters. They are driven, disturbed, unsettled from the beginnings to the ends of their journeys. With Milkman Dead in *Song of Solomon*, Morrison culminates her pattern of reversal and simultaneously allows Milkman to find meaning in a territory that her previous characters have shunned or escaped.

Few characters in African-American literature chart their courses from north to south, for the myth informing their actions invariably pictured the North as the freer place, where money was plentiful and liberty unchallenged. So they usually went north, to that earthly land of milk and honey.[17] In *Song of Solomon*, therefore, Morrison debunks one myth and creates another. Born in the North, and heir to the material advantages that generations of blacks identified with that territory, Milkman Dead must find meaning for his life by reversing the pattern, by going south, back into the territory of his ancestors. There must also be a reversal in his expectations on that soil. Initially, he goes searching for gold, as many generations of blacks came north in hopes of improving their material wealth. But the South is not the land of riches, of physical, tangible goods waiting for those seeking their fortunes. It is the land of blood and death, of slavery, of countless generations of Africans tied to brutal and unrewarding labor, of intangible instead of tangible wealth. Milkman ultimately returns to the South for things that he can carry away only in his mind, in his conception of self, in his contentment with communal and familial history, and in his satisfaction with knowing and being who he is.

Milkman's journey is one that works because he forges out of it a blueprint for knowing himself. By going against the traditional archetypal movement and structuring a more personally rewarding one, Milkman earns our respect as he discovers his identity. Though his journey may share certain features with some of the mythological quests, it is nevertheless more distinctive than imitative.

Milkman's major problem is that he has been too complacent in his northern, middle-class existence, far removed from the stock of black people in the South who were tied to his ancestors who moved north. In order for Milkman to appreciate those roots, to become receptive to his past, he must be stripped of external symbols of separation. His city ways and attitudes have to change; Morrison effects the change by showing their uselessness on southern soil. Milkman undergoes a devolution from which he can be reborn as a sensitive human being. The stripping process begins with his arrival in Danville, Pennsylvania, where he hopes to find leads on where Pilate has left the gold. His emotions, clothing, accessories, and manners are all signs of the distance between him and the people whose help he needs.

Emotional readjustment signals the onset of many changes. For the first time, he is put in the position of trying "to make a pleasant impression on a stranger" (229) when he goes to Reverend Cooper's house asking about Circe. That slight discomfiture gives way to tale swapping when Milkman discovers that Cooper has known his father, yet it is nonetheless a prediction of the adjustments Milkman will have to make on his journey.

His trip to Circe's house and to the cave induce physical discomfiture to match the earlier emotional one; the literal stripping process begins. His city hat gets ripped off by tree branches. He must take off his shoes and socks in crossing the stream to the cave, and his bare feet are "unprepared for the coldness of the water and the slimy stones at the bottom" (249). He soaks his fancy pants and cigarettes, and breaks the "gold Longines" watch his mother had given him: "the face was splintered and the minute hand was bent" (250). His fancy shirt becomes soaked with sweat, as does his face, for which he uses his tie as a handkerchief. Upon discovering no gold in the cave, he screams in anger, and the bats in the cave startle him into a run, "whereupon the sole of his right shoe split away from the soft cordovan leather" (252). He uses his tie to strap the shoe together and lashes his way through branches and weeds back to the stream and the highway where he has been scheduled for a pickup. His watch now gone, he can only gauge by the sun that his ride has probably come and gone.

Although he has been stripped of several items of his city clothing, Milkman has not learned much from his adventures. His disrespectful manners show that he is still insensitive to Southern hospitality. The man who prides himself on being able to give the worn and tattered Milkman a ride back into Danville has his gesture thrown in his face when Milkman tries to pay him for one of his Cokes. The man's face "changes" as he insists that he "ain't got much," but he "can afford a Coke and a lift now and then" (255). His love for gold has blinded Milkman to the little courtesies of life, to the small favors that poor people relish performing for one another. His greed is his only motivation: "The fact was he wanted the gold because it was gold and he wanted to own it. Free" (257). A long way from the changes that will be necessary for his growth, Milkman has at least begun the physical movement that will eventually be matched by an emotional and spiritual change.

Milkman's sojourn in the wilderness of Danville has been difficult for him emotionally and physically, almost as if the very environment thwarts the unhealthy motives he has in looking for the gold. At this stage, the journey backfires more than it moves forward. Yet Milkman discovers some things in the process. He knows that the gold is no longer in the cave, and he surmises that Pilate had probably returned with it to her ancestral home in Virginia. Though he moves in that direction without a clear sense of where he is going or a significantly altered psyche, his willingness to continue the journey is itself noteworthy, for he has at least not been deterred by the obstacles he has encountered. They are mere preludes to what he must overcome the closer he gets to the object of his quest.

Journeys, by their very nature, pose obstacles for questers. There must be some test to gauge that the seeker is worthy of reward, as well as to determine if he or she has the stamina and the will to continue the quest. Whether posed by humans or gods, the tests, if passed successfully, earn respect for the seeker and enable him or her to make progress on the journey. For Milkman Dead, northern black rich man, the tests involve humiliation designed to teach him that his status does not separate him from the national corpus of black humanity. They show that his pride is disproportionate to his achievements, that he must learn to value those toward whom he is disdainful, and that he needs more assistance than his previous independence has allowed for. Because of the extent of his arrogance and the height of his separation from the blacks he meets, his tests have to be especially humbling. The black men in Shalimar, Virginia, are more than willing—and able—to effect his reassessment of his position in the world.

Milkman insults their ways and denies their humanity within a few minutes of his arrival in town. Bred to insensitivity concerning the customs of the South, his very ignorance is a weapon he wields against the men. He casually mentions that he will buy a new car if the old one cannot be repaired, thereby making the men dwell intensely upon their poverty and limited abilities to take care of their families. "He hadn't bothered to say his name, nor ask theirs, had called them 'them' . . . his manner, his clothes were reminders that they had no crops of their own and no land to speak of either" (266). His money highlights their poverty, and his easy survey of their women threatens the fragile bonds they can still use to claim their manhood. When he locks his car, in a town "where there couldn't be more than two keys twenty-five miles around," they know he is like the white men for whom they sit and hope for a day's work: "They looked at his skin and saw it was as black as theirs, but they knew he had the heart of the white men who came to pick them up in the trucks when they needed anonymous, faceless laborers" (266).

A man whose mere presence calls into question their own claims to manhood can only be tested in the same arena. Milkman has the power, manner, clothes, and money the black men identify with white men; therefore, they focus their first test on his sexual capacity—is he as much a man in sexual matters as the signs suggest, or can he be a "faggot"? If they can humiliate him with insinuations about homosexuality, and perhaps embarrass him or drive him away, they can restore to themselves some of the lack of manhood his presence makes them feel. The ritual of transference is old, though its specific manifestations may be unique. If Milkman leaves the scene, then the men will feel justified in not helping or accepting him. If he can hold his own and somehow survive their insults, then they will stop the ritual testing and tolerate him, perhaps even accept him into the community.

The men in Solomon's General Store begin their test with a verbal assault, in the tradition of one of the oldest forms of contest within black communities. Rather than playing the dozens, which would reflect subtle, less direct attacks, they confront Milkman with insults aimed not at his mother but specifically at him. From the assertion that "pricks is . . . wee, wee little" in the North, they seek confirmation from Milkman and move on to insults about homosexuality and sexual perversion:

> "That true?" The first man looked at Milkman for an answer.
>
> "I wouldn't know," said Milkman. "I never spent much time smacking my lips over another man's dick." Everybody smiled, including Milkman. It was about to begin.
>
> "What about his ass hole? Ever smack your lips over that?"
>
> "Once," said Milkman. "When a little young nigger made me mad and I had to jam a Coke bottle up his ass."
>
> "What'd you use a bottle for? Your cock wouldn't fill it?"
>
> "It did. After I took the Coke bottle out. Filled his mouth too."
>
> "Prefer mouth, do you?"
>
> "If it's big enough, and ugly enough, and belongs to a ignorant motherfucker who is about to get the livin shit whipped out of him." (267)

More mouth than ability, Milkman pleases the spectators by succumbing to the physical battle they have all anticipated, but he is little match for his knife-flashing opponent: "Milkman did the best he could with a broken bottle, but his face got slit, so did his left hand, and so did his pretty beige suit, and he probably would have had his throat cut if two women hadn't come running in screaming . . ." (268). Having given his adversary a "jagged cut" over his eye, sufficient to induce profuse bleeding, Milkman is left in the hot sun, tending his wounds and reflecting on the incident as the others casually go their way.

Milkman's ability to hold his own with the bottle earns him a tinge of respect, but not enough for the fun to end. The measure of his worthiness continues in the older men's invitation to him to join them in a night hunt. Milkman cannot walk away from the challenge and still claim superiority, so he boasts that he is the "best shot there is" (269). The claim is a vestige of pride held on to in an impossible situation. The pride has to be tempered at the same time that the men must reevaluate their feelings toward Milkman. Change on his part will bring him closer to them and, on theirs, will encourage them to respect him at a mutual, horizontal level rather than a hierarchical one. As Dorothy H. Lee comments, "the older men take over the initiation rite from the youths. The names of the men—Omar,

King Walker, Luther Solomon, Calvin Breakstone, and a giant called Small Boy—seem to indicate that Milkman has entered the circle of village elders, of poets, kings, and men of God."[18]

The coon hunt tests Milkman's courage and endurance, simultaneously forcing him to be dependent upon individuals he has scorned. Their familiarity with the territory, equipment, and procedures highlights Milkman's greenness. He does not foresee the noise that loose change in his pocket would make during a hunt, and he shows his lack of night sight by bumping into Calvin as they walk along a trail listening for the dogs. Milkman's city body, worn down by the earlier testing and his general fatigue, eventually gives out, and he finds himself alone in the dark woods, too weak to do anything but sit and reflect upon the circumstances that have brought him to that point. The hunt therefore assumes a triple purpose. It is a part of Milkman's journey south, a part of the ritual testing, and most important, a part of his journey inward, his "hunt" for the best within himself. His reflections show some of the strongest signs of growth, among them his recognition that he has treated his family and Pilate's badly. He literally experiences a dark night of the soul in which he realizes that none of the things separating him from the men hunting with him are of any use to him:

> There was nothing here to help him—not his money, his car, his father's reputation, his suit, or his shoes. In fact they hampered him. Except for his broken watch, and his wallet with about two hundred dollars, all he had started out with on his journey was gone: . . . His watch and his two hundred dollars would be of no help out here, where all a man had was what he was born with, or had learned to use. And endurance. Eyes, ears, nose, taste, touch—and some other sense that he knew he did not have: an ability to separate out, of all the things there were to sense, the one that life itself might depend on. (277)

Milkman is learning lessons that he will not truly be able to value until later, but his current predicament has caused a previously unmatched reflection on his part. Guitar's attempt to strangle him to death shortly after these reflections makes Milkman realize even more the fragile nature of the material goods he has clung to throughout his life.[19]

That brush with death seems to sharpen Milkman's desire to live. He is able to find his way in the darkness to the spot where Calvin and the other men have treed a bobcat. A more expansive symbol of Milkman's newfound awareness than a coon would perhaps be, the bobcat becomes a measure of Milkman's acceptance into the group of hunters, into the kind of courage that has taken him through his path in the woods. The bobcat also culminates the ritual of acceptance; by allowing Milkman, the initiate, to pull out its heart, the men incorporate him into their fraternity and forgive him his former superiority over them.[20] He can now joke easily with them, admit that he was "scared to death" (280), describe that condition graphically for them, and enjoy becoming the butt of their jokes.

This coon-turned-bobcat hunt has additional significance from the perspective of African-American folklore and culture. "Coon," like "nigger," is a derisive name for blacks, one of which most insiders to the culture are aware. To be called a coon is to be reduced in value, made more thing than human. The pattern of Milkman's life has been one in which he has not lived up to anyone's conception of manhood—not his father's, or Guitar's, or Pilate's, or even his own. Going on the coon hunt, then, is a metaphorical way for him to shed the negative connotations of his lack of manliness, the negative connotations of his lack of commitment to black community and black people, and to gain a victory from that confrontation with absence.

His position is not unlike that of the black man in the folktale, "Coon in the Box."[21] John the slave convinces his master that he can tell fortunes, after which the master bets his entire plantation on John's skill. The bettors test John by putting a raccoon under a box and guarding it until the time he is scheduled to reveal the contents. Knowing that he has listened outside his master's bedroom to predict previous events, and knowing that he has no knowledge of what is under the box, John is in a predicament when the time comes for him to show his clairvoyance. After much posturing, puzzling, and head-scratching, he accepts his presumed fate by simply saying: "Well, master, I guess you got the old coon at last." Having been reduced to relying on nothing but their natural wits, John and Milkman make the right choices, utter the right words, and survive. And survival is all that matters at the test point, for the game for both characters (Milkman bragging that he knows hunting, and John bragging that he can tell fortunes) has become more dangerous than either intended. John turns the potentially negative situation positive by equating himself with the derisive epithet for blacks, and Milkman eludes his course of self-destruction by realizing that he has indeed been "niggerish" in his treatment of all the people in his life. Both survive by arriving at the point of vulnerability and *accepting* that potentially destructive condition.

At the literal level of the hunt, however, Milkman has again held his own, and the men are fair-minded enough to recognize it; they now share food and company with him and provide him with the first lead to finding information about his grandmother, Singing Bird. Finally, they send him to a woman who completes his process of initiation into their community.

Sweet, as she is more than appropriately named, is one of the "pretty women" Milkman has been brash enough to observe upon his arrival in Shalimar. Now that he has proved his manhood on their terms, the men judge him to be ready to sleep with one of the local women. She becomes one of the rewards for the quester having successfully completed his quest. Hers is a ritual of reclamation for him, which involves purification before lovemaking. She washes away the blood of the fight and the dirt and grime of the evening's hunt, thus formally baptizing him into official acceptance in Shalimar. And she willingly presents herself as the prize he has won for battles endured. Such a formulaic analysis, however, is mitigated by Sweet and Milkman thoroughly enjoying their sharing, especially Milkman, who is awakened to a new sense of awe in physical contact with a woman. "What she did for his sore feet, his cut face, his back, his neck, his thighs, and the palms of his hands was so delicious he couldn't imagine that the lovemaking to follow would be anything but anticlimactic" (285). It so far exceeds his expectations that he offers to give her a bath in return, an action far removed from anything he has done for Hagar and, in its sharing, anything he has done for any of the women in his life.

Having been tested verbally, physically, emotionally, and sexually, Milkman is better prepared, more sensitized to recognize that his family history is more important than any gold he could seek. His tests have taught him that human beings are not to be dismissed or ill treated with impunity. As a part of the tie that binds him to all living beings, especially people of African descent, he can no longer use his money to separate himself from the Sauls of Shalimar, or his city-slicker shoes to separate him from the Calvins, or his condescension from the Sweets of the world. They all tie him to a communal and familial heritage that goes back to Africa, and they represent, in their various states of development, some portion of his grandfather's journey from Virginia to Pennsylvania. The first Macon Dead's hope for better things drove him from the stifling South, a hope shared by the people who are still living there and being similarly stifled by poverty. And his travel on a wagon, so far distant psychologically and economically from Milkman Dead, reflects the very soil and work to which the people of Shalimar are rooted. Milkman has been shocked into the recognition that he will not be allowed to break the circle of connectedness extending generations before his own existence.

His rediscovery of his humanity makes him sensitive enough to Susan Byrd's information to realize that the children in Shalimar are singing about his great-grandmother, Ryna, and his great-grandfather, Solomon. He deciphers names and connects their songs to Pilate's blues song about Sugarman. The puzzle of family history becomes more engaging than searching for gold. Knowing one's name, being able to call it in spite of personal or institutional distortions, becomes all important to Milkman. He understands that names have "meaning," as Pilate has understood by putting hers in her ear. He comes to understand why people in Michigan insist upon calling the street on which he lives Not Doctor Street, why they value the nicknames he has heard in the pool halls and barbershops all his life. The names, taken "from yearnings, gestures, flaws, events, mistakes, weaknesses" (330), all "bear witness" to the concreteness, the reality of black people's lives in spite of the census bureau or the post office or drunk recorders. Inherent in the tradition of which the names are a part is the penchant of black people to adhere to their own reality in spite of almost insurmountable obstacles. By arriving at this state of awareness, Milkman can link his own family names to others representing black history and struggle. The golden threads tying him to his family history are far more valuable than the original gold he has sought.[22]

Milkman's growth on his journey is measurable. He changes from a self-centered, middle-class bore to a man genuinely able to share in a physical relationship as well as in societal and communal interchanges. He realizes how wrongheaded he has been about his father and mother and how he has used all the women in his life, especially Hagar. He had put his whims and desires before those of his sisters and had discounted their needs to be more than the older siblings of Macon Dead's chosen offspring. He had judged his mother harshly and had ignorantly tried to chastise his father. He had violated Pilate's home by stealing from her and continued that violation by journeying hundred of miles to find gold he believed she had hidden. Yet in the darkness on the coon hunt and in later scenes, Milkman comes to know many of his limitations and faults in human relationships. He has been especially abusive to Hagar:

> He had used her—her love, her craziness—and most of all he had used her skulking, bitter vengeance. It made him a star, a celebrity in the Blood Bank; it told men and other women that he was one bad dude, that he had the power to drive a woman out of her mind, to destroy her, and not because she hated him, or because he had done some unforgivable thing to her, but because he had fucked her and she was driven wild by the absence of his magnificent joint. His hog's gut, Lena had called it. Even the last time, he used her. Used her imminent arrival and feeble attempt at murder as an exercise of his will against hers—an ultimatum to the universe. "Die, Hagar, die." Either this bitch dies or I do. And she stood there like a puppet strung up by a puppet master who had gone off to some other hobby. (301)

In his egotistical focus on self, he had "gone off and left" Hagar in the same way that his great-grandfather had gone and left Ryna. In fact, Milkman's reflections upon Hagar spur his recognition of his family in the song sung by the children. In his remorse over Hagar, he begins to feel a sense of family responsibility and commitment negated in his great-grandfather's action of flying away from his family.

Throughout his life, Milkman has been "leaving" his family—through his disdain and hatred for his mother and father, through his condescension toward his sisters, and through his now recognized mistreatment of Hagar. He has left a string of bodies like his great-grandfather left Ryna and Jake, Milkman's grandfather. Where the paths converge signals a new beginning for Milkman, but it may be an ambiguous one. The exhilaration he feels upon learning that Solomon could fly is matched by the tragic circumstances surrounding that fantastic event. The celebration of flying simultaneously highlights Ryna's insanity and the fatherlessness of Solomon's twenty-one sons. Happiness in the knowledge of flight leads to the enigma of unhappiness in the consequences of the flight. Flying, then, becomes a selfish celebration of the freedom of an individual judged against the enslavement of twenty-two people.[23] The selfish path Milkman has followed throughout his life parallels the flight of his great-grandfather and its symbolic implications.

When Milkman arrives at the discovery of his great-grand-father's flying abilities, he has two options. He can continue the path of Solomon (celebration without commitment), or he can use the kinship as a sign to renew his ties to his family. The journey cannot work for Milkman unless some reversal occurs; flight itself must be made secondary to commitment. If he merely celebrates flight, then he runs the risk of separation and of continuing to follow in his great-grandfather's flight pattern. If he puts commitment first, then he will show allegiance to Pilate, who has repeatedly maintained that "You can't just fly on off and leave a body" (147, 332, 333). Emotionally, it is clear that Milkman, through his reflections and seeming changes of attitudes, follows Pilate. But the attraction to flying makes him confront Guitar in what may be a fatal end to the lessons he has just learned.

In confronting Guitar, Milkman may be flying off and leaving a body again (Pilate has specifically asked him to look after Reba), but he does so with a desire for commitment, an understanding of what his role should now be in his family. And perhaps he understands his communal role as well, if we view his soaring toward Guitar as an act of love. He does take Guitar with him; if their flight ends in death, it can be viewed as Milkman having saved Guitar from himself and from the gradually warping executions he carries out. The death could also be viewed as vengeance, thereby creating a situation in which Milkman acts for family—because Guitar has killed Pilate—instead of neglecting them. The problem with this latter view is that it would mean that Milkman has adopted Guitar's eye-for-an-eye philosophy, which is unacceptable under any circumstances.[24] What is clear from the final scene is that Milkman is thoroughly changed from the selfish little creature he started out to be; he has reevaluated himself and his relationship to his family, and he has progressed in healthy ways.

The transfer of value from material to immaterial things, from things to people, and from directionless activity to purposefulness all suggest that Milkman's journey has worked for him in ways that no other journey in Morrison's novels has worked for any other character. He finds in the South, in the land of his African forebears, the key to appreciating his family and to understanding how he came to be. His enlightenment, no matter the cost, is well worth the trip.[25]

Female Sacrifices for Male Identity

The success of Milkman's journey depends in large part on the string of female bodies, figuratively and literally, that he leaves along his path. The women form a long line of mothering and nurturing that culminates in Milkman's renewed sense of himself; they become sacrifices on the altar of his possibilities. Comparable to the blood sacrifices in *Sula*, those in *Song of Solomon* are striking in that female characters are consistently the victims. That victimization begins with Ruth, whose deviant actions to get pregnant are not enough to save her future relationship with her husband or her son. In order to give birth to Milkman, Ruth must forever give up physical relations with Macon. In order to keep Milkman alive, she must intensify her role as mother, only to relinquish it forever when he becomes an adolescent.

Ruth's primary function in the novel is to give birth to Milkman, not to establish a relationship with him—certainly not beyond the long period of nursing. She is important to his story only as long as her body serves his needs (or as long as she can nurse him without discovery); once those needs are served, he casts her aside emotionally, as he will later similarly discard Hagar. Ruth has very little reality for Milkman, and she is not drawn so that our sympathies are overly aroused in favor of different treatment. Yet here is a woman who lives somewhat of a martyred life, or certainly a cloistered one, for Macon's rejection of her after Milkman's death essentially turns her into a nun. She has given her all on the altar of her male off-spring, whose future, set beside hers, is judged to be significantly more worthy of consideration. Not exactly a pathetic figure, Ruth is nonetheless a sacrificial one, for her life must fade into the back-ground as Milkman's rises to the forefront.

In the language of fairy tales, she becomes an expendable helper who gives safe passage to Milkman from conception to birth, but whose importance lessens as Milkman learns to fend for himself.[26] Her emotional sacrifices for her son are perhaps more stultifying than those of Corinthians and Magdalene, but the sisters nonetheless find their futures compromised to Milkman's. Their father becomes bored with them when he gets the opportunity to begin shaping Milkman in his image of entrepreneur. Though Macon sends Corinthians to college, that does not signal any intrinsic evaluation of her worth on his part; it is simply what a man of his means can do for his children, even if they are female. He sees the image of what being middle class means; he is unconcerned about his daughters as girls or as women. He will continue to take care of them, as the weaker, more useless sex, but they do not spark his interest, and they hold out to him no promise of the family line being continued. Also, as an extension of the war with his wife, he would more naturally identify with Milkman, a potential convert to his viewpoint, than with his daughters.

From the time Milkman urinates on Lena's dress during the family's customary Sunday drive, his desires take precedence over those of his sisters. Even before he is consciously aware of his power as male, he is able to get his way as the youngest child in the family. When he learns that his father wants him to collect rents and become his apprentice, he quickly adopts the same attitude toward his sis-ters that Macon has. He allows them to wash, cook, clean, and care for his other housekeeping needs without any consideration for them as individuals who may wish to do something else with their lives. When Milkman knocks Macon down for hitting Ruth, and when he tells of Corinthians's affair with Porter, he is not doing so out of love for his mother or his sister. As Lena says of the fight with Macon, Milkman was not protecting his mother: "You were taking over, letting us know you had the right to tell her and all of us what to do" (216). On the night of their conversation, when she is thirty-one, Milkman finds himself talking to a sister "to whom he had not said more than four consecutive sentences since he was in the ninth grade" (211).

Another set of Morrison's "twins," Lena and Corinthians are almost as ineffectual as the deweys. Corinthians is unable to determine her destiny until she is well into middle age, and Lena is never able to determine hers. Buffeted by external forces, they are unwilling helpers in the destiny that awaits Milkman, but helpers nonetheless.[27] Without the vividness of their deprivations and constrictions, we would have less of a sense of Milkman being his father's chosen one. Either to win their father's approval, or his tolerance, or because they have no choice, Corinthians and Lena are trapped in the house on Not Doctor Street. Their entrapment leads in part to Milkman's growth and freedom; they therefore become other victims symbolically and literally sacrificed on the altar of Milkman's quest for manhood and identity. Like Florence Grimes upon the arrival of Gabriel in James Baldwin's *Go Tell It on the Mountain* (1953), Lena and Corinthians must be sacrificed to the future that only the male offspring can have. Though Corinthians escapes in middle age, the little happiness she may now find has been undermined by years and years of subservience to someone else's definition of reality.

Milkman meditates at one point upon what he has "deserved" (276) or not as his lot in life, and he has acted throughout as if his mother and sisters were put upon earth because he deserved their services. They are almost nonentities, except when he needs a clean towel or fresh linen. Servants more than sisters in the height from which they are condescendingly viewed, Lena and Corinthians content themselves for most of their lives with existing in the tiny spaces into which Macon and Milkman have shoved them. Without value to brother or father, and without any animating love for their mother, Lena and Corinthians exist as shadows whose substance can be measured only by its fading from them into their brother's future.

Of all the female sacrifices made for Milkman's growth and development, Hagar's is the most pathetic and Pilate's the most tragic. Milkman essentially destroys Pilate's family, for once Hagar and Pilate are dead, Reba is lost; unable to care for herself, she will probably be institutionalized. Still, the women make no effort to stop the destruction of their family, which begins with Hagar. Their leniency and desire to give Hagar whatever she wants combines with Milkman's selfishness to ensure her downfall. While her desires might be simple enough to see Milkman as her quintessential fulfillment, Hagar fails to recognize that he cannot be counted on to reciprocate her passion or her love. She is an adventure for him, a toy he is content to play with over the nearly twenty complacent years of his adult adolescence. When he tires of the toy, he dispassionately tosses it aside. His proclivity for white women and for black women of his own social standing relegates Hagar to a small niche in Milkman's life; "she became a quasi-secret but permanent fixture" (97–98). The relationship of the two families to each other also dictates the quasi-secret status. Certainly Ruth would be appalled to know that Milkman is sleeping with his first cousin's daughter, and Macon would be livid not only about this son having gone into Pilate's house but having become Hagar's lover. By contrast, Reba and Pilate simply accept life as it is. Though coquettish at first, Hagar shortly becomes Milkman's for the taking, a priceless jewel diminishing its own value by its failure to value itself. She is one of the reasons Milkman is able to "stretch" "his carefree boyhood out for thirty-one years" (98). Hagar is his expected sexual outlet in the way that his sisters are his maids—convenient and exploitable. When she centers her whole life upon Milkman, placing "duty squarely in the middle of their relationship" (98), he tries "to think of a way out."

Like Plum, Hagar has acquiesced in the ritual of destruction in which she is victim. Having granted to Milkman total control of her life, she similarly grants him control of her death, which his termination of the affair amounts to. His decision to remind her that they are cousins, that "she needed a steady man who could marry her" because "he was standing in her way," is the pouring of kerosene on an already burning mind. His hypocrisy disguised as concern is a transparent rationalization designed to effect his own freedom, which he does by sending Hagar a dismissal letter:

> He went back to his father's office, got some cash out of the safe, and wrote Hagar a nice letter which ended: "Also, I want to thank you. Thank you for all you have meant to me. For making me happy all these years. I am signing this letter with love, of course, but more than that, with gratitude." (99)

Guaranteed to gall any self-respecting woman, the letter reeks of distance and emotional coldness; Milkman can send it to Hagar only because he does not value or respect her. In the absence of any sense of family or communal commitment, Milkman dismisses Hagar as easily as he perhaps dispossesses his father's tenants.

Macon Dead has put Milkman in training to be callous, and Reba and Pilate have unconsciously assured Hagar's victimization:

> Neither Pilate nor Reba knew that Hagar was not like them. Not strong enough, like Pilate, nor simple enough, like Reba, to make up her life as they had. She needed what most colored girls needed: a chorus of mamas, grandmamas, aunts, cousins, sisters, neighbors, Sunday school teachers, best girl friends, and what all to give her the strength life demanded of her—and the humor with which to live it. (307)

Without encouraging her to see some reality outside of Milkman, some reality outside of their taking care of her, she is destined to acquiesce in her own destruction just as Milkman is destined to execute that destruction. Her "graveyard love" ("Anaconda love," Morrison calls it) for Milkman literally becomes that. As sacrificial victim, her fate is sealed. As victimizer, Milkman has other choices. Certainly Macon has taught him to value money above people, but he and Guitar, who is concerned about people, have been friends for more than twenty years by the time Milkman dismisses Hagar. Guitar's concern and the antimaterialistic philosophy he has spouted off to Milkman for years have at least ensured his exposure to something other than his father's sentiments. While Hagar has little choice in the path she follows, Milkman does not wish to make the choice that would suggest responsibility and caring. He continues carefree and unattached, finding and taking sexual favors wherever he pleases. His immaturity contains an inherent viciousness antithetical to Hagar's desire for a more committed relationship.

Hagar's sacrifice is complete when she makes Milkman's will superior to her own. As Milkman lies in Guitar's apartment, unmoving as Hagar approaches with the knife, she knows at last that she can no longer evoke any emotion from him, not even the fear that has driven her to pursue him month after month, and certainly not the pity she deserves. Yet the insensitive Milkman can only see her failure to kill him as a triumph of masculinity over femininity, of his incredible sexual powers over the susceptible Hagar. His final words to her are striking in their utter callousness:

> "If you keep your hands just that way," he said, "and then bring them down straight, straight and fast, you can drive that knife right smack in your cunt. Why don't you do that? Then all your problems will be over." He patted her cheek and turned away from her wide, dark, pleading, hollow eyes. (130)

It is ironic that Guitar, the executioner, is more sympathetic to Hagar than Milkman. When he takes the nearly comatose woman from his apartment after her attempt on Milkman's life, he maintains that Hagar has been "pitiful. Really pitiful" and asserts that "it had to be something more" that Milkman has done to her, because "that girl's hurt—and the hurt came from you" (152). Incapable of feeling the pity that Guitar does, Milkman claims that his friend is "meddling" and "criticizing" him unfairly.

By the time Milkman pauses in those dark woods to think about Hagar, many emotional light years and hundreds of miles away, she is already bringing her ritual of death to an end. He concedes that "if a stranger could try to kill him, surely Hagar, who knew him and whom he'd thrown away like a wad of chewing gum after the flavor was gone—she had a right to try to kill him too" (276–77). The accurate image of having thrown her away like chewing gum comes too late to help Hagar, but it serves its purpose in pushing Milkman toward maturity. The pattern is set in a way that Milkman thrives in direct proportion to Hagar's demise. As he learns more about his relationship to her and the rest of his family, her physical essence decreases in value. For each stage on the journey that brings enlightenment to Milkman, that enlightenment comes directly from Hagar's lifeline. When he discovers—in Shalimar, Virginia, sitting in front of Solomon's General Store—that the children are singing about his great-grandfather, he moves into a realm of self-awareness that makes it impossible for him to treat anyone else as he has treated Hagar. Almost in keeping with that progression, Hagar dies. Another victim on his search for self, she has helped Milkman in substantial ways by being an outlet for his negative emotions and a symbol around which he gathers his reflections. Once he truly understands and accepts that people cannot be ill treated with impunity, then she is no longer needed. Her purpose served, she dies before Milkman can return to act out any of his newfound knowledge about how to deal with his family and with people in general.

A helper who has not known the extent of her assistance, and whose giving leads to her own death, Hagar presents her body as one of the bridges over which Milkman walks into his own humanity and manhood. Her physical sacrifice is the culmination of Pilate's prophetic prediction on the occasion when Ruth has come to her house to ensure that Hagar would not attempt to kill Milkman again. As Hagar and Ruth stood arguing about their value to Milkman, Pilate has said: "And he wouldn't give a pile of swan shit for either one of you. . . . He ain't a house, he's a man, and whatever he need, don't none of you got it" (137, 138). More specifically related to Hagar's death, Pilate comments to Ruth: "Ain't nothin goin to kill him but his own ignorance, and won't no woman ever kill him. What's likelier is that it'll be a woman save his life" (140). Her comment needs some modification, for it is not a woman, but several who save Milkman's life.[28] Hagar is one of them; she dies in order that he might grow—and perhaps, too, because there is no realistic place for her. Even if Milkman returns to the North, enlightened, with a proposal of marriage to Hagar, chances are they would not be able to execute that desire. Also, the extent of Milkman's transgressions warrants a more striking lesson than a mere forgiving and making up. Hagar's death points out the emotionally destructive binge Milkman has been on all his life. Morrison does not spare him from having to confront the trauma resulting from that crime.

Hagar, another body Milkman has left in his "flying" pursuit of his great-grandfather, is like Ryna or one of the twenty-one children Solomon left on his flight to Africa. Like Ryna, the desertion leads to insanity and death. But, also like Ryna, who lives on in the tales of Ryna's Gulch, Hagar will live on in the lessons she has taught and in the box of her hair Pilate gives to Milkman as an indication that he must take responsibility for "the life he had taken" (332). Victims in the examples of their fates, both Hagar and Ryna enable Milkman to transcend the possibility for future victimization.[29]

These pathetic women and the losses do not measure up, in the

final balance, to the loss of Pilate's life in Milkman's quest for identity, family, and value beyond gold. Teacher, nurturer, surrogate
mother, keeper of the blues tradition, Pilate has always placed value
on altruistic human relationships. In all of these roles, she gives
voice to the value of human connectedness. In singing "O Sugarman," she serves as the herald for Milkman's birth. In singing with
Reba and Hagar, she articulates the pain Macon feels and soothes his
wounds. In singing at Hagar's death, she voices the pain of loss in
sound rather than lyrics. And in singing the "Song of Solomon," she
places stress on the intricate ties to African and black American
history that unite all generations of those scattered in the Diaspora.
In her voice is the blending of secular and sacred traditions, natural
and supernatural concerns.[30]

She values human relationships, but she recognizes human limitations. When the absence of a navel finally "isolates" Pilate, "she
gave up, apparently, all interest in table manners or hygiene, but
acquired a deep concern for and about human relationships" (149).
When Guitar shoots her, her only regret is: "I wish I'd a knowed
more people. I would of loved 'em all. If I'd a knowed more, I would
a loved more" (336). That this tower of selflessness should fall, even
for an enlightened Milkman, is difficult to acquiesce to. Yet it is
consistent with Pilate's prediction about who would save Milkman's
life, and it is consistent with the traditional demise of the helper/
guide once the initiate has learned all the helper has to teach. Milkman has definitely learned the value of family and of human relationships, and he has learned that escape from a situation does not
lessen responsibility for it: he is as guilty for Hagar's death as
Solomon has been for Ryna's insanity and for whatever happened to
his twenty-one sons. He can now effectively take his teacher's place,
become the guru rather than the seeker after knowledge held by the
guru.

Such a refined interpretation, however, does not alter the evaluation that Pilate joins the other women in Milkman's life in being
made a victim to his health, to his growth into a positive sense of
self. Milkman's inability to convince Guitar that there is no gold,
combined with Guitar's warped sense of community commitment,
brings about the ironic circumstances surrounding Pilate's death.
Pilate and Guitar have believed in essentially the same things, in

commitment and human relationships. Guitar has approached the motherly in his feelings for Hagar, and he has deeply sympathized with the destruction wrought upon her. That he should kill Pilate in his effort to shoot Milkman makes her the victim of communal, familial, and individual values, brought together in the man who loves community enough to kill for it and the one who loves family enough to die for it.

A free spirit whose body has never weighed her to the earth, Pilate is triumphant in that, by sacrificing her own life, she will bring to an end the sequence of events, both historical and contemporary, that have divided her family and caused so much grief in it. And by setting in motion the events in which Guitar is ready to die for his cause, she also succeeds in eliminating the driving force behind the hatred practiced by the Seven Days. Her victimization, therefore, might have its worth in the larger picture of familial and communal good. And in the folk patterns that inform the novel, it is frequently a good, much-to-be-missed person whose sacrifice has the power to renew. Thus Pilate can do for Milkman what no one in *The Bluest Eye* could do for Pecola Breedlove and Lorain, Ohio. Not only does she sing the lore of her culture, she lives it as well.

5

Tar Baby

Transforming the Tar Baby Story

The title of Toni Morrison's fourth novel, *Tar Baby* (New York: Knopf, 1981), was obviously intended to evoke comparison to the famous story of the same name. In that story, as in the novel, a forbidden territory is invaded by an outsider who attempts to get away with valuable property. When the intruder is halted in the traditional folktale, he effects an escape. There the ties to the novel begin to be transformed, because it becomes increasingly less clear in Morrison's work whose territory is being invaded, who is the tar baby, who is trapped, who needs rescue from whom, and whether or not he (or she) effects an escape.

The tale is informed by the trickster tradition in African-American folklore, in which an animal or human "hero" succeeds in besting a larger or more powerful adversary.[1] The trickster relies on his or her wits to avoid difficult situations, or to escape from them if unable to avoid them. In some trickster tales, and that is certainly the case with the story of the tar baby, the hero can play two roles simultaneously or in succession. The hero can be triumphant or victimized, having power over the adversary or being reduced to a powerless state by the opponent.[2] Brer Rabbit begins many versions of the tar baby story by being the aggressor; he then degenerates to victim; and he finally succeeds in escaping or ends up being eaten by the animals he has tried to trick. This element of uncertainty ties in well with Morrison's persistent lack of unchallenged conceptions of absolutes; there is always room for equivocation.

To see how the story evolves and is transformed in the novel, it would be useful to consider the most common African-American versions. In one such tale, Brer Rabbit enters the farmer's garden to steal cabbages. He is caught by the tar baby, from which disadvantageous position he succeeds in freeing himself and escaping to the famed briar patch. In the black American version of the tale related by Hughes and Bontemps in *The Book of Negro Folklore*, Brer Rabbit refuses to share in the digging of a well with other animals, and there begins his trouble. The tale recounts the ensuing complications:

> So when the well was done Rabbit he was the first one to git some of the water. He went there at night an' git de water in jugs. The other animals see Rabbit's tracks from gittin' water in jugs. So all the animals git together an' see what they goin' to do about Brother Rabbit. So Bear say, "I tell you, I'll lay here an' watch for it. I'll ketch that Rabbit." So Bear watched but Rabbit was too fast for him. So Fox said, "I tell you, let's study a plan to git Brother Rabbit." So they all sit together an' study a plan. So they made a tar baby an' put it up by the well. So Brother Rabbit come along to git some water. He see the tar baby an' think it is Brother Bear. He say, "Can't git any water tonight; there's Brother Bear layin' for me." He looked some more, then he said. "No, that ain't Brother Bear, he's too little for Brother Bear." So he goes up to the tar baby an' say, "Whoo-oo-oo-oo." Tar Baby didn't move. So Rabbit got skeered. He sneaked up to it an' said, "Boo!" Tar Baby didn't move. Then Rabbit run all aroun' an' stood still to see did he move. But Tar Baby kept still. Then he moved his claw at him. Tar Baby stood still. Rabbit said, "That must be a chunk o' wood." He went up to see if it was a man. He said, "Hello, old man, hello, old man, what you doin' here?" The man didn't answer. He said again, "Hello, old man, hello, old man, what you doin' here?" The man didn't answer. Rabbit said, "Don't you hear me talkin' to you? I'll slap you in the face." The man ain't said nothin'. So Rabbit hauled off sure enough an' his paw stuck. Rabbit said, "Turn me loose, turn me loose or I'll hit you with the other paw." The man ain't said nothin'. So Rabbit hauled off with his other paw an' that one stuck too. Rabbit said, "You better turn me loose, I'll kick you if you don't turn me loose." Tar Baby didn't say anything. "Bup!" Rabbit kicked Tar Baby an' his paw stuck. So he hit him with the other an' that one got stuck.

Rabbit said, "I know the things got blowed up now; I know if I butt you I'll kill you." So all the animals were hidin' in the grass watchin' all this. They all ran out an' hollered, "Aha, we knowed we was gonna ketch you, we knowed we was gonna ketch you." So Rabbit said, "Oh, I'm so sick." So the animals said, "Whut we gonna do?" So they has a great meetin' to see what they gonna do. So someone said, "Throw him in the fire." But the others said, "No, that's too good; can't let him off that easy." So Rabbit pleaded an' pleaded, "Oh, please, please throw me into the fire." So someone said, "Hang him." They all said, "He's too light, he wouldn't break his own neck." So a resolution was drawed up to burn him up. So they all went to Brother Rabbit an' said, "Well, today you die. We gonna set you on fire." So Rabbit said, "Aw, you couldn't give me anything better." So they all say, "We better throw him in the briar patch." Rabbit cry out right away, "Oh, for God's sake, don't do dat. They tear me feet all up; they tear me behind all up; they tear me eyes out." So they pick him up an' throw him in the briar patch. Rabbit run off an' cry, "Whup-pee, my God, you couldn't throw me in a better place! There where my mammy born me, in the briar patch."[3]

The briar patch looms large as the comfortable realm of the trickster, the well-mapped territory in which he has no rival. A comparable inequity looms behind the interactions of Morrison's characters; Son is clearly out of place on Isle des Chevaliers and in New York, and Jadine is out of place in Eloe, Florida.

The motivation for the trickster is also worthy of consideration. In the story cited above, Brer Rabbit is lazy and wants water. Other tales show him violating somebody's space for the purpose of getting food. In still other tales, he is simply insulted that the tar baby will not speak to him. The latter is the case in the more literary version of the tale as recounted by Joel Chandler Harris's Uncle Remus and called "The Wonderful Tar-Baby Story."[4] The tar baby is constructed by Brer Fox to capture Brer Rabbit for some past indiscretion. When Brer Rabbit encounters the tar baby and greets it without getting a reply, he determines to teach it some manners (not unlike Son with Jadine). The tale ends when Brer Rabbit has been stuck at the traditional five points of contact (hands, feet, and head), and it is unclear whether or not he escapes.[5] By implication he does because of his appearance in numerous other of Uncle Remus's tales.

The significant thing about the Harris version of the tale is that Uncle Remus refers to the tar baby as "she." While this reference might be indicative of the Gullah people's lack of consistency in delineating pronoun and gender, which could have influenced the Georgia-born Uncle Remus, it nonetheless connects with centuries-old African versions of the tale, in which the tar baby was consciously conceptualized as female.[6] This history will provide additional context for viewing Jadine.

When we think of the folkloristic patterns of interaction in *Tar Baby*, we usually interpret Jadine *and* Son as tar babies. Both of them have some irresistible attraction for each other that could potentially bring about their downfall. Jadine recovers soon enough to be transformed from tar baby to trickster, in that she lands initially in the briar patch of New York and later in the briar patch of Paris, with the possibility of escape from the relationship more a certainty than it could ever be with Son. While Son and Jadine both exhibit traits of the tar baby, we usually assert that Jadine is more identified with the powers that create the tar babies, that she is more in control than controlled in the relationship.[7]

I would contend, however, that a close reading of the novel would show that Son initially has as much power and control as Jadine, if not more; indeed, he shares more traits with Valerian than with the victims who usually get caught in the traps that master "farmers" like Valerian set for pesky "rabbits" like Son. In the simultaneity of role playing, we can ascribe as much trickery (or godliness) to Son, as much desire to shape other people's lives and impressions of him, as we can ascribe to Valerian, or as we can ascribe trickery to the pesky Brer Rabbit who invades the well dug by other animals, steals their prized water, and escapes when he is caught.

From the minute he enters L'Arbe de la Croix, Son matches wits with Valerian. Theirs is the primary level of competition; his interaction with Jadine can only occur if Valerian consciously chooses to overlook it. Son has an arrogance that borders on amorality in the same way that Brer Rabbit and other tricksters characteristically respond to the situations in which they find themselves. Just as Brer Rabbit claims water from a well he did not share in digging, so too does Son assume proprietary rights over the property and people at L'Arbe de la Croix. He claims the territory by virtue of his night-creeping; his hunger transcends judgments of right and wrong. The food he finds, he believes, is his for the taking.

But, as with Brer Rabbit, food is only one indication of the extent of Son's proprietary rights. When he finds his way into Jadine's bedroom, he is claiming freedom of access sexually as well. While he certainly does not rape anyone, he lays claim to the territory and the private spaces that would enable him to do so if he desired. In this regard, he has more power than Valerian, for Valerian has been shut out of his wife's bedroom, and he surely has not given thought to entering anyone else's.

Although Son never attempts to rape anyone in the Street house, his body does figure in the aggressive stance that defines power. From Jadine's perspective, his hair is "physically overpowering, like bundles of long whips or lashes that could grab her and beat her to jelly" (113), and he does not hesitate to restrain her ("He uncrossed her wrists and swung her around, holding her from behind in the vise of his arms. His chin was in her hair"—121) or to press his smelly body and forceful private parts against her as a levelling strategy in their encounter in her bedroom. In other words, Son exhibits the amorality of the trickster by refusing to recognize any limitations on his movements or his behavior.

His appearance here also suggests one of the points at which roles once again get merged. Son's unkempt state could very easily be compared to that of the black tar baby (with a stereotypical connection between blackness, animality, and dirtiness), and in fact Morrison uses imagery to emphasize the connection: "he barely had time to breathe into her the smell of tar and its shiny consistency before he crept away hoping that she would break wind or believe she had so the animal smell would not alarm her or disturb the dream he had placed there" (120). In her irresistible attraction to Son, Jadine is drawn toward the forbidden just as easily as Brer Rabbit and others who stand before the tar baby are tempted to slap it/him/her. Just as her sexuality will later be the "stickiness" that attracts him so irresistibly, what Jadine senses underneath his physically disgusting appearance is also a potentially engulfing, "sticky" situation for her.

In his current ostensibly powerful state, Son exhibits a kind of "at home" quality in all of his actions in the Street household. When

Jadine escapes from her bedroom, Son assumes further proprietary rights by selecting her shower for removing the twelve days of dirt and filth from his body and by leaving his filthy pajamas on her bathroom floor. A violator of community norms who echoes Brer Rabbit's violations, Son is an uncontained force loosed in a world that respects boundaries. That contrast enables him to get away with his antisocial actions, for no one on the island, other than Valerian, is equipped to deal with someone so obviously in the raw (and we will discover later that Valerian falters as well). By not playing by the rules, Son is second in power only to Valerian. Margaret is clearly afraid of him, and Sydney, Ondine, and Jadine cannot do anything without Valerian's consent. By assuming traits of the "crazy nigger" or "bad nigger" of oral tradition, Son carves out a freer space for himself than anyone else in Valerian's household manages to do.

As the manipulative trickster, Son recognizes the value of sizing up the situation in which he finds himself and using it to his advantage. Consider his interaction with Valerian on the morning after his arrival at the island. Knowing that Valerian could indeed become antagonistic and have him jailed or deported, Son slides easily into a stereotypical role and performs for Valerian. The greatest potential threat is that of an accusation of rape, thus when Valerian asks Son what he was "really doing" (146) in Margaret's bedroom, he becomes the ignorant, hunger-driven, asexual "coon" running from his own shadow. He becomes in dialect and posture something that exists only in Valerian's head:

> I uh thought I smelled oyster stew out back yesterday. And it got dark early, the fog I mean. They done left the kitchen and I thought I'd try to get me some, but before I knew it I heard them coming back. I couldn't run out the back door so I run through another one. It was a dinin room. I ran upstairs into the first room I seen. When I got in I seen it was a bedroom but thought it belonged to the one y'all call Jade. I aimed to hide there till I could get out, but then I heard somebody comin and I ducked into the closet. I was just as scared as your wife was when she opened that door and turned that light on me. (147)

For anyone accustomed to stereotyped black dialect and to the stereotyped behavior emanating from its usage, a clear picture of Son's performance comes to mind. We can imagine the posture, as well as the gestures, and some cross between Stepin Fetchit and Mantan Moreland comes to mind.

Valerian knows that Son is performing, and Son knows that Valerian knows that he is performing, but the fiction of his own image as a white person unalterably in control of every situation will not allow Valerian to destroy this current fiction (that is his mythological heritage as surely as the trickster guise is Son's). In order for him to retain a semblance of power, he has to accept Son's explanation. And Son ensures that acceptance by casting himself as a frightened darky who does not have control of the controller's language. Any glimpse at Son's speech in other sections of the novel will confirm the differences between those and his performance in this instance. By stroking the stroker, so to speak, Son is assuming further proprietary rights, granted to him by virtue of the racial and cultural patterns of interaction between blacks and whites in the United States. By wearing the mask, playing a different kind of trickster role, Son ensures his own safety and ensures that he can continue to disrupt the Street household in other ways. In this scene, he and Valerian match wits so subtly that the power play might escape the casual reader. For like many verbal contests in the tradition of the dozens, where the power of words enhances status and one-upmanship, the trickster's power of words here makes it clear that Son can compete at Valerian's level whenever necessary. It is not surprising, therefore, when things begin to fall apart later that Son can openly defy Valerian's request that he leave the house.

Son's understanding and manipulation of Valerian is also clear in this same scene when Son relates a joke about "the three colored whores who went to heaven" (148) and evokes laughter from Valerian loud enough "to beat the band" (149). Playing on the white master's desire to be entertained by his black servants, Son gives Valerian what he wants. Also, in relating a joke just after being questioned about being in Margaret's bedroom, Son is able to extend the stereotype of the happy, grinning, asexual darky and divert Valerian's attention even further away from any possibility of a serious threat to Margaret. This process enables him to redirect sexual assumptions as well; Son restores the chaste white woman (Margaret) to her pedestal by implying that it is black women (not black men) who are sexually promiscuous. The black women become an abstraction that can be insulted from a distance, whereas Margaret's immediate presence makes references to her potentially dangerous. Son's motive in being willing to insult the black women he praises in other circumstances might simply be credited to expediency, but it nonetheless evokes ambivalent responses. This ambivalence, however, does not ultimately detract from the power he wields in the situation.

The power that Son has is also clear in his assessment of Valerian's handling of Thérèse's theft of the Christmas apples. Unlike Valerian, whose power resides in his ability to shape lives in a very public way, Son's power emanates from his understanding of human nature as well as from a sense of outrage that evokes comparison to Cross Damon in Richard Wright's *The Outsider* (1953). Son is just as offended by Valerian's firing of his servants as Cross is by the Fascists in his apartment building. He imagines Valerian as a part of a vast conglomerate of white males whose sole purpose in life is to defecate on the world (203). Son's power at this point presumably resides in a clarity that enables him to separate his own actions from those of Valerian, but what he has recently done has already undercut that assumption. He has been just as willing to defecate on Jadine, to dirty her and therefore control her, as Valerian is with his servants; his self-righteousness is therefore suspect, but it nonetheless continues to highlight the amorality and ambiguity inherent in the actions of animal and human tricksters.

Son's power begins to erode when he adds an element to the trickster guise. Sex is not the usual objective of the trickster. Even in those situations in which tricksters must enter the vagina and break the male-destroying teeth located there, the focus is less on the sexuality of the female than on the power of the male. In those contests in which a female is the object of a conflict between the trickster and an adversary, the prize is not tied to her value as a female but to the trickster's ability to defeat his opponent. When Brer Rabbit declares to Miss Meadows that he uses Brer Fox as a riding horse and sets out to prove it, he does so less out of a sense of Miss Meadows's innate value than out of a sense of insult because the Fox has challenged him for Miss Meadows's attention.[8] If we follow this line of analysis in the trickster dynamics Morrison has set up in *Tar Baby*, it becomes clear that Son loses his power in direct proportion to his focusing upon Jadine as having intrinsic value in and of herself.

The folkloristic dynamic changes, and Son moves from being trickster to victim, for Jadine's value as the tar baby comes to the fore, her sexuality becomes the stickiness that attracts Son, and he begins to exhibit the error-prone ways that have proven the downfall of many tricksters. In his interactions with Jadine once they leave the island, Son is never as clearly in control as Soldier asserts that he is accustomed to being in relationships. He goes into Jadine's briar patch in New York, where she is trickster *and* tar baby. He must conform to her world and her values. He is the prized stud that she parades before her friends. She manipulates him into taking examinations and applying to schools he has no interest in attending.

Son's downfall is assured when he insists upon taking Jadine to Eloe, Florida, where his relatives reside. Again, in a nonconventional move for the trickster, he seeks a traditional relationship and therefore continues to value female as female instead of female as medium of exchange or impetus to contest. When Son gives over his destiny to Jadine, that is the final step in his transition from trickster to victim. By abdicating his position of power, he might become more human, but he also becomes more vulnerable. Detachment has been his salvation; involvement is the key to his downfall.

It is appropriate that the message of downfall centers upon sexuality, for in the original versions of the tar baby story, those from India and Africa, that message is central. In India, it is Buddha who must escape the temptations of the flesh; in Africa, a female tar baby is set to capture a culprit. Although American versions of the tale have only rarely included an explicit female in the role of tar baby, that connotation can sometimes be implied. The "stick-fast" motif, in which Brer Rabbit strikes the tar baby at five different points, can perhaps be viewed as a kind of penetration, and the tar baby is forced to play a traditionally submissive, nonresistant role to this male violation.

The point is that Son gives in to the temptation—not to what the tar baby *represents*, but to what the tar baby *is*—which makes him even more vulnerable. Because he re-centers the contest from Valerian and himself to Jadine and himself, he loses whatever objectivity, whatever control made it possible for him to be the subject of desire.

By transferring that to Jadine, he delivers himself into her less-than-tender hands. Absolute judgment is irrelevant here, for Jadine and Son have been equally attracted to each other, equally willing to use and abuse the other, equally anxious and willing to control the other. Morrison manages to subvert whatever unqualified sympathy may be directed toward either character by casting them in molds of ambivalence.

Our understanding of the traditional tale would lead us to expect that L'Arbe de la Croix is the invaded territory, the prized garden or paradise into which Son comes in the guise of rabbit trickster. This analogy would lead us to expect that Jadine is the prized possession (and certainly she is from Sydney and Ondine's point of view) stolen from that forbidden territory. Another possibility would be to consider Eloe (the garden of cultural heritage) the territory into which Jadine comes to steal away one of its most prized possessions, namely Son. In this reading, she plays around in the garden (with her camera and her attitudes), is there only because of the value she places on Son, takes what he has to offer (sex, a temporary diversion from her boredom), tries to reshape him, and leaves when he proves intractable.[9]

If we view Jadine in this context as taking on characteristics of the trickster, then these traits center upon her identification with systemic power. She wants to trick Son into acceptance of the emasculating (for black males) values of the American economic and social system, which shows the merging of her roles. Son sees her as the "gatekeeper, advance bitch, house-bitch, welfare office torpedo, corporate cunt, tar baby side-of-the-road whore trap" (219–20) for black men like himself. He extends that analogy later by again identifying Jadine with forces set in motion to trap black men. When the rabbit comes eating the white farmer's cabbages, Son tells Jadine, "he got this great idea about how to get him. How to, to trap . . . this rabbit. And you know what he did? He made him a tar baby. He made it, you hear me? He made it!" (270). In spite of his assertion that Jadine was set in motion and is yet controlled by whites, Son is unable to resist her. Jadine may be the glue that could bind him to a sense of his place in the society, but she is manipulative enough to direct him to the glue (the trickster role) as well as to bind him there (the tar baby role). Her femininity makes her a tar baby, but her color makes her a trickster (identified with the white farmer to whom Son refers).

She maintains the amorality of the trickster by being able to dismiss Son from her life as easily as she buffs a "tiny irregularity" (290) in a fingernail to instant perfection as she is on her final flight to Paris. She moves on to other adventures because she has understood more clearly than Son the rules of the game they have been playing. Unlike him, she has allowed nothing to touch her in a possibly permanent way. Her ability to detach herself emotionally, to claim her destiny for herself, becomes almost masculine in the trickster analogy. She keeps the center of value focused upon herself and is therefore never seriously threatened by Son; indeed, we might say that she forms a community of one, complete unto herself. In retaining the negative traits of the trickster without mitigating positive ones, Jadine can only continue to be an ambivalent character, not a heroic one.

Son's permanent spiritual attachment to Jadine presupposes that he will never be in control of his own destiny again. Once he realizes that she has indeed left New York for good, he concludes: "Whatever she wants, I have to do it, want it. But first I have to find her" (273). Since he has obviously not wanted to be and do everything she wanted, his expression of that willingness amounts to a defeat, a resignation to lack of control over his own life. That abdication enables Thérèse to step in where Jadine has left off and make a decision for Son. She therefore leads him to the opposite side of the island when he requests help in getting there, and leaves him in the realm of myth and legend. In his running "lickety-split" and "looking neither to the left nor to the right" (306) at the end of the novel, he has either joined those lost souls he observed in New York in that they too have given up the better part of themselves, or he is running with the purposefulness of a man who has at last made a decision to reclaim himself.[10]

Morrison's use of the tar baby folktale in her novel allows for provocative mixtures of tricksters, tar babies, and victims. As is true with all of her works, she makes it impossible to delineate clearly agents of good and evil; qualification of some sort is always necessary. By assigning Son, Valerian, and Jadine overlapping parts of the tar baby and trickster interactions, Morrison gives new dimensions to the racial and sexual dynamics inherent in that folktale. More important, she saturates her novel with a folkloristic base designed to illustrate that the powerful and the powerless are as much victims of their own imaginations as they are of the trickster-generated actions in which they are sometimes caught.[11]

Of "Ancient Properties" and Other Misnomers

While we can read Jadine into the role of African-American tar baby or trickster, other possibilities exist for interpreting her as well. Just as there can be simultaneity in the interpretation of tricksters/victims, Morrison also offers simultaneity in the layering of folkloristic forms. If we focus on the novel within the heroic tradition of the African-American toast or from the perspective of a fairy tale, those patterns reveal Jadine as antithetical to, rather than belonging within, African-American folk traditions.

From these angles of vision, therefore, critics who have read Jadine Childs in the context of a woman who has somehow lost contact with her cultural properties may be on the wrong track in assessing her.[12] Instead of reading the novel in an effort to reclaim Jadine for black people and black culture, it might be more fruitful to let her go. Jadine has been happily outside of African-American folk culture all of her life and clearly does not wish to be claimed by anyone who resembles or descends from the inhabitants of a place like Eloe, Florida, which provides our only contrast to the "Philadelphia Negroes." Her encounters with the women of eggs and breasts are perhaps less about culture than they are about femininity. Her disturbed reactions to them are located in personal discomfort more so than in guilt for failing to identify totally with black people. Her middle-class upbringing, her schooling, and her profession have all separated her from the masses of black people. The culture she bears is not that with an African base, but that with a basis in notions of realizing the American dream. Her place in the novel's society, therefore, is with Franklin, Emerson, and Thoreau, as Ellison would say, not with cornpone and trickster tales. The upward mobility that has been carved out for her by Sydney and Ondine has long since eliminated the possibility that she would ever see Son, the people of

Eloe, or their culture as anything but quaint and curious—good for brief, possibly entertaining, interludes, but ultimately boring beyond endurance.[13]

It is easy to be unsympathetic to Jadine. Here is a black woman who turns her back on family, denies her heritage, profanes her love relationship, and haughtily departs for another country. Our lack of sympathy for her is cued into the cultural symbols surrounding the conceptualization of her character. Understanding these symbols clarifies why Jadine can never be heroic. Culturally, we are unprepared for Jadine. In defying the things we value, she looms as an arrogant person, Alice Walker's Myrna turned seasoned rebel, without caring or concern for anything. Our negative reaction to Jadine, however, is predicated upon the inability of members of the culture to applaud the traits she has when they appear in feminine guise; we would readily accept all that Jadine is, and most of her actions, if the doer of the action were male instead of female. In other words, African-American folk culture has not prepared us well for a female outlaw, or for a beauty queen with the traits of an outlaw. The burden placed upon Jadine is that of ties to the women of breasts and eggs. When she denies that role, indeed assumes her individuality, she evokes negative rather than positive reaction. We can applaud Milkman even when he is immoral because we have so many masculine models for the individual resisting the pressures of community. We can see traits of Stagolee in Milkman as well as in Son, but we have no models for accepting Jadine as a "bad woman."

In the lore, women who attempt to be bad are subdued by the men with whom they dare to compete. The immoral women of the fornication contests always seem to meet their match. Females in trickster tales frequently serve as prizes for the men. Women who dare to assert individualistic values over communal ones are summarily put in their places. Men who follow individualistic paths are deemed heroic; that remains so even when they are consciously iconoclastic outlaws such as Stagolee.

Stagolee's exploits do not occur in an arena where he confronts a recognized enemy of the community, at least not initially. He insults and kills other black men. He disrespects older black women, and he sexually exploits the younger ones. He recognizes no laws except those generated by his own code of survival. He defies societal courts and laws by extending and solidifying his marginality not only as a black human being, but as a mean-spirited, death-dealing black man. Totally responsible for the set of circumstances he creates, he accepts the consequences of perverted creation. He neither seeks nor accepts sympathy or partnership in his ventures. The ultimate destroyer of values, Stagolee nonetheless reaps the approbation of the hero because the values finally are not those of his community, but those of the larger society. Tellers of Stagolee's exploits believe that those values, often antithetical to the life and health of the black community, deserve to be upset; they therefore side with Stagolee in his temporary triumph over the almost unbeatable foe of white power. This victory seems to outweigh in the tellers' minds the fact that Stagolee's aggression is initially turned against his own community.

Historically documented African-American heroic figures, such as Morris Slater, similarly share the community's values even when they perpetuate "criminal" or unacceptable behavior. Slater killed a white policeman in self-defense and eluded authorities in Alabama for three years in the 1890s. He "became well known for breaking into crates on trains, removing their contents and throwing them out along the tracks only to return later to pick them up. He then sold his bounty to poor African Americans who lived along the railroad tracks. His train robbing exploits earned him the name of 'Railroad Bill.' "[14] Railroad Bill became heroic because he acted in favor of community, not against it, and he did so by undermining the power and authority of the larger white community

Jadine is not only an outlaw in a world where male outlaws are more readily tolerated than female ones, but she is a communal and familial outlaw, not a societal one. By directing her passive-aggressive behavior at people like herself, without the broader challenging or upsetting of the status quo, Jadine looks more like a monster than Stagolee, even without murdering other blacks. More to her detriment, she "kills" family, community, and culture, which are infinitely more significant than the loss of a single individual's life.

Sydney, Ondine, Valerian, and Margaret have all shared in the paving of Jadine's road to individualism. Initially, as an orphaned child, she elicits everyone's sympathy. The feelings Ondine and

Sydney hold toward her are augmented by her making up for the child they can never have: "She crowned me" (193), Ondine asserts to show how much she values Jadine. Thus elevated, Jadine early learns that Sydney and "Nanadine" are willing to make excruciating sacrifices for her. In the tradition of the "Philadelphia Negro" with which he claims kinship, Sydney wants only the best for his niece.[15] In the process of lavishing things and attention upon her, and expecting very little in return, Sydney and Ondine give Jadine the license to trample on their hearts, as she will later do. They raise her in the tradition of a "chosen one," a little black girl who, through the advantages heaped upon her, should always know the distinction between her kind of black folks and those who masquerade in the same skin color.

In raising Jadine in the Street household, Sydney and Ondine are not appreciably different from the many black servants who taught their children to prefer the paths and values of the master to those of their own culture (and in contrast to most black homes, the Street home really is like a castle). That stream of indoctrination extends from characters like Mammy Jane and Jerry in Chesnutt's *The Marrow of Tradition* (1901) to Granny and Rosie Fleming in Kristin Hunter's *God Bless the Child* (1967) to the unspoken models in Morrison's *The Bluest Eye*. Jadine is taught that she is *different*, by association with and by virtue of having privileges made available by the Streets. If there is royalty in the black community, then she is taught that she deserves a throne. The inculcation of such values for self-improvement do not have negative implications in the abstract, but when Jadine tries to associate with other black people on practical levels, as in Eloe, it is clear that, for her, difference has also meant permanent spiritual separation.

Valerian and Margaret also help mold Jadine into a princess who loses the ability to sympathize with her own people. Especially is this true of Valerian. Indeed, the fact that Jadine evokes an analogy to fairy tales such as "Sleeping Beauty" emphasizes her oppositional relationship to black culture. In her illustration, once again, of where a fairy tale pattern meets black life and clashes with it, Morrison portrays Jadine as a creature of comfort, one who prefers things to people and who does not value the culture or the people who have nourished her enough to embrace them instead of those values antithetical to them. Jadine is a princess in a world where the price of the kingdom is the price of identity, where coats made of the hides of ninety baby seals are preferable to those "ancient properties"—even if she knew what they were—that would link her to black people in her own family as well as globally.

Early on, when Valerian contributed to Jadine's education, he was acting in many ways as a fairy godmother would. Jadine was the chosen one by virtue of her ties to Sydney and Ondine, and Valerian had the power and money to ensure that her future would be bright. His altruism was perhaps not selfishly motivated, but it definitely had advantages for Valerian. With Jadine resembling a white mainliner as much as possible, she could become the companion to his much younger and restless wife. If Jadine, after initial training, could become Margaret's "social secretary," then perhaps Margaret would be more content with her position as the rather useless wife of a candy magnate. Simply by being who he is—a powerful white man with the ability to influence a number of lives—Valerian can exert control over Jadine. It is not within his sensibility to encourage a sense of blackness in Jadine, for that is antithetical to his own experience and utterly useless in his environment. So his molding of her takes the form of that with which he is most familiar—his own background and values. He indoctrinates Jadine to the value of education without placing it in the same liberating vein in which most black people view it. He teaches her the value of business solely for the sake of making money, not because there is some intrinsically character-forming quality to it. He thus gives her advantages without the altruistic attitudes toward race and culture that should inform them; consequently, she develops allegiances to things and people unlike Son and those she encounters in Eloe (she will also ultimately turn away from Sydney and Ondine).

Prior to her meeting the black woman in yellow in Paris, Jadine has been asleep to black culture and to any value of or commitment to black people, and she has erroneously assumed that she is a near perfect, *total* woman. She has pursued school, modeling, and French recipes and social gatherings without any concern for a past or a future not in the same glittering mold. Indeed, her geographical movements translate into her embracing of a Eurocentric view of the world and her abandonment of a potentially Afrocentric perspective. Jadine extends the traditional pattern of movement from South to North in the quest for freedom all the way to Paris, where the outer ranges of the pattern become indistinguishable from traits alien to African-American culture. Paris is the Old World European cultural base Jadine values in preference to things American or black. There, she can be the colorless or "white" model whose slightly dusky features invite intrigue and curiosity rather than raising issues of color and discrimination. So she wallows in luxury, unaware of any black world that could be relevant to her—until the black woman in yellow spits out her disgust for high-yellow black women (46).

A sympathetic response to Jadine would be to assert that the woman victimizes her; that possibility, however, is mitigated by Jadine's staring at the woman, detachedly observing her in the same way the whites do. Her visual vantage point therefore aligns her with the evaluators of blackness who would assign it a lesser value. The woman senses this in Jadine—the curiosity instead of the kinship—and responds accordingly. She, like other blacks, knows that she can direct her irritation at being observed toward Jadine, who is less likely to retaliate, indeed is less capable of retaliating, than the whites in the store. By recognizing a shared powerlessness, the woman places Jadine in a category with herself, while she simultaneously rejects her with the spitting gesture, which reminds Jadine that she has been outside of blackness as she has stared at the woman.

The eggs the woman carries, her expansive baby-producing hips, her regal demeanor all suggest to Jadine that there is an essence of femininity and fertility that the woman represents that she can never claim as her own: "that woman's woman—that mother/sister/she; that unphotographable beauty" (46). Both traits get tied into blackness because Jadine cannot separate out what she finds most fascinating. Is total womanhood also tied to being a *black* woman? Must beauty always be made an exception in someone who is so strikingly black? Can blackness ever be detached from its perceptions by a staring world? As a black woman, is the relationship she has with Ryk merely a game in the presence of this *real* thing? Are efforts to suppress blackness useless, when it will "pop out" even in the midst of predominantly white Paris?

The encounter with the African woman begins Jadine's awakening from her carefree, deliciously irresponsible slumber. A bit more rude than a prince's kiss, the jolt sends her briefly on another path. She is disconcerted enough to go back to her "roots," so to speak, during which her plan will be altered, and she will eventually be forced to think through some of the cultural issues of blackness and whiteness. Preferring retreat to transformation, she originally intends to draw strength from Sydney and Ondine and reassurance from Valerian and Margaret, and to leave without really explaining to them why she has come. In that place so conducive in its natural lushness to whatever fairy tale notions she wants to maintain, Jadine can perpetuate whatever myths she wants; the only truths she needs are the ones that support her philosophy.

The geographically based, Eurocentric ethic that touts individuality over community begins to emerge as Jadine shows her insensitivity to the people who have nourished her. She clearly wants to avoid commitment and responsibility when Ondine declares: "Don't you ever leave us, baby. You all we got" (40), and she sees herself as "playing daughter" (68) to Sydney and Ondine. When the fights between Valerian and Margaret become vicious, she is unwilling to attend to the problems of her benefactors. When Margaret rushes from the table just before she discovers Son in her closet, and Valerian rambles to Jadine about his relationship with Michael, Jadine is too self-centered to notice that Valerian and Margaret both have regrets about Michael. Instead, Jadine is the polite, superficial creature they have created, giving an ear—and barely that—to their problems. She sits passively bored as Valerian remembers his relationship to Michael:

> Another cup of coffee, another glass of port—nothing could bring her alive to the memories of an old man. I ought to be saying something, she thought. I ought to be asking questions and making comments instead of smiling and nodding like a puppet. Hoping there was a residue of interest in her eyes, she held her chin toward him and continued to smile—but only a little—in case what he was remembering was poignant but not happy. Long ago she had given up trying to be deft or profound or anything in the company of people she was not interested in, who didn't thrill her. Gazing at her stem of crystal she knew that whatever he was saying, her

> response was going to miss the point entirely. Her mind was in
> automatic park. (77)

Having contributed to the creation of the princess who has turned
from passivity to active control of her life, Valerian evokes no more
pity from her than do her blood relatives. They have all trained her
well, given her the money and the support to acquire skills that will
enable her to live without them, to dismiss them as insignificant to
her future.

Her self-centeredness makes clear that, as a woman and as a
black human being, Jadine had only been shocked, not substantially
changed, by the reaction of the woman in yellow in Paris. She needs
a greater jolt to awaken fully from the narrowness of her cultural,
racial vision. When Margaret discovers Son in her closet, Jadine realizes that everything the woman in yellow represented about blackness has invaded her island paradise, fairy tale world. Son picks up
where the African woman left off in making Jadine confront what
she has blissfully ignored for so many years. Through her interactions with him, her rejection of blackness and her questionable identity as a woman become clear. Refusing to accept the escape route
from insipidity that Son offers her, to become in spirit the beauty
that she is physically, she decides instead to retreat into the lair of
the beast, to sleep once again among dangers to her people if not
specifically to her person.

Jadine's realization of what the faint duskiness in her skin ties
her to in terms of black people like Son and the inhabitants of Eloe
makes her renounce them forever. The renunciation properly begins
and ends with Son, whose striking, unapologetic blackness comes
through from the moment Sydney ushers him at gunpoint into the
Streets' dining room. Initially unsettled by his color and his general
unkempt appearance, Jadine is no less unsettled by the unobtrusive
arrogance she senses in the man. Here is someone who should perhaps be on his knees, begging and pleading for understanding and
sympathy, yet Son defies all forms of humility and subservience
even as he stands with a gun at his back and his hands clasped
above his head. Black without compromise, male without the polish
to which Jadine is accustomed, Son assaults directly everything the
African woman has hinted at in spitting at Jadine. The little "white"

girl who has forgotten that she is black can return to her "whiteness" only by suppressing that blackness forever. She denies passion, spiritual affinity with black people, history, and the power of the past to influence the present or the future.

Beyond her initial disgust in the dining room scene, Jadine finds herself physically, sexually aroused by Son, perhaps in one of those stereotypical responses to the presumed sexual prowess of black males, but also in genuine attraction. If she would win the security of being the irresponsible princess again, then she must contain that passion, or, if it is unleashed, find the strength to walk away from it. Passion must be controlled and manipulated in the world represented by Paris; it must be made into an art where one lover understands if the other has an occasional fling with a third party, as Ryk makes clear to Jadine. If passion becomes all-consuming, as Jadine concludes about what she witnesses and becomes a part of in the black community, then it is potentially too destructive to exist. Feeling, self-expression, emotion, and commitment are what Jadine sees threatening with Son; resistance means keeping all of those feelings in contained spaces.

Her image of containment is represented by dogs on a leash; if she can contain the lightning movement suggested by their silver feet, then perhaps she has a chance to come through the encounter with Son unscathed (the leash is a magical talisman, suggesting an extranatural—restrained, nonhuman—quality). But to control Son is to deny herself, to ignore the freedom of feeling and expression that she identifies with black people. She feels her first "bolt of fear" when she realizes that there is probably more to the man than his hiding around the house has suggested: "As long as he burrowed in his plate like an animal, grunting in monosyllables, but not daring to look up, she was without fear. But when he smiled she saw small dark dogs galloping on silver feet" (94). He arouses in her whatever feelings of spontaneity she has left after the art and modeling worlds in which she has spent her life; symbol of fertility and sexuality, the dogs can only inspire Jadine to try to leash them again and again. Her relationship with Son wavers between when she holds the reins securely, that is, when she can resist him, and when she cannot.

Control (the impulse to individuality; making Son respond to her on her terms) versus lack of control (bowing to communal wishes; being irresistibly receptive to Son) dominate Jadine's interactions with Son. The "small dark dogs galloping on silver feet" (113) must be restrained when Son wanders into her bedroom. Responsive feelings toward him initially take her voice. When the conversation reaches a manageable level—around a question about Gideon—Jadine "smiled, searching for the leashes of the small dark dogs" (115). When Son asks for a cigarette, a neutral, nonthreatening subject, "Jadine grabbed the leashes" (115). When the subject becomes personal again, about Valerian's support for her, she makes sure that "the leather was knotted tightly around her wrists" (119). She works desperately to check her feelings and save the image she has of herself.

When that image is upset, when Son maintains that he "smells" her there in the bedroom just as she smells him, she is reminded of her childhood in Baltimore in which a dog in heat was pursued by several males. The intensity of the natural urge clashed with the public witnessing of the pursuit to teach Jadine that such passion should always be controlled, for the female, the "bitch," was the one knocked over the head and blamed for something that was not within her natural power to control. Determined not to be like the female dog, to be used at the mercy of males, Jadine had resolved that she would never allow her basic femaleness to be her downfall; she will retain control at all costs. Her years of schooling had cultivated an exterior manner, "but beneath the easy manners was a claw always ready to rein in the dogs, because Never" (124) would she be used, abused, and discarded.

The clean-shaven Son presents more of a threat to Jadine than the unkempt one. When he asks to play the piano, "he did not know that all the time he tinkled the keys she was holding tight to the reins of dark dogs with silver feet. For she was more frightened of his good looks than she had been by his ugliness the day before" (158). She connects him to the woman in Paris; he "distracts" her from the insult she had felt with that woman. And she wonders at this point if she can remember his name and "would she say it out loud without reaching for the leash?" (159). Ultimately Jadine relaxes the leash, and she gives in to Son—for a time. When the affair is over, however, when she is about to board the plane to Paris, she concludes of her

New York experience that "the dogs were leashed in the city but the reins were not always secure" (288). She has run away from Son in part because she doubts her ability not to give in to the passion he represents, but also because the pull of Paris is safer; it can be controlled without the same kind of exertion.

In her personal involvement with Son, Jadine rejects spontaneity for control, feeling for art. In the trip to Eloe, she rejects spiritual affinity with black people as well as the history that ties her specifically to black women. She cannot see in a woman like Rosa, who has built the room in which Jadine sleeps, the same kind of desire for independence that she ascribes to herself in being a model. She sees the morality of the women as the height of the primitive and cannot see that their assumed poverty is really their refusal to give up self-control for welfare. She prefers to see herself in an earthy competition with the women instead of sharing roles and aspirations with them. Whatever they do, whatever they want, is to her mind at an elementary stage in the evolutionary cycle to the sophistication with which she characterizes herself.

Her life, therefore, is not about having forgotten her ancient properties; it is a refusal to recognize the existence or value of such properties. Jadine cannot give up what she has never had, has refused to learn, and has rejected before understanding. The opposition in the novel between elitism and folk culture, as well as between European values (Old World, high culture) and American values (popular culture) places Jadine on the side of the former in each category. It is impossible, given her training, inclination, and extreme independence, for her to embrace anything that would threaten either of those categories. She therefore rejects those nurturing women because of their giving nature; she rejects the African woman because her basic existence is not accounted for in the European conception of art; and she rejects Son because he wants to change her attitude toward her education, toward Paris, and toward her notion of her commitment to other people, but especially to him. Finally, Jadine is indeed an Orphan Woman, free to create herself from whatever snippets of whatever cultures she desires, but she succeeds in fashioning a model of uselessness to all of them.

Magical Realism and the African-American Folk Tradition

It might reasonably be argued that, whereas God shaped man in His image, African-Americans have in turn shaped the supernatural and the inanimate portions of this world in the image of human beings. As creators of a vibrant lore, they have made it replete with beings from all realms of planetary interaction. Perhaps reflecting their origins in agrarian countries and their first occupations in the United States, black Americans have willfully drawn their imaginative conceptions from nature, consciously seen themselves as a part of the natural world, and based their healing traditions in the organic arts. These tendencies reflect an acceptance of humankind's place as one of many creatures on the planet, a kind of democracy that recognizes a continuum of existence, shared origins, and the absence of barriers between humankind, animals, and nature. It is no accident in African-American folklore that God speaks in a southern dialect, for that is what most creators of black American folklore spoke; nor is it unexpected that God is concerned about mosquitoes or the tradition of "Christmas gift," for the landscape and the customs of the South similarly influenced the world view that black people created in their lore.[16]

The general anthropomorphism assigned to God pervades African-American folklore and is perhaps captured most vividly in literature in James Weldon Johnson's *God's Trombones* (1927), where God walks, talks, smiles, and shows pleasure with His handiwork in the same way that human beings might. But clearly God is not the only supernatural being who has been afforded speech and movement in the lore; so have Saint Peter and other angels, along with the devil and his cohorts. In fact, the African-American folk world view makes allowances for frequent cooperation between God and the devil, for the devil serving as the impetus to certain heavenly phenomena, or for God serving as the impetus to certain devilish practices.[17] African-American storytellers feel little need to dichotomize their world view. As numerous scholars have pointed out, there is an established interweaving of the good and the bad, the secular and the sacred, in African-American culture. Indeed, that interweaving works well in explaining Morrison's consistent refusal to stratify her works into absolutes; evil can perhaps reside in good human beings just as goodness can in those presumed to be evil. Who knows, as the presumably evil Sula points out, if she has not been the good one in the relationship between herself and staid, churchgoing, status quo–supporting Nel.

The anthropomorphism assigned to God, angels, and the devil extends as well to elephants, owls, rabbits, raccoons, and every now and then a tree or two. Humankind, according to this world view, is not solely privileged on the planet; it is just one of many species of creatures who can cross superficial boundaries and communicate with each other. Anthropomorphism, personification, animism, sentience—whatever term is preferable, African-Americans have made the concept pervasive in their lore.

This folkloric background, then, provides the springboard from which to begin a discussion of Morrison's incorporation of sentience and speech for nonhuman beings in *Tar Baby*. Instead of considering Isle des Chevaliers a tainted or "perverse" Eden, as some critics do,[18] it could just as easily be considered a prelapsarian incarnation of folk imagination, where beings are not bound by their later prescribed natural proclivities. Or it could be considered a reclamation of folk mythology, in which it is just as natural for trees, butterflies, and reptiles to communicate and to experience pain as it is for human beings. The river that runs raging through a pained earth on the island is not so far removed from the hills and valleys that round out and shape themselves at God's command in the folk account of the creation of the world.

On Isle des Chevaliers, sentient rivers are not the aberration; people are. People have created an opposition in the novel where there should be harmony, that is, an opposition between humankind and nature. The talking, feeling, nonhuman beings are the vestiges of that harmony and offer the key to possibly reclaiming it. Those people who created the rupture between humankind and nature have long gone, but their descendants—the Streets, Sydney and Ondine, Jadine, and Son—are in a position to rethink that rupture and to try to repair it. Characters like Valerian and Jadine, who have no interest in the natural world, are ultimate losers in this bid for reconciliation. Margaret, Sydney, and Ondine would all prefer Philadelphia to the island. Son, who proves to be most sensitive to the natural order of things, has the greatest potential to restore harmony and eliminate the strife.

The mythic world of Isle des Chevaliers shares with other myths the formation of a civilization or race or place because of a wrong that has been done to it, some pain that has been caused.[19] The luxurious world of L'Arbe de la Croix has come into being upon the back of a wounded earth and its creatures; it cannot therefore expect to thrive overly long. As Morrison tells the story, the building of "winter houses" on the island led the clouds and fish to believe that "the world was over" (9), a message they communicated to the parrots, who sought another refuge. The initially serene champion daisy trees were finally convinced that "the world was altered" when the river began to run wild from the reshaping of the earth for excavation for the houses.

> The men had already folded the earth where there had been no fold and hollowed her where there had been no hollow, which explains what happened to the river. It crested, then lost its course, and finally its head. Evicted from the place where it had lived, and forced into unknown turf, it could not form its pools or waterfalls, and ran every which way . . . until exhausted, ill and grieving, it slowed to a stop just twenty leagues short of the sea. (9)

And the champion daisy trees, assaulted by men, became "wild-eyed and yelling," and "broke in two and hit the ground" (10). The disruption of the natural world leads to an elegy for the river, the source of life: "Poor insulted, brokenhearted river. Poor demented stream. Now it sat in one place like a grandmother and became a swamp the Haitians called Sein de Vieilles. And witch's tit it was: a shriveled fogbound oval seeping with a thick black substance that even mosquitoes could not live near" (10). The center of personification in the tragedy of defilement, the river shares traits with human beings who have been violated in some way and discarded, or rendered useless, like a grandmother, victimized by unyielding, unthinking forces intent upon their own conception of the world.

The quality of suffering assigned to the river echoes that of humans who have suffered acute losses. As in the human world, however, the natural beings count their losses and go on with their existence. This somewhat reduced state of being is what Son encounters when he arrives on the island and what Jadine will encounter after her picnic with Son. The island has been good to Son before his discovery by Margaret; he has been wrapped in the cover of darkness, protected against discovery as long as he depended upon the natural habitat to cloak his movements. It is when he ventures into the artificial structure, the house, and overstays his sojourn there that he is discovered. Like Brer Rabbit in his briar patch, Son can manipulate the impressions of darkness, but he loses that ability in direct proportion to his willingness to identify with the inhabitants of L'Arbe de la Croix, to be transformed from a natural to an unnatural state.

Unnaturalness in the novel takes a variety of forms, affecting most of the characters. It is unnatural for Valerian to wall himself off from the bountiful growth of the island, unnatural for him to ignore the sea (water—again the source of life) except as it brings mail (a human invention) into his life. It is unnatural for him to carve out an artificial garden in the midst of an abundant natural garden, and unnatural for him to try to keep natural creatures, like ants, out of that garden. It is unnatural for him to force manmade bricks into the resistant dirt in front of the greenhouse. In preferring artifice to life, art to vibrancy, Valerian resembles the creatures on Keats's Grecian urn; they have attained beauty at the price of life. When Valerian's artificial world is reclaimed by nature near the end of the novel, he does not recognize that as the potential for restored harmony, but as the dissolution of the world as he knows it.

Margaret and others in the household are also unnatural in the sense of having lost touch with the organic growth around them as well as with those parts of themselves that are most closely bound to nature. With Margaret, that tendency might be capsulized in her taping of the "frownies" between her eyes; she tries to delay the effect of these natural aging marks, cultivating her artifice of beauty—typified in her "beautifully manicured" (24) hands and her designation as the "Principal Beauty"—just as Valerian cultivates his garden. Her masking her eyes in sleep and protecting herself from the sun while sunbathing are equal attempts to place a wall between her conception of herself and what she really is: a part of nature. And that cultivation of her unnatural status has perhaps culminated in her relationship to Michael, toward whom it has been difficult for her to be an unqualified success as mother. Of the relationship between Margaret and Michael, Ondine comments: "I didn't say he didn't love her; I said he don't want to be near her. Sure he love her. That's only natural. He's not the one who's not natural. She is" (36). A mother who abuses her child, rather than protects and nurtures him, is as much an aberration of human nature as the winter houses on Isle des Chevaliers are an affront to its organic system.

Even Sydney and Ondine view the natural beauty of the island more as oppression than possibility. Ondine seemingly prefers not to work outside the house, just as it is difficult for her to understand why the "Marys" prefer that outdoor world. Clothed in somebody else's notion of civilization, Sydney and Ondine have for years been willing to allow their relation to the natural world to be formed by their employer. Unable or unwilling to separate their identity from his, they are just as caught in the unnatural perpetuation of their existence as he is. That unnaturalness toward the organic world is mirrored in the strained relationship between them and Jadine, who can never really conceptualize what it means to be a responsible niece/daughter/woman.

Jadine's profession as a model, with its connotations of art and artifice, cleanliness and purification, consciously removing the funkiness from life (as Geraldine does in *The Bluest Eye*), is well chosen to illustrate the problematic position she holds in relation to natural states. The human body is a naturally smelly organism; it is no wonder that the greatest insult to Jadine is Son's assertion that she smells. For a model to smell is perhaps comparable to a debutante loudly expending gas during her formal presentation—just too much for anyone who has eliminated the funkiness from life. No wonder, then, that the insult from Son evokes the fighting response that it does from Jadine. And no wonder that Jadine is able to appreciate natural beauty only when it has been sanitized into the artifice of the hides of ninety baby seals.

The funkiness of smelling is tied to the key area in which Jadine wishes to remain unnaturally in control: sex. For Son to smell her reminds her of the scene she had witnessed of a dog in heat when she was twelve years old. Rather than ever being so humiliated by males, Jadine had determined to keep the dogs of sexuality firmly on leash. By smelling her, Son "had jangled something in her that was so repulsive, so awful, and he had managed to make her feel that the thing that repelled her was not in him, but in her" (123). That uncommonly repulsive thing is simply uncensored, natural sexual attraction, something that the artful, restrained Jadine will not allow herself to experience.

To further illustrate how oppositional the characters are in relation to their environment, Morrison sets up the picnic scene with Jadine and Son. Jadine takes her sketch pad to freeze images from nature (just as she will later use her camera to freeze images of the black people in Eloe); indeed, she is unable to sketch Son unless he is still, thereby bending his naturalness to her will. His spontaneous laughter at one point is "disarming" (170) because he lifts his head to the sky and disrupts the studied, controlled image she would prefer. She concludes that she cannot become involved with Son because he is not "manageable" (180). He displays such human emotions as anger when driving his car through the house where his wife was being unfaithful with her adolescent lover, whereas Jadine would prefer to keep entangling emotions, such as Son displays in admiring her feet, safely hidden.

Jadine's desire to escape from everything not subject to her intellectual control becomes even clearer when she is caught in the swamp following the picnic. The tar is not simply an inconvenience for her; it is anathema. It becomes a metaphor for possible emotional entrapment. Consequently, Jadine is unable to identify with the spirit of femaleness, exemplified by the women in the trees, that such involvement might represent. Instead of reaffirming the essential femaleness in herself, she remains in a state of rejection. She is shown thus to be a violator in a world that would embrace her if her attitude were different; the spirit of femaleness represented in the trees again shows the possibility for harmony between humankind and nature, a possibility to which Jadine remains willfully blind. Jadine does not realize that the trees for whom she shows no respect are really the source of her rescue from the pithy swamp (182), just as the natural spirit of femaleness could rescue her from the materialistic, nonculturally black life-style that she leads. The women in the trees, in their "exceptional femaleness," marvel at Jadine's "desperate struggle" "to be something other than they were" (183). In being something other than they are, something not of nature, Jadine continues to choose the semblance of feeling over its true expression.

By centering sentience and understanding of basic femaleness in the trees, and showing Jadine holding herself willfully, angrily outside that knowledge, Morrison makes clear where the lacks are that create the disruption between the human and natural worlds. As earlier with the woman in yellow in Paris and later with the women who haunt her by exposing their breasts in Eloe, Jadine's lacks are shown to be suppressed parts of her basic nature, the "smells" that she will not admit into her consciousness.

Jadine, Valerian, Margaret, Sydney, and Ondine are therefore outside the basic conversation that goes on in the novel, the conversation between the various forms of nonhuman beings. The humans can be subjects of that conversation, but only in a disparaging way. The emperor butterflies, for example, have a more highly developed sense of propriety and morality than Jadine does. They "don't believe" that she has the coat "the angel trumpets had described to them: the hides of ninety baby seals stitched together so nicely you could not tell what part had sheltered their cute little hearts and which had cushioned their skulls" (87). She makes them blush at her unabashed caressing and celebration of the loss of some of their fellow creatures. She parades nude shamelessly before them as well as before the bougainvillea.[20]

Of the human characters, Son is the one who has the most potential for bridging the gap between humankind and nature. Having spent eight years at sea, essentially in the womb of the earth, he had known a kind of "fraternity" (168) with his fellow sailors. That fraternity had made up for a kind of homelessness he had acquired as a result of killing Cheyenne and escaping from Eloe:

> He was dwelling on his solitude, rocking in the wind, adrift. A man without human rites: unbaptized, uncircumcised, minus puberty rites or the formal rites of manhood. Unmarried and undivorced. He had attended no funeral, married in no church, raised no child. Propertyless, homeless, sought for but not after. (165–66)

The rites of earthbound humanity that he has escaped have led to rituals of incorporation with other "undocumented men" (166) whom he has met in his travels. And perhaps those undocumented

men are finally more at one with nature than their landed counterparts. Certainly they have an appreciation for the beauty and the
danger of nature, as Son does on his swim from his ship at the
beginning of the novel; the current, or water lady, can save him or
kill him.

Coughed up from the sea, Son experiences a kind of rebirth into
the natural setting on the island. Like Milkman Dead in *Song of
Solomon*, he is denuded of the trappings of civilization—clothing,
shoes—during his swim to the boat that Margaret and Jadine have
borrowed (and, like Milkman, though he has a questionable and
ambivalent past, he still has the potential for heroism). Released
from the womb of the boat to the lushness of the island, he spends
more time in the pristine state of nature—searching for food and
sleeping. His hair grows, and he reverts to the natural state of a man
in the wild who is recognized primarily by his smell, as are other
animals. The sensitive Thérèse picks up the smell: "Like a beast who
loses his animal smell after too long a diet of cooked food, a man's
smell is altered by a fast" (105). Son becomes nocturnal, perhaps
even with heightened eyesight. He is thereby more sensitive to
sights and sounds than the other inhabitants of L'Arbe de la Croix,
already in a stage that identifies him more with the champion daisy
trees and the emperor butterflies than with the less sensitive human
beings. In this state, Son has as much reason to fear people as the
river or the diamondbacks.

His metamorphosis from alignment with natural to human
world, his rite of incorporation into the Street household, disrupts
for a time his place in the natural world, although he certainly still
understands its workings. Inexplicably but appropriately, he can ad-
vise Valerian on the correct strategy for deterring the soldier ants
from entering the greenhouse (147), as well as the correct process for
getting his cyclamen to bloom (148). Even the fact that Son "smells"
Jadine, immediately after she has taken a shower, is further testament to his heightened perceptions in a world usually limited to
obvious sensory stimuli. Son is viewed as having "brought luck to
the greenhouse" (187), and his success with the cyclamen and hy-
drangea is viewed as a kind of "black magic" (189). Notions of luck
and black magic are not far removed from the extranatural quality
associated with healers and rootworkers, who are traditionally

viewed as having some special relationship to, or understanding of, nature.

In trading the island for New York, or his solitude for Jadine, Son deserts what is best for him. His story becomes that of a young man who strays from his best path to one antithetical to his very being and eventually ends up back on the right path. In returning from New York to the island, and being led to its opposite side by Thérèse, Son arrives at his destiny. He joins the legendary horsemen of the island, becomes one with myth and nature, in essence takes from the human world to give back to the natural world in atonement for previous human trespasses. If the champion daisy trees are "marshaling for war" (274) after thirty years of being overrun by humans, if the soldier ants have entered the greenhouse, then it is only appropriate that this process of reclamation take its human toll as well. Of all the men on the island, Son is the likeliest candidate to make the journey from human to natural worlds. Valerian's ability to exert his control is certainly diminished, but neither he nor Sydney is as viable a specimen for the reverse process of conquering/claiming as is Son. He can indeed become a "son" to nature as well as a "son" and companion to the older, perhaps tiring horsemen. Like an aging sorceress who claims the body of a younger woman, so can the spirit of the horsemen claim Son. It does not matter that he is initially unwilling to go the path Thérèse outlines; neither the river nor the champion daisy trees have been volunteers to what they have suffered. And in contrast to potential short-term suffering, a mere thirty-year interlude, Son, unscathed, is being offered the option of immortality in the realm of myth and legend; he, like the champion daisy trees and the rain forest they inhabit, can become "scheduled for eternity" (9). Thérèse locates the horsemen as racing "all over the hills where the rain forest is, where the champion daisy trees still grow. Go there. Choose them" (306).

One signal that this reclamation process has been possible for Son is his never having bought into the system of materialism represented by L'Arbe de la Croix and Jadine's successes in New York and Paris. He has consistently maintained that all he has wanted is his "original dime," a designation of value that has centered upon the unglamorous and "undocumented" people. The human interactions that led to his earning the dime have been elemental, people helping people without overtones of exploitation. This basic, natural interaction has shown that Son prizes the responsible ties that human beings have to each other, ties that show them most closely aligned with the natural world around them.

It takes Thérèse, the wise woman guardian of folk traditions and the intermediary between humankind and nature, to shed further light on Son's place in the novel and his potential for repairing the rupture between the two worlds. In the tradition of many such wise women, she is understandably misunderstood, assumed to be raving, or otherwise taken for granted as she lives and interprets the intersections between the two worlds. Several events in the novel make clear that she is capable of seeing without seeing (by using the eye of the mind) and knowing without knowing. Her near-blindness highlights the fact that she is more intuitive than empirical in her understanding of the world, that she shares ties with the forces around her that transcend rational, scientific explanations.

In addition to smelling Son's presence on the island, Thérèse "hears" the soldier ants in their march toward the greenhouse; she knows that they are following the trail of chocolate wrappers that Son has left. She has seen him in a dream (104) and characterizes him as being "as silent as a star" (105). His quality of stealth brings to mind trackers of tradition, who are able to merge into the natural world without disturbing it, as John Washington is taught to do by Old Jack in David Bradley's *The Chaneysville Incident* (1981). Thérèse immediately assumes that Son is a "horseman" with a special destiny on the island; while she may not be able to articulate precisely what that destiny is, she wavers between couching it in myth and legend, and romance.

Because Thérèse seems a part of the island, more native in the sense of being tied to the land and culture, than even Gideon, her sentiments arrest our attention. Her "magic breasts" (108), which have given milk long beyond her child-bearing years, also identify her with the essence of fertility in nature and make her capable of assuming the nurturing, mothering role for Son's rebirth comparable to that of Pilate with Milkman. The tales of the blind horsemen, who had hidden from their enslavers and now ride freely through the hills of Isle des Chevaliers, carry the same connotations for spiritual rebirth for Son as the tales of the flying Solomon carry for Milkman

Dead. Thérèse perpetuates the tales and claims to have seen the horsemen; therefore, she is again more attuned to her natural environment than the whites and most of the native blacks.

Thérèse's passion also ties her to the natural world. Just as the champion daisy trees are marshalling for war against the wrongs that have been done to them, Thérèse asks Son to kill the Streets for having fired her. Her passionate reaction to them harks back to the hyperemotional way in which she has concocted tales of the true relationship of Son to the Street household, as well as to her generally high level of enthusiasm about everything—from shrieking with delight when Son kisses her hand to drooling over apples. She has not allowed so-called civilization to neutralize or mute her basic emotions, just as Son has not allowed possible punishment to stifle his reaction to his wife's infidelity. They are both passionate people, both uncensored in their loves and lives, which makes it doubly appropriate that Thérèse become Son's escort on his final journey.

When Thérèse leaves him, Son crawls from water to rock to land in yet another transformation or rebirth. The rightness of his action is made clear when "the mist lifted and the trees stepped back a bit as if to make the way easier for a certain kind of man" (306). That certain kind of man, whose racing "lickety-split" into the woods reminds us of Brer Rabbit, is being endowed with sight beyond sight and knowing beyond knowing. In his decision to go forward instead of turning back, Son embraces the world Thérèse has offered. Any hint he might have of the possibility of error on her part in leading him to L'Arbe de la Croix is more than made up in his movement, which is a movement into the unknown, a movement that initiates a receptivity to myth. Even if he were to reach the house, it would not be the house he left. It, too, with its reversal of roles for Sydney and Valerian, and Valerian and Margaret, has begun to progress toward a different kind of human myth, and the champion daisy trees and the soldier ants are already reclaiming it for the natural realm. Either destination for Son, then—the house or the horsemen—will bring him to the same place of myth and legend, for his relationship with Jadine has been more mythical than real. The text suggests fairly clearly, however, that his destination is with the horsemen. As Keith E. Byerman asserts, "*Tar Baby* marks the final step of immersion into the black folk world. Son achieves his truest nature by becoming one, not with the tellers of tales, . . . but with the tales themselves."[21]

The mist that lifts (thus picking up the theme of the various ways of seeing/knowing in the novel and recalling the "maiden aunts" of fog who always seemed to make life so unpleasant for Jadine, Margaret, and Valerian—62, 64, 65, 194) and the trees who make way for Son provide the final punctuation, the period, in his many stages of transformation and retransformation. In recognizing Son as a kindred spirit, in preparing the way for his road to be easier, the trees claim him by giving him the space to claim himself. They appear patient and receptive, ready for this long-lost one who is now being returned to them. Without weeping or images of suffering, they suggest a newer, stronger future for their world. Their calmness at this point is a culminating contrast to the agitation many of their kindred have felt earlier.

At several prior points in the novel, natural sentience serves, as in many literary episodes of the natural world mirroring the events of the human world, to comment upon, express shock about, or mourn with human disasters.[22] Just as the emperor butterflies are struck by Jadine's coat, the avocado trees are equally struck by her cursing (127). After the Christmas dinner fiasco, the angel trumpets sense the pain of the island; they shrivel and die in Valerian's presence because the air is too poisonous for them to breathe (231). More important than mirroring human disasters, therefore, natural sentience mirrors human insensitivity; it is a measure of how far humans have transgressed against their own potential to be a part of the world beyond their petty concerns. The calmness of the trees suggests that reparations for those transgressions are being made.

One of the striking things about the nonhuman beings who converse in the novel is that they never make Son the subject of any of their disparaging observations. The potential significance of this omission is that they recognize no disrupter in Son. Perhaps there is enough of his natural essence still about him—even as he tries to make the transition into the Street household—that they never have anything to fear from him, indeed that they recognize him as one of their own. He never does anything to shock them, and he never violates them. He appreciates what they have to offer in the way of food during his days of foraging. He is content to nestle in the bosom of the earth rather than rip hollows in it or take it for granted. When they finally make way for him as one of their own, they are welcoming the potential for the best in themselves, the potential to sing a song of unity that will resound through the hills of the island in a blend of humanature and naturekind.

6

Beloved

"Woman, Thy Name Is Demon"

If we think of Toni Morrison's work on a continuum from *Sula* (1974), where she begins the transformation of woman from human being to something other than human and where she experiments with sentience beyond death, through *Tar Baby* (1981), with its talking trees and butterflies, then *Beloved* (New York: Knopf, 1987), with its emphasis on the temporal transcendence of the grave, is a natural extension of those ideas. The ancient tree mothers who would claim Jadine as their sister by drowning her in tar if necessary are not so far removed from the single-mindedness of Beloved, who would kill Sethe as quickly as she would claim her as mother. In exploring the novel's basis in folk traditions, some prevailing ideas about the female body, especially those grounded in myth and fear, are especially illuminating.

Stereotypical conceptions of the female body as "Other" have pervaded oral and written literature. In contemporary times, athletes are warned against intimacy with women before important competitions, some husbands believe their wives poison food if they are allowed to cook while menstruating, and yet others believe their penises could literally be engulfed by women's vaginas. We could document a host of additional persistent and often destructive images of women; underlying these notions is a basic clash between the masculine (those who have power and voice) and the feminine (those who are acquiescent and silent but potentially destructive), which is also worked out in Morrison's novel. These folk and popular stereotypes about the female body have often been bolstered by "scientific" research.

For example, in 1968 psychiatrist Wolfgang Lederer published a volume called *The Fear of Women*.[1] It is a storehouse of information on the control of female images throughout the ages, on how the female body was used to account for a plethora of problems in the world. As early as medieval times, woman stood as Frau Welt ("Mrs. World"), a deceptively beautiful damsel from the frontal view, who, upon being viewed from the rear, showed a disgusting, maggot-filled eruption crawling with snakes, frogs, and other vile creatures with whom she shared inclinations to make man's righteous path in the world difficult if not impossible. The ability to engulf and destroy, as well as to poison the air, were commonplace notions about women. Lederer documents those practices in certain cultures where menstruating women were encouraged to walk over newly plowed and planted fields in order to poison the insects and ensure the growth of the crops.

The blood that flowed every month concentrated the distinguishing differences between men and women that Lederer documents so carefully. And not only was woman the bleeder, but she was also insatiable in her desire for blood. Kali, the Indian goddess, is the epitome of the bloodthirsty female on the rampage against human, especially *man*-kind. Tales about her illustrate the recurring ambivalence of the traditions. On the one hand, woman is the mother/nurturer; on the other, she is the goddess/destroyer.

As recently as 1986, a song played repeatedly on black radio stations was the Isley Brothers's "Insatiable Woman." Its upbeat tempo, coupled with the soothing voice of the male singing the lyrics, quickly lulled one into forgetfulness against its evil intent. The female body, the singer complained, could never be satisfied; no matter what he gave—probably sperm donations—she wanted more. Obviously he could not keep delivering the donations at the rate at which she could receive them, so he could only verbally affirm: "Baby, I'm yours," and perhaps hope that she would let him be. The song and the verbal tradition it perpetuates of the engulfing, never-satisfied woman recalls the tale of the preacher and the pretty young woman. Preacher tales, a special subcategory of African-American folk narrative, frequently debunk the authority and prestige of ministers. Preachers are invariably painted as greedy; they especially love fried chicken, alcohol, and money. They are also impious and sexually unrestrained. As the story goes, a preacher who thought he would take advantage of her parents' absence and seduce a young woman gets the tables slightly turned on him. He sends her upstairs to the bedroom and maintains that he will be up shortly to "scare" her, his euphemism for sexual intercourse. He discovers, however, that her receptivity is longer than his stamina. After three trips upstairs and increasingly weaker, near crawling returns, when she requests that he come upstairs and "scare" her yet another time, he responds: "Well, BOO, goddamn it!"[2]

The female body, as it has been written in the oral tradition and in sexist literature, is in part a source of fear, both an attraction and a repulsion, something that can please, but something that can destroy. The tricksters of tradition find one of their chores the task of bravely entering the vagina to break those teeth that tradition has long identified with it. Such actions are considered heroic—and at times helpful even to the woman herself, for the poor dear never realizes what difficulty she is in until some man tells her and proceeds to rescue her. And in *his* ending to the tale, she usually appreciates the rescue and indeed becomes more decorous in her sexual habits. Witchlike, Other, Strange, Fearful—that is how the female body has been characterized. In many instances the attributes center upon the demonic, as indeed many of those traditions I've described would encompass. Women could be witches or healers—depending upon point of view—only because they were in some way in league with the devil. Or indeed, just the nature of being female was considered evil—without the specific connotations of satanic contact.

The nature of evil—the demonic, the satanic—those are the features of the female body as written by Toni Morrison in *Beloved*. We can describe the title character as a witch, a ghost, a devil, or a succubus; in her manipulation of those around her, she exerts a power not of this world. In her absence of the tempering emotions that we usually identify with humankind, such as mercy, she is inhumanly vengeful in setting out to repay the one upon whom she places the blame for her too-early demise. We should note that this is not the first time that Morrison has called woman Demon.

In *Sula*, she begins the transformation of woman from human being to something other than human. The people in the Bottom make Sula into a witch whom they believe to be in league with the forces of evil if not with the devil himself. They believe that she makes Teapot fall off her steps, that she causes Mr. Finley's death when he chokes on a chicken bone, and that she is a witch who can make herself appear much younger than she is. Her suprahuman qualities lead them to ostracize her to the point of circumventing the rituals that usually apply to death and funerals in black communities. Sula's demise, however, points to another source for comparison with Beloved. Sula's sentience beyond death, presented briefly in the book, is enough to signal that Morrison has drawn no final lines between the planes of life and death. Indeed, Morrison has asserted that the call of one of the stories that inspired Beloved worked on her so strongly that it may have surfaced unwittingly in her earlier novels: "... I had been rescuing [the dead girl] from the grave of time and inattention. Her fingernails maybe in the first book; face and legs, perhaps, the second time. Little by little bringing her back into living life."[3]

Following the African belief that the demise of the body is not the end of being, which David Bradley develops so vividly in The Chaneysville Incident (1981), Morrison hints with Sula what becomes her major preoccupation in Beloved. During her life, Sula has given some insight into the actions of those who are set apart or deemed demonic. They owe allegiance only to themselves; Sula is interested only in making herself, Beloved is interested only in claiming and punishing her mother. Their desires are foremost; the wishes of others are inconsiderable. Sula sleeps with her best friend's husband without compunction; Beloved sleeps with her mother's lover. Though one is alive and the other returned from the dead, at several points the actions of the two characters are strikingly similar in motivation and execution.

The world view in Sula prepares us for the seeming topsy-turviness of Tar Baby, with its racing blind horsemen and mythic life forms, for the otherworldliness represented by Pilate's lack of a navel in Song of Solomon, and for the emphasis on the temporal transcendence of the grave in Beloved. Remember, too, that Eva talks to Plum after his death (he comes back to tell her things) and that Valerian sees Michael's ghost in the dining room on the night that

Son intrudes into the island world. Morrison has well prepared her readers, therefore, for complete suspension of disbelief in the human and natural worlds. The female body reduced to desire makes Sula kindred in spirit and objective to Beloved. Consider, too, that Ajax, Sula's lover, leaves her when he begins to fear her body as woman, when he judges that she wants to trap him into marriage, or at least domesticity.

Woman's body is a threat to men in *Beloved* as well; that is the vantage point from which we see what happens in the novel. Paul D's arrival at Sethe's house brings with it the ancient fear of women. When he enters the house haunted by Beloved's ghost, it becomes the enveloping enclosure of the vagina; the vagina dentata myth operates as Paul D *feels* the physical threat of the house. The red light of the baby's spirit drains him, makes him feel overwhelming grief, feminizes him. Sethe and Denver live in the presence of the spirit; they may be annoyed by the spirit of the "crawling-already?" baby, but they have little to fear from it as females. Indeed, there is evidence that Beloved may be nurturing them into acceptance of her later physical, human manifestation. They comment at one point that "the baby got plans" (37).

For Paul D, however, the house is immediately his enemy, a veritable threat. He perceives that it bodes no good for him, and he senses—more than he knows—that the contest is between male and female spirits. Walking through the "pulsing red light," "a wave of grief soaked him so thoroughly he wanted to cry. It seemed a long way to the normal light surrounding the table, but he made it—dry-eyed and lucky" (9). To cry is to be broken, diminished as a man. Holding himself together against such a feminine breakdown, Paul D already views the house as a threat to his masculinity. He therefore enters it like the teeth-destroying tricksters of tradition entered the vagina, in the heroic vein of conquering masculine will over female desire. The competition, as it develops, then, seems initially unfair—a grown man against a baby. The supernatural element of the baby's spirit neutralizes the inequality somewhat, but the spirit of maleness in this initial battle seems stronger even than Beloved's supernaturalism. In his confrontation with the house, Paul D *wills* Beloved's spirit away. His vocal masculine will is stronger than her silent, though sometimes noisy, desire. The power of his voice to command behavior, even that of spirits, is ultimately stronger than the spirit's desire to resist.

Or at least that is one possible reading of the confrontation. Another would be to explore it from the perspective of Beloved's demonic nature. In this seeming rite of exorcism, it is not Beloved who is removed, but Paul D who is lulled into a false sense of victory. The demonic Beloved voluntarily leaves the scene in order to prepare for a greater onslaught of female energy. In seemingly forcing Beloved to leave, Paul D, like the heroes of tradition, gives to Sethe and Denver the peace that they have been unable or unwilling to give to themselves. Presumably he has made the society better. The house is quiet, he and Sethe can pretend to be lovers, and the women can contemplate such leisure activities as going to a circus.

By blending the temporal and the eternal planes of existence, however, Morrison gives Beloved the upper hand for most of the novel. As the shapeshifter who takes on flesh-and-blood human characteristics, Beloved introduces a logic and a world view into the novel that defy usual responses to such phenomena. Certainly in the black folk tradition, a ghost might occasionally appear among the living—to indicate that all is well, to teach a lesson, or to guide the living to some good fortune, including buried treasure. There are few tales, however, of revenants that actually take up residence with living relatives. One such tale, "Daid Aaron," which is from the Gullah people, centers upon the theme of revenge. Aaron refuses to go to the dwelling of the dead because his wife is already showing signs of her intention to have other suitors. But then, that's a male/female conflict as well. The widow finally gets rid of Aaron when he requests that her fiddler suitor provide dance music. Aaron dances gleefully and madly, faster and faster, until he comes apart, literally bone by bone.[4] Whether she knew of such tales or not, Morrison has asserted that she and her family members "were intimate with the supernatural" and that her parents "told thrillingly terrifying ghost stories."[5]

Beloved has a brief experience that brings to mind the possibility of disintegration comparable to Aaron's. She pulls a tooth, then speculates:

> Next would be her arm, her hand, a toe. Pieces of her would drop maybe one at a time, maybe all at once. Or on one of those

mornings before Denver woke and after Sethe left she would fly apart. It is difficult keeping her head on her neck, her legs attached to her hips when she is by herself. Among the things she could not remember was when she first knew that she could wake up any day and find herself in pieces. She had two dreams: exploding, and being swallowed. When her tooth came out—an odd fragment, last in the row—she thought it was starting. (133)

But Beloved does not decay. Like a vampire feeding vicariously, she becomes plump in direct proportion to Sethe's increasing gauntness. Vengeance is not the Lord's; it is Beloved's. Her very body becomes a manifestation of her desire for vengeance and of Sethe's guilt. She repays Sethe for her death, but the punishment is not quick or neat. The attempt to choke Sethe to death in Baby Suggs's clearing and the lingering pain of that encounter is but the beginning of Beloved's taking over the women's lives. Before she can accomplish that, however, she must extricate the most formidable opposition, Paul D. In another demonic parallel in the male/female clash, she becomes the traditional succubus, the female spirit who drains the male's life force even as she drains him of his sperm. Beloved makes herself irresistible to Paul D, gradually forcing him, through each sexual encounter, to retreat farther and farther from the territory she has claimed as her own. Her "shining" or sexual latching on to him causes him initially to sleep in a rocking chair in the kitchen, then in Baby Suggs's keeping room behind the kitchen, then in the storeroom, and finally in the "cold house" outside the main house. "*She moved him*," and Paul D "didn't know how to stop it because it looked like he was moving himself" (114—emphasis added). Their three weeks of sexual encounters in the cold house result in a guilty Paul D trying to confront Sethe with the news only to find that he cannot; Beloved's control over him, together with his discovery of Sethe's killing of her baby, force him off the premises altogether. After all, what option does he have? To stay is to contemplate the violations he has committed—sleeping with a woman who has been much abused and abusing her further by sleeping with her daughter/ghost. To go or to stay is to contemplate a possible further evil—having slept with the devil—either in the form of the mother or the daughter.

Paul D's departure makes clear that Beloved has not only used her body to drain him physically, but spiritually as well. He becomes a tramp of sorts, sleeping where he can, drinking excessively, literally a shadow of his former self. From the man who was strong enough to exorcise a spirit, Paul D reverts to his wandering, unsure of his residence from day to day and unclear about what kind of future, if any, he has. The picture of him sitting on the church steps, liquor bottle in hand, stripped of the very maleness that enables him to caress and love the wounded Sethe, is one that shows Beloved's power. There is no need for her to kill Paul D; she simply drains him sufficiently to make him one of the living dead, in a limbo-like state from which he cannot extricate himself as long as Beloved reigns at 124 Bluestone Road. For this male warrior, therefore, the demonic female has won over him in the very realm he has used to define himself; his sexual fear of woman is justified.

But the parasitic Beloved is not content to destroy maleness; she also attacks femaleness. Or, I should say it is perhaps less femaleness that she attacks in Sethe than motherhood, another symbol of authority almost masculine in its absoluteness. We could say, then, that as far as Beloved is concerned, Paul D and Sethe are in some ways shaped from the same mold—those who have the power to command, those who have power over life and death. In her resolve to escape from slavery, Sethe, like Jean Toomer's Carma, is "strong as any man."[6] In the resolve that keeps her going during the ordeal of Denver's birth she is again, stereotypically, strong as any man. In her determination to kill her children to keep them from being remanded to slavery, she is again as strong as any man. Beloved's anger with Sethe for having killed her may be centered in mother love, but it is also centered in the patriarchal authority that Sethe assumed unto herself in killing Beloved, in becoming the destructive, authoritative mother/goddess. Beloved's war against Sethe, then, can be read from one perspective as a further attack against masculine privilege, against the power over life and death that is stereotypically identified with males or with those masculine mother/goddesses.

Think, too, about how Sethe is viewed in the community. Comparable to Sula, she is too proud, too self-sufficient, too independent, generally too much on her own for the neighbors. Her rugged individualism is more characteristic of males than females of the time.

The more feminine thing would be for her to need help from the community. She neither seeks nor accepts any before Beloved arrives; later, she is too transformed to care.

Perhaps we are sufficiently encouraged, then, to see Sethe as a masculine presence that the female demon seeks to exorcise. Beloved symbolically begins feeding upon Sethe as the succubus feeds upon males; she takes food from her mouth, eats whatever there is to eat, and inspires Sethe to leave her job, thereby relinquishing her ability to feed herself, and causing her to shrink, to become diminished in stature as well as in self-possession. By denying to Sethe the power to support herself, Beloved initially attacks Sethe's spirit of independence. She sends her into a stupor comparable to that of Paul D. But Beloved is not content to stupefy Sethe; she is after her life force. She drains her by slowly starving her and, as the neighbors believe, beating her (255). The apparently pregnant Beloved blossoms, glows, and continues to get plump as the shrinking Sethe literally becomes a skeleton of her former self. Like Paul D, Sethe loses will power, thereby losing the ability to control her own body or her own destiny. She and Paul D are assuredly slaves to Beloved's desire as Sethe and the Pauls were literally slaves earlier. Beloved becomes the arbiter of life and death, so playfully so that Sethe acquiesces in her own decline.

It is in part the playfulness of the situation that tones down its potentially destructive side. With Beloved, Sethe has the opportunity to live out two fantasies. First of all, she can be mother to the daughter she has never known. Giving all her time and attention to Beloved makes it easy for the demon to execute her desire. On the other hand, by giving all to Beloved, Sethe becomes childlike, pleading for acceptance by a harsh "parent" who is more intent upon cruel punishment than understanding forgiveness. By relinquishing her will to survive, Sethe again becomes Beloved's willing victim.

Their relationship raises questions about Morrison's intentions in the novel. Is guilt the central theme, thereby making it understandable how Sethe acquiesces in her own slow destruction? Does the guilt deserve the punishment of the demonic? Is infanticide so huge a crime that only otherworldly punishment is appropriate for it? If, on the other hand, we understand, accept, and perhaps even approve of the dynamic that allowed a slave mother to kill rather than have her children remanded to slavery, would not the dominant theme be love? After all, Sethe has precedence in her action; her own mother killed some of her children rather than allow them to be slaves, or to recognize her own forced depravity in having given birth to them (62). If the theme is love, what warrants allowing Sethe to be so violated for her love of Beloved?

As the novel develops, it would seem that Beloved's *desires,* irrational as they are, are the acceptable force driving the story. I emphasize desire as opposed to will simply because Beloved is not to be denied in what she wants. Her desire is for a mother, and she will have that mother even if it means killing her in the process of claiming her. She desires Paul D and takes him in spite of her mother's involvement with him. As it manifests itself in the novel, desire is unbridled id, self-centered and not to be easily denied.[7] Will, on the other hand, can be altruistic; Paul D wills Beloved out of 124, it can be argued, in part to bring a measure of peace to Sethe and Denver. The destructive, irrational force, is pure desire, which in turn is perhaps the most otherworldly. It is out of desire for something that spirits are able to make the journey between the two worlds. Beloved, the personification of desire, thus epitomizes the demonic.[8] Her lack of caring is spiteful retaliation for not being allowed to live; she is the unleashed force of the childish mentality at which her life ended. Twenty years in body, but eighteen months in mind, she is the objective, physical distillation of desire.

Beloved's characterization ultimately makes her "Thing," unhuman, unfeeling, uncaring except in the perpetuation of what she wants. Like Frau Welt, she cannot live up to the promise of herself; to become involved with her is to be destroyed. As Thing, Beloved has no consistently seen reflective trait; the point of view of the narrative encourages us to see her as the traditional vampire. We see her inner thoughts for only brief moments, which do not evoke undue sympathy for her. We are left to judge her objectively, to infer motive from a distance, and thereby to solidify our evaluation of her as demonic. Her actions suggest that she has ultimate power of judgment, that vengeance is indeed hers, that her brand of justice has no guiding morality to temper it with mercy.[9]

In her amorality, Beloved shares kinship with some of the tricksters of tradition—ever guided by personal desires and frequently identified as masculine. Such figures are recognizable by the power they wield, without consideration for those being affected by that power. Brer Rabbit kills the elephant simply to escape detection for a crime he has committed, or he avenges himself on the entire alligator family because of an insult by Brer Alligator. Unleashed and unrestrained, Brer Rabbit is limited only by the power of imagination that conceived the cycle of tales in which he stars. With her supernatural dimension, Beloved has no obvious limits. Nonetheless, she ultimately seems subject to a force greater than herself.

A potentially troublesome part of the novel is how Beloved is exorcised from 124. Paul D's initial driving of her spirit from the premises is merely temporary. She is finally exorcised not by individuals working in isolation but by a community of effort directed against her presence. And that community of effort comes from a group of women, women who call upon ancient and contemporary messages, murmuring incantations and singing songs, to control Beloved. Is Morrison suggesting finally that women, who may themselves be demonic—or *because* they are demonic—are the only force with sufficient power to control that evil? Is it a question of good versus evil? Are the women who send Beloved away in any way identified with the forces of good? Most of them are certainly not the image of stereotypically traditional churchgoing black women. Nor do they pursue the exorcism from altruistic motivations. Rather, like Richard Wright's District Attorney Ely Houston pursuing the murderous Cross Damon in *The Outsider* (1953), they are simultaneously attracted to and repulsed by the evil in their midst. They see in it tiny mirrors of the selves they have suppressed, and they want it extracted before it touches them too greatly or even has the potential to reclaim them. And they are offended. They "didn't mind a little communication between the two worlds, but this was an invasion" (257).

In other words, Beloved is a threat to them in the psychological sphere as effectively as Sula is a threat to the women in the Bottom in the sexual sphere. Extending the philosophy from that novel, where the community is content to recognize evil and let it run its course, the women in *Beloved* cannot afford that detachment. Letting Beloved run her course may mean the destruction of them all. They must exorcise that part of themselves, therefore, that is a threat to them. If thy right eye offend thee, pluck it out. This is not a far-fetched philosophy when we consider that throughout history it is frequently women who cast sanctions most vehemently upon other women.

Exorcising the demonic part of the self so that all women are not judged to be demons—that is what the women are about in getting Beloved to leave 124. And how do they accomplish this? With a combination of pagan and religious rituals. They initially find power in numbers as they gather in a group of thirty to move toward 124. They raise their voices in singing and in religious murmurs as they march along the road. The comparative images that come to mind are straight out of *The Golden Bough*. The voices raised serve the same function as the sticks and pans villagers of pretechnological cultures might have used to drive evil spirits from their midsts. The act of singing itself serves as a chant, perhaps as the proverbial "witch doctor" of ancient times might have used to implore or command that some living/hearing evil take its leave from the environs of the innocent and the helpless.

What the pregnant Beloved sees then, as she comes to the front door of 124, is that those with whom she identifies as well as despises are organized against her. The mothers are multiplied many times over, as are the breasts of the women in Eloe, Florida, whom Jadine confronts in *Tar Baby*; against the demands of that immutable force of potential mother/goddesses, who seem to represent justice without mercy, Beloved can only retreat. The vengeance of parents punishing recalcitrant children is ultimately stronger than will or desire.

But Beloved's retreat may in reality be a departure from a battlefield where she has won, accomplished what she set out to do. Consider what happens as the white Mr. Bodwin drives up. In the near-reenactment of what happened at Beloved's death, it becomes clear that Sethe is nearly deranged. She is decidedly no longer the figure of authority and independence that she has been before Beloved's arrival. When she takes the ice pick in hand to save Beloved once again, the same set of imperatives does not apply. Slavery has ended; the man approaching is a rescuer rather than an enslaver; Sethe needs rescue *from* Beloved rather than rescuing her from someone else. Reduced to irrationality engendered by the wiping out of eighteen years of her life, Sethe is now the recalcitrant child, in need of correcting and nurturing (252). In this reading of the scene, Beloved can leave instead of being sent away because she has accomplished two things. First, she has caused Sethe to become temporarily deranged. Second, the result of that derangement is that Sethe acts without thought, instinctively, to save Beloved. What Beloved could not see as a "crawling-already?" baby, she is now able to see as an adult: that her mother's action, many years before and in its current duplicate, was indeed one of love. This reading does not mean that the demon changes her nature, but that she achieves her desire: tangible evidence that her mother loved her best of all. Ironically, to achieve that goal is simultaneously to risk eventual destruction of the individual of whom the evidence was required.[10]

Again, Beloved either leaves voluntarily or is driven out. Whatever interpretation we accept, one thing is clear: Sethe and Beloved cannot exist on the same plane. If Sethe is to live, Beloved must depart. If Beloved stays, Sethe can only die. The trip from beyond, though, is apparently a one-time thing. Once removed from 124, the undelivered, restless Beloved roams the neighboring territory, her footprints a reminder that she is there but her desire fulfilled sufficiently so that she cannot return all the way to 124. Her inability to return is attested to in the return of Here Boy, the dog, to 124 and in the return of Paul D, the masculine presence. Of the animals traditionally believed to sense ghosts and evil spirits, dogs are perhaps first on the list.[11] When Here Boy takes up residence again, that is the folkloristic signal that Beloved will not be returning. When Paul D finds the energy to pursue Sethe again, to experience the returning of sexual desire as well as general concern for another human being, that is also a signal that Beloved will not be returning. Paul D's presence means health for Sethe, the opposite of what Beloved's presence meant. With the novel ending on a sign of health, there will at least be calm at 124.

And what of Beloved? The demon comes and goes. Humans interact with it, but it ultimately transcends them, returns to another realm of existence controlled only by human imagination. Morrison lifts Beloved from a void and returns her there. Her footprints relegate her to kinship with Big Foot and other legendary if not mythical creatures. Beloved goes from imagination to humanoid to legend, basically unchanged in her category as demon, the designation of Other that makes it impossible for her to be anything but eternally alone.

Shaping the Tales in the Tale

In *Beloved*, Toni Morrison concocts a sequence of events in which she shares with her characters the creation of her novel. In the tradition of storytelling and composition, they are as much artists as she. In fact, it could be argued that there is a single master mind and that parts of that entity tell various parts of the tale. The story of Denver's birth provides the prime example of this multiple composition. Denver relates a part of the story (29–30, and especially 77-78). Sethe recounts another portion (31-32). And the omniscient narrator provides more (32–35, 78–85). Each teller carries the burden for her particular portion, which is frequently shaped by the audience before whom it is created. Consider the power of audience in the instance in which Denver feeds on Beloved's reaction to her story of the pregnant Sethe roaming through dog- and patteroller-infested woods. Inspired by her audience of one, Denver allows her creative imagination to leap far beyond the mere fact of her mother's experience:

> Denver was seeing it now and feeling it—through Beloved. Feeling how it must have felt to her mother. Seeing how it must have looked. And the more fine points she made, the more detail she provided, the more Beloved liked it. So she anticipated the questions by giving blood to the scraps her mother and grandmother had told her—and a heartbeat. The monologue became, in fact, a duet as they lay down together, Denver nursing Beloved's interest like a lover whose pleasure was to overfeed the loved. (78)

Denver may know part of what Sethe relates, but she does not usurp Sethe's authorship by recounting in any great detail the part of the story that Sethe relates in detail. And Sethe takes up her portion of narration where Denver leaves off. They know, or seem to know instinctively, what is needed to complete the story; therefore, Morrison imbues them with a portion of her omniscience, a trait that makes them somewhat otherworldly and intuitive, or at least a trait that suggests the interconnectedness of the lives, minds, and hearts of the three women. The single controlling narration gives Morrison at some level the same relation to her story as her characters, while at another it is obvious that Morrison as author of the text ultimately controls the story. When she does share narration with her characters, Morrison shows an intuitive respect for their collective experience, one that binds them as strongly to each other as they are bound to her as their creator.

The story of Denver's birth is as much rumor and conjecture as it is fact, or so the townspeople believe. It is too fantastic to be taken at face value and thus borders on folktale. As she was trying to escape from slavery, so the story goes, Sethe, then six months pregnant, met the white girl Amy Denver, who not only laid healing hands upon her lashed back and swollen feet, but also attended at Denver's birth. These basic details get embellished depending upon who is relating the story to whom. In a time when patterollers were rampant and white people were believed to be instinctively hostile toward blacks, Sethe's story violates the rules of interracial interaction with which her fellow blacks are familiar. The more logical expectation would have been for Amy to turn Sethe in. This seeming discrepancy, combined with Sethe actually escaping in her condition, leads some of the locals to speculate that there is something unnatural about her even before she kills Beloved and pridefully shuns them all. The tale, then, already has components of legend, myth, and outright lying before it begins to get reshaped in the minds and memories of Sethe, Denver, and their neighbors. When the other events ensue, the townspeople reject Sethe not only because of her pride, but perhaps because she is too witchlike or too otherworldly for them.

As they tell this and other stories to each other, therefore, Sethe, Denver, and Beloved form a small folk community in which they all have distinct roles to play. Sethe discovers as quickly as Denver does how much Beloved appreciates stories: "It became a way to feed her. Just as Denver discovered and relied on the delightful effect sweet things had on Beloved, Sethe learned the profound satisfaction Beloved got from storytelling" (58), so she tells Beloved about her "diamonds." Oral history joins hands with fiction and rumor in basing the stories in a germ of truth; that germ is quickly reduced—or elevated—to motif as, through repeated tellings, the stories are modified and reshaped to suit the imagination and needs of the teller and her audience. The women are inseparable in their bid to create the stories and in their need to perpetuate the lore about their existence. Their family folklore binds them to a bone-chilling, destructive interaction that may have historical parallels at its most basic level but soon transcends the traditional.

The *process* of storytelling as presented in the works of such folklorists as Zora Neale Hurston is a pleasant communal affair. In their roles as tradition bearers, narrators can weave a tale individually or with participation and encouragement from their communities. Even when the community does not actively contribute to the telling of the tale, it nevertheless contributes actively by listening to the tale, for there can be no storytellers without audiences. The community of three women that Morrison creates in *Beloved*, therefore, is a dynamic storytelling one in which the tellers and their tales have a direct impact upon the lives of those around them. Denver estimates her value in direct proportion to the way in which the stories Sethe relates focus on her birth. Other stories about Sweet Home send her into periods of depression and loneliness that drive her to her secret place in the boxwood trees. Beloved's well-being, if we can call it such, exists in direct proportion to the stories that Sethe relates, no matter the topic; the *act* of storytelling itself is what pacifies Beloved and emphasizes the childish part of her being.

For Beloved, Sethe's willingness to tell stories is a measure of Beloved's obsession for and desire to possess Sethe, an indication of her unbridled id at work. The ownership component of their relationship, which becomes so apparent later, is presaged in Beloved's attempt to control Sethe's creative imagination. From the control she exerts in this arena, it is easy for her to make the transition to control of Sethe's body. Storytelling in this context, therefore, is about power, one sometimes sinister in its manifestations. Sethe weaves a story, but Beloved weaves a web of tangled parental responsibility and morality from which Sethe is barely able to escape.

Sethe is willing to satisfy Denver's desire for information about herself, but she stops when the stories make the past live again much too vividly for her. Her whole life is about "beating back the past" (73). That past can be kept at bay if the stories are untold, the memories sheathed. The paradox of Sethe's position is that both of her daughters desire the stories, but for compellingly different reasons. And they each have different powers to exert in urging her to tell the tales. Beloved relies upon Sethe's less blemished memories of Sweet Home, and later, upon the guilt Sethe feels for having killed her. Denver also appeals to Sethe's more pleasant memories of Sweet Home as well as to Sethe's sense of guilt for excluding Denver from a history in which she clearly had a vital role. Thus for Sethe, Denver, and Beloved, storytelling is an active rather than a passive art, for it has the power literally to heal or kill.

To give such power to stories is one of Morrison's extensions of the function of folklore. She elevates the narratives beyond the entertaining, psychological, and educational functions they usually serve. Beloved may be entertained by the stories, and she certainly learns a lot about her family history, but she is also drawing her very lifeblood from them; they are creating a memory for her, filling in the gaps in her life that she cannot remember. For Denver, the stories enable her to fill in a history from which she had been excluded by virtue of her youth and forbidden from entering later by virtue of Sethe's vow to continue "keeping the past at bay" (42) and "beating back the past" (73). The stories provide self-definition in the way that legends, anecdotes, and personal experience narratives define their subjects.

Denver's geographical location at the point of storytelling makes this idea clearer. She lives at 124 Bluestone Road in Cincinnati, Ohio, in a house whose porch provides the boundary for the "edge of the world." As a secluded, psychologically immature, and functionally illiterate person, she is as much heir to the horrors of falling off the edge of the world as those early explorers who believed that the world was flat. Left with an imagination uninformed by the reality beyond her porch, she can create whatever monsters she wishes. An early participant in her history but without the maturity to register it, Denver has to find means to place herself within her own life, within her own family; she must flesh out her life from one dimension to multiple dimensions, from isolation to involvement, from a house to the world. Storytelling is her continual birth process, her continual bid to find herself in the family portrait and to

find value within the family. Consider how she imaginatively concocts stories about an absent father who will one day rescue her
from the difficult situation she sometimes believes she is in with
Sethe; evocations of fairy tales, with the passive princess waiting to
be rescued, immediately come to mind. Denver's fantasy, like those
of many children, locates her squarely at the center of value in her
family portrait.

Her contacts with people during Baby Suggs's lifetime were not
sustained enough for her to develop a sense of what is normal. She
may well have grown up thinking that spending time in jail with her
mother was not unusual if Nelson Lord had not asked the question
that brought on her deafness. Certainly her becoming deaf is an
indication that she believes she is somehow stigmatized, but she is
able to judge that only in relation to her rejection by the other children. She has not previously thought that her situation was somehow wrong, that her mother's act was an unlawful, immoral, isolating one.

Denver is a tablet upon which her own life can be written. The
stories of her birth are the chalk for that creation. Stories, for
Morrison, then, are much more vibrant and viable forces in the lives
of her characters than they are in historic folk communities. They are
not just effects; they are effects with consequences. The consequence
of Denver learning about herself is that she can begin to form the
basis upon which to grow into an adult human being. The consequence of Beloved learning about herself is much more destructive;
it enables her to exert more control over the lives of those around
her, and indeed the knowledge she gains through the information
provided by storytelling could enable her to become a murderer.
Morrison therefore strips the word down to its original, creative
essence; it can be made flesh, or it can destroy.

It is no wonder, then, that Morrison describes Denver's telling of
her birth story to Beloved as a creative act of godly proportion.
Denver gives "blood," a life force, to the "scraps" of stories she has
gotten from her mother and grandmother. Her infusion of blood
thereby grants a "heartbeat" (78) to what she relates. We are immediately reminded of Ezekiel and the dry bones, with God asking,
"Son of man, can these bones live?" (Ezekiel 37:3). Through imagination (faith), the power to create what did not exist before—or

existed only in a half-formed state—Denver and the other women reiterate the power of words.

Morrison thus draws upon biblical implications of the word as well as upon those connotations of creation that pervade the African-American folk bible. From Genesis comes "And God *said*, 'Let there be light'" (Genesis 1:3), "And God *said*, 'Let us make man in our image'" (Genesis 1:26), but from the pages of James Weldon Johnson's *God's Trombones* we get the specific folk impetus for what God said. The world is here *because* God *said*, "I'm lonely—I'll make me a world," and with each creation, he proclaims, "That's good." The anthropomorphic God who responds to the wishes of his people, as in the tale of the black Adam and Eve climbing up to heaven to ask God to reconcile the discrepancies in male and female power,[12] connects the human and extranatural realms in ways comparable to those Morrison devises. The invitation to appear at 124, combined with Paul D's voice, are the words that name the flesh that Beloved becomes, just as the supernatural Jesus is made flesh. "In the beginning was the Word, and the Word was with God, and the Word was God" (John 1:1). Just as the word can bring forces not of this world to life, *sound*, the pre-word condition we might say, can have equally effective consequences. It is sound that eventually drives Beloved out of 124 just as it has been the word that has made her flesh. Words, then, are an active force in the novel (and they have just as much shaping force as hands).

These single entities become even more potent when they are shaped into the larger units called stories. Consider the story—as told by whites and printed in the newspaper—of Sethe's killing of Beloved; it is almost as destructive to Paul D as stories other than those of her birth are to Denver—they diminish her. In the minds of the whites who arrest and try Sethe, and those who record her story, she is a horrible statistic, an indication of the inhuman acts of which blacks are presumably capable. Their power of the press, along with the horror it relates, diminishes her in the eyes of the black community as well as in Paul D's eyes. They use a narrative to shape a life.

The operative dynamic between Denver, Sethe, and Beloved is one in which they have the power to replenish or diminish each other by the sheer sound of their voices (remember Janie Crawford discussing the potency of lying thoughts in *Their Eyes Were Watching*

God). This power is comparable to that we see in some folktales in which there is a magical component to the spoken word. Consider, for example, the ability of various conjurers to command inanimate objects to come to life (to speak, dance, or perform some other action). I think especially of the tale in which crafty John the slave has a short stint as a fortune-teller by commanding a cowhide to come to life and do his bidding.[13]

The emphasis upon the power of words becomes another way for Morrison to break down the barrier between planes of existence in the novel, to show once again that powers assigned to one realm or the other may or may not adhere to their assignments. It also stresses the blurring of lines between human and supernatural acts, which is a corollary to the breaking down of planes of existence. We might expect Beloved to act (and she does) in many ways like a demon—or a goddess—but Morrison makes it clear that Sethe's and Denver's intuitive powers, as well as the power of their voices, may also cross over the human/divine marker and become extranatural in what they can accomplish. This is also obviously the case with the women who drive Beloved out of 124; their voices combine in their power to fight the demon/devil, and who can wage such a battle successfully if not a divine/creative force? Not only do the women call upon God, but they assume the power of godhead. Ella has made the decision about the limits of activities for spirits (that they may have legitimate reasons for returning but they do not have the right to punish the living), which is a divine decision, and she follows through on it in her control of the extranatural force (Beloved) that has made the decision necessary.

Thus Morrison adapts the dynamic of storytelling and the power of the word to create, alter, and destroy personalities. Hers is a world of friendly competition, polite verbal contests, turned dangerous. Getting the best of an opponent is apparent in storytelling sessions where teller and audience interact without restraint, but other considerations come into play with the novel.

As many scholars have recognized, the transition from oral to written necessarily distances the author/teller of a tale from the reader/listener. They maintain that the written form loses the immediacy that registers audience response to teller;[14] it also eliminates the corrective, participatory option for audiences. I would contend that Morrison succeeds in closing that gap by creating a story that insists upon response from readers. She does that by politely assaulting our acceptance of certain cultural assumptions. Initially, she challenges beliefs about morality, about the absoluteness of good and evil; she has done so in all of her books, but the challenge is more intense in *Beloved*. Killing a child is certainly antithetical to the basic roots of our society, but Morrison forces us to ask again and again what we might have done under the circumstances. And she succeeds in making Sethe so simply human and American (the God-given right to motherhood, love of one's children, desire of a better life for them, love of freedom, nonconformity) that we cannot easily condemn her act even when we clearly do not condone it. The moral issues, therefore, lock us into participation in the novel. We are constantly encouraged to ask questions: "Is Sethe right to kill Beloved? What would I have done under the same circumstances? Are some conditions of life worse than death?"

Morrison also draws us into active intellectual participation in the novel by challenging our beliefs about ghosts. In western societies, where we are taught that the demise of the body is the end of being in this realm, it is difficult to conceive of a ghost taking up residence in someone's home for more than a year. Yet Morrison treats that as a probable occurrence and invites us to suspend disbelief long enough to see where she takes us with the possibility.

We are also drawn into the active suspense of the tale. We know very early on *what* happened, but we don't know *why* or *how*. We read on to learn the answers to those questions. I suspect that there is also a kind of voyeuristic enterprise at work; we read on to see if Morrison's imagination will overstep the bounds of good taste and provide us with some of the specifics of the atrocities of whites' inhumanity to blacks during slavery. The titillation in suspense is thus not only centered upon plot, but upon the very nature of what it means to be human, how slavery alters that status, and how characters—black and white—respond to that alteration.

Reading the novel is more than an intellectual experience; it is a physical one. This is especially true with many mothers of young children. They bring to bear their identification with Sethe, their hope that mother and child can somehow be saved even when they know that Morrison will not allow them that possibility. What they feel as mothers is wrapped up in their superficial bonding with Sethe as well as in their love for their own children. Reading the novel is also a physical experience for those who are naturally squeamish about violence and brutality, and who suffer some physical discomfort as a result of reading about them.

The author/reader interaction for this text may be delayed, therefore, but it is only minimally less powerful than if Morrison were sitting in our living rooms telling us the story of Margaret Garner and the research she did to create Sethe's story. The emotions and reactions Morrison is able to evoke in us as she tells her tale place her in the best tradition of oral performers who weave magical and unusual worlds for us to contemplate, applaud, evaluate, condemn, or stare at in wonder. As Morrison herself has asserted, she wants her readers actively involved in her narratives. In order "faithfully to reflect the aesthetic tradition of Afro-American culture," she observes that group involvement is essential; "the text, if it is to take improvisation and audience participation into account, cannot be the authority—it should be the map. It should make a way for the reader (audience) to participate in the tale."[15]

For Morrison, then, storytelling is the form as well as the substance of her creation of *Beloved*. By developing her novel associatively, that is, by narratively duplicating the patterns of the mind, the way it gathers tidbits of experiences in *seemingly* random fashion, she achieves a structural effect that evokes the process of oral narration.[16] She thereby weds folklore to literature with a finesse uncharacteristic of most writers seeking such a blend. On close examination, it becomes clear that her novel is as much folklore as fiction, as much oral history as legend. In drawing upon folk forms, characters, styles, and ideas, Morrison provides an arena for scholars to work out some of the intricacies of the ties between folklore and literature.

When the Called Rescinds Her Calling

The power of words is manifested not only in storytelling events in *Beloved*, but in the specific textual verbal art of preaching—or, I should say, of calling people together for preaching-like sessions. As the convener of the sessions, and the person anointed in such traditions, Baby Suggs is the closest the novel comes to a traditional Christian world view, and she does not allow it to come very close.

In African-American folk religion, preachers are "called" to their profession, that is, they get some sign from God that He needs their energies; accordingly, they become workers in His vineyard. While Baby Suggs is certainly in the tradition of being called, she points more to the folk imagination in her anointing than to biblical traditions. With the blessings of her community, she anoints herself out of her own experiences of suffering and shame, as well as out of appreciation for the fact that she can now call her body her own. She becomes "Baby Suggs, holy." Yet in another of Morrison's intertwinings of the secular and sacred traditions in African-American culture, Baby Suggs uses the *form* of religious rituals to impart secular advice.

Baby Suggs is a "woman of words," which puts her on par with the godly, creative power of words noted earlier. From the preaching tradition documented by James Weldon Johnson in *God's Trombones*, to the toast tradition depicting characters like Shine ("The Titanic"), to Muhammed Ali's diatribes against his opponents, to contemporary rap music, the man or woman of words has held a place of respect in African-American communities. Verbal artistry is an enviable, much-admired trait. The respect given Baby Suggs is not only attested to in the crowds that gather at the Clearing, but in her house being a way station on the underground railroad and a general community center. The fact that her neighbors become angry with her later does not erase the significance of the position she has historically held among them.

In her interactions with the crowds that gather in the Clearing (on *Saturday* afternoons, not Sunday mornings), Baby Suggs draws upon the call-and-response tradition informing almost all of African-American folklore. And the responses to her invocations are so intense that they give substance to what in many instances has degenerated into polite reactions. Unlike an audience whooping politely in response to a blues singer, the blacks in the Clearing expend heartfelt emotions at Baby Suggs's direction. They cry, dance, and laugh in celebration of the humanity they have bestowed upon themselves (87–89). In telling them that "the only grace they could have was the grace they could imagine" (88), Baby Suggs solidifies the notion that their fate is in their own hands. Like their slave ancestors who took to their feet and the woods, they must carve out for themselves a space and a place to be. In the traditional inspirational guise of the master wordsmith, Baby Suggs blends the best of the sacred and the secular worlds. Two comments from Morrison seem especially relevant here: "It's always seemed to me that black people's grace has been with what they do with language."[17] Once asked what she considered distinctive or good about her fiction, Morrison replied: "The language. . . . It is the thing that black people love so much—the saying of words, holding them on the tongue, experimenting with them, playing with them. It's a love, a passion. Its function is like a preacher's: to make you stand up out of your seat, make you lose yourself and hear yourself."[18] With a few words, selectively chosen, Baby Suggs is able to offer a transcendent experience for those who believe in her voice.

Baby Suggs becomes a communal poet/artist, the gatherer of pieces of her neighbors' experiences and the shaper of those experiences into a communal statement. Her role is in many ways like that of a ritual priestess.[19] At appointed times, she summons the group, motivates it to action, and presides over its rites of exorcism; the pain and grief of slavery are temporarily removed in a communal catharsis. Having given up seven of her eight children to slavery, Baby Suggs knows what it means to have to put the heart back together after it has been torn apart valve by valve. As a medium who gives voice to unvoiced sentiments, Baby Suggs, like Claudia MacTeer, articulates what many of her people cannot. She is therefore participant and observer, the subject and the object of creativity. Transplanted to the soil of Cincinnati, Ohio, in the northward progression typical of blacks, Baby Suggs is the archetype for leadership among those sometimes drifting masses.

Her role in the community, therefore, makes her larger than life. She becomes hope-bringer and visionary, suggesting to her neighbors that the possibilities on the northern side of the Ohio River may indeed be realized. As a holy woman, a sane and articulate Shadrack, an unselfish Eva, Baby Suggs uses her heart to become the heart of the community. People expect her to be superior to them, yet they find it hard to forgive the "excess" of the feast she gives upon Sethe's arrival on Bluestone Road. They want their goddess to keep her feet of clay visible, so they wrongly interpret the feast event. It is a ritual of possibility, a rite of incorporation for Sethe, not a slap at their poverty.[20] It is a larger version of the Saturday afternoons, of what freedom can mean. Unfortunately, Baby Suggs's neighbors can acquiesce in the routine transcendent rites, but not in the elaborate one.

By denouncing her calling, Baby Suggs rejects the power of folk imagination, which has clearly served a constructive purpose for her and the entire community along Bluestone Road. Giving up means she denies the possibility for transcendence that is inherent in folk religion as well as in the blues. She therefore finally short-circuits tradition by lifting herself away from the bonds of caring; whereas Pecola was forced out, Baby Suggs leaves voluntarily, a choice that seems to undercut her role as an ancestor figure.[21] To give up voice for silence returns Baby Suggs to the passive, acquiescent role that defined her character during slavery, and indeed makes her a slave to life rather than a master of it. Instead of remaining one of the shapers of the tales in the novel, of the destinies of its people, she chooses instead to become an object for contemplation by her neighbors and the readers. By abdicating her creative role, Baby Suggs descends from the legendary status that has defined her to become just another victim of slavery, a victimization all the more tragic because she clearly had the power not to adhere to such a fate.

The Myth of Sweet Home

In Paul Laurence Dunbar's "The Party" and in the popular folktale "Master's Gone to Philly Me York," the image of slavery is unlike that in most revisionist history books. Dunbar depicts black people as having a delightful ball to which four plantations of slaves have been invited. They have plenteous quantities of mouth-watering food, leisure time for games and dances, and the unmatched good humor to appreciate the wonderful lives they lead. "Master's Gone to Philly Me York" is a tale of classic slave wish fulfillment. The master goes away for a few days and leaves a faithful slave in charge with the expectation that the plantation business will be run as usual. Seizing his opportunity, the slave slaughters a number of the master's livestock, invites slaves from surrounding plantations for a barbecue, and assumes the throne of power the master previously held.[22]

The worlds depicted contrast strikingly to the beatings, separation of families, inadequate diet, and other atrocities that characterized slavery, yet in concept they bear striking similarity to the world created on the Garner plantation in *Beloved*; there are no beatings, food is plentiful, and freedom of judgment and action are not only allowed, but encouraged. Sweet Home—before the arrival of schoolteacher—is every slave's dream of how that intolerable condition can be made tolerable. Women are not raped; men are not beaten like mules; and Garner is willing to allow slaves to hire their time and purchase their families and themselves.

From a relative perspective, the place is as sweet as its name. In remembering what it was before schoolteacher arrived, Sethe and other of its inhabitants imbue it with an aura of myth, of folktale larger than life, and the persons who inhabit it in turn become larger than life.[23] Schoolteacher's appearance is significant in contributing to this image, for as he destroys what once was, that former state is highlighted even more in the memories of those who knew it earlier. The mythical Sweet Home, then, assumes such proportions in direct relation to the memories of atrocities that spoiled its paradisiacal state. And these memories in turn shape the narrative structure of the novel. Defying linearity, memory and imagination combine to give an oral quality to the telling of the tale, just as they give a folkloristic bent to the perception of characters and the territory on which they reside.

Garner has been very much god in that paradise of Sweet Home. Like Eva Peace, he appropriates to himself the power of naming as the tangible symbol of his godhead; he goes further than Eva, however, for where she was content to name individuals, he names a species. He can call slaves men in the world that he has created, in his plantation paradise, just as Valerian Street can invite Son to dinner in the world in *Tar Baby* where he plays with shaping everyone's life. Before the satanic schoolteacher arrives, Garner has clearly given unprecedented license to the slaves and has won the enmity of his neighbors. In designating his slaves men, he has vio-

lated the boundaries of master/slave interaction (most of his fellow
slaveholders consider their charges less than human), and he has set
himself apart in a world where the maintenance of the system depends upon conformity from slaves as well as from masters.

Garner's unorthodox position, though, elevates him to legendary status with his neighbors as well as with his slaves. His forced
physical contests with other white men are a constant reminder to
them that he is different and a constant challenge to himself to live
up to the physical prowess implied in that difference. As the following exchange illustrates, Garner seeks challenges from his neighbors:

> "Y'all got boys," [Garner] told them. "Young boys, old boys,
> picky boys, stroppin boys. Now at Sweet Home, my niggers is men
> every one of em. Bought em thataway, raised em thataway. Men
> every one."
> "Beg to differ, Garner. Ain't no nigger men."
> "Not if you scared, they ain't." Garner's smile was wide. "But
> if you a man yourself, you'll want your niggers to be men too."
> "I wouldn't have no nigger men round my wife."
> It was the reaction Garner loved and waited for. "Neither
> would I," he said. "Neither would I," and there was always a pause
> before the neighbor, or stranger, or peddler, or brother-in-law or
> whoever it was got the meaning. Then a fierce argument, some-
> times a fight, and Garner came home bruised and pleased, having
> demonstrated one more time what a real Kentuckian was: one
> tough enough and smart enough to make and call his own niggers
> men. (10–11)

By implying that slaves designated as men are capable of violating
the sexual taboo between the races, perhaps with the consent or
invitation of the white women, Garner marginalizes himself from
white society, then reclaims his place in it by showing what a *man* he
is—rugged, individualistic, capable of insult, and capable of defend-
ing himself physically against the implications of his insult.

The man who makes a name for himself among his neighbors,
therefore, is as much legendary to them for his physical prowess as
for what they avow as his stupidity in not treating his slaves as they
treat theirs. A man capable of broad gestures, such as escorting Baby
Suggs across the river to Ohio when Halle's purchase of her is com-

plete, Garner is a dangerous enigma to his neighbors. In the tradition of legendary perpetuation, they elevate and/or kill that which they do not understand.[24]

Garner is not the only larger-than-life personality at Sweet Home. The slaves and their interactions with Garner as well as with each other are equally legendary. Sethe, for example, is able to experience a period of sexual abstinence and courtship undocumented in the annals of slave history. In leaving the young virgin to herself, the Sweet Home men exhibit almost superhuman control. Other than Sixo, they have no human sexual outlet. For them to allow Sethe the year it takes for her to choose one of them is perhaps reflective of a larger definition of manhood than that Garner has assigned to them. They elect to be human in a world that usually gives them permission to act like dogs.

The respect Paul A, Paul F, Paul D, Sixo, and Halle show to Sethe and what that means within self-imposed definitions of manhood is comparable to how Sethe later responds to being a mother. In spite of that larger world around her that has attempted to usurp her status as mother, she vows to remain one. In her actions, and in those of the men toward her, slaves show that masters cannot ultimately control the values of interaction among and between them.

These dual definitions of manhood (Garner's and the black men's themselves) enhance their legendary status, as do their individual actions. Sixo, for example, borders on folk characterization in several ways. His name sets him apart just as the repetition of names singles out the Pauls. But Sixo has an aura of mystery surrounding him comparable to many heroes of legend. He has mysterious origins; indeed, others refer to him as "the wild man" (11). He engages in solitary rituals that partly explain his unusual behavior: "Sixo went among trees at night. For dancing, he said, to keep his bloodlines open, he said. Privately, alone, he did it. None of the rest of them had seen him at it, but they could imagine it, and the picture they pictured made them eager to laugh at him—in daylight, that is, when it was safe" (25). His "flame-red tongue" and "indigo" (21) face mark him in the way that conjurers of tradition have had some distinguishing feature. He exhibits a kinship to the natural world and respects the spirits of the dead, especially those of Native

Americans, whose permission he requests for use of a deserted lodge for a rendezvous (24). He chooses silence over language and gifts of interaction (baking sweet potatoes for the Pauls and Halle) over physical expressions. He executes single-minded devotion to nearly superhuman feats, such as walking thirty miles in between his field obligations to see Patsy, who becomes known as the Thirty-Mile Woman.

Sixo's solitude, occasional preference for nature over human beings, unusual behavior, and aura of derring-do bring to mind such folk figures as Big Sixteen and Stagolee. His spirit cannot be conquered even if his body is destroyed. He is the ultimate man, as illustrated in his laughing during the burning death perpetrated against him by schoolteacher and his nephews. Schoolteacher may whip him, may burn him, may kill him, but Sixo still triumphs. He triumphs physically in laughing rather than howling in pain when he is lynched, and he triumphs spiritually in knowing that Patsy is pregnant with his child. His yell of "Seven-O" (226) as he is dying makes clear that this breed of man, Garner or no Garner, cannot be contained by a system called slavery.

And his howling laughter—as if he is on his way to better things than the demise of his body—links him to the themes that Morrison develops with Beloved. This plane of reality may be intolerable, and others may be equally intolerable, but perhaps there is one (where the blind horsemen of Isle des Chevaliers reside?) where Sixo can fully exploit those parts of his personality that we see only in glimpses.

Patsy's nickname, like Sixo's, makes her equally larger than life. By her designation as the "Thirty-Mile Woman," her indication of value becomes greater than that assessed by the slave system under which she lives. She is the possibility for family ("Sixo was hell-bent to make [a family] with the Thirty-Mile Woman"—219) and freedom, concepts antithetical to slavery but clearly the guiding forces in the lives of those enslaved. With this value attached to her, it is somewhat surprising to learn that the Thirty-Mile Woman is a girl of fourteen—a prize, certainly, during slavery, but the elevation of her before we know her age leads us to anticipate something more, perhaps that she is a wise older woman, capable of extraordinary feats. Her ordinariness highlights the process of transformation into legend that takes place in the novel.

Sethe also assumes her share of the legendary status of Sweet Home residents. It is difficult for most people to understand how she managed to escape from the Garner plantation without provisions and six months pregnant. There must have been something superhuman, if not otherworldly, in her determination. That quality is reflected in her eyes, which are frequently depicted as being totally black to indicate how absorbed Sethe can become in the tasks or memories at hand. It is a quality that Sethe exhibits in her insistence that she is a mother in a world that would declare otherwise. She lives that determination, thereby giving Denver a chance to see her legendary attributes in the next generation. Denver's image of Sethe is that of a "queenly woman" who controls herself, responds calmly to emergencies, and stares everything, including death, in the face:

> The one who never looked away, who when a man got stomped to death by a mare right in front of Sawyer's restaurant did not look away; and when a sow began eating her own litter did not look away then either. And when the baby's spirit picked up Here Boy and slammed him into the wall hard enough to break two of his legs and dislocate his eye, so hard he went into convulsions and chewed up his tongue, still her mother had not looked away. She had taken a hammer, knocked the dog unconscious, wiped away the blood and saliva, pushed his eye back in his head and set his leg bones. (12)

Legendary status becomes, to some extent, the nature of survival for slaves and newly freed blacks. To desire to live as a free person was in itself something extraordinary, and to reach that objective— through one's own initiative— was beyond the imaginations of most slaves; those who did so could only be viewed as larger than life.

Not only are people from Sweet Home made into legends, but inanimate things and animals are as well. Just as Sweet Home is almost a tangible memory to Sethe, so are specific places and trees on the plantation; the very air is special, almost bewitched.

> . . . [T]here was Sweet Home rolling, rolling, rolling out before her eyes, and although there was not a leaf on that farm that did not

make her want to scream, it rolled itself out before her in shameless beauty. It never looked as terrible as it was and it made her wonder if hell was a pretty place too. Fire and brimstone all right, but hidden in lacy groves. Boys hanging from the most beautiful sycamores in the world. It shamed her—remembering the wonderful soughing trees rather than the boys. Try as she might to make it otherwise, the sycamores beat out the children every time and she could not forgive her memory for that. (6)

Brother, one of the trees, not only provided shade (21, 224) for the Pauls, Halle, and Sixo, but it was anthropomorphized into one of them. The tree became a brother, fit partner in conversation as Miss Jane Pittman talked to trees in Ernest Gaines's *The Autobiography of Miss Jane Pittman* (1974). When Paul D is taken away to prison, his last look is toward Brother (106); in prison, he cultivates another tree, a small sapling, unlike the "old, wide and beckoning" (221) Brother, but serving a purpose nonetheless. Brother is the objectification of love, a tangible substitute for the absence of women at Sweet Home, as well as a method of communing with forces larger than Paul D. The sapling in Alfred, Georgia, is a way for Paul D to focus on something to love just a little bit in order to retain some semblance of his humanity. The value Paul D places on trees is clear in this elevating conclusion he draws about Brother and Sixo at one point: "Now *there* was a man, and *that* was a tree" (22).

Mister, the rooster at Sweet Home, is an objectification of freedom and a metaphor for manhood. As the rooster swaggers around the barnyard, strutting for the hens present, he has more freedom and control over his existence than Paul D. As that freedom and sexual interplay get interpreted, Mister is also more "man" than Paul D, more human—in the sense of having a separate, individual identity—than human beings who are slaves. In popular definitions of maleness, Mister is ultimately the "cock" that Paul D can never become. It is that irony that makes the sight of Mister so painful for Paul D when he is wearing the iron bit in his mouth. Memory for Paul D is the image of a rooster who is freer than he has been, a rooster who has been helped out of his shell because he had been abandoned by his mother. That failing notwithstanding, Mister had reached—and perhaps extended—his full potential as a male member of his species, something that has been unavailable to Paul D. Mister established his place in the barnyard lore by whipping "everything in the yard" (72).

The particularly poignant scene of Mister sitting on a tub and gazing at Paul D when he is wearing the bit is an occasion when inequality is made tangible and when spatial positioning signals to Paul D how incredibly devalued he is.

> "Mister, he looked so . . . free. Better than me. Stronger, tougher. Son a bitch couldn't even get out the shell by hisself but he was still king and I was . . ." Paul D stopped and squeezed his left hand with his right. He held it that way long enough for it and the world to quiet down and let him go on.
> "Mister was allowed to be and stay what he was. But I wasn't allowed to be and stay what I was. Even if you cooked him you'd be cooking a rooster named Mister. But wasn't no way I'd ever be Paul D again, living or dead. Schoolteacher changed me. I was something else and that something was less than a chicken sitting in the sun on a tub." (72)

As he relates his memories of Sweet Home to Sethe, Paul D is remembering Mister's metaphysical position in that world as much as he is remembering a neglected chicken carving out a space for himself. Mister had been able to compete on an equal level with the other roosters in the barnyard; Paul D is forced outside the arena of competition, without the ability even to respond to those who are manipulating him.

Mister, like Brother, acquires a quasi-human status for Paul D when he describes the world that has had such an impact upon his life. As memory gets meshed with imagination, it perhaps looms larger than fact, and it leads more naturally to the shaping of legends. Imagination also serves to explain the demise of Sweet Home. Others may claim that Garner had a heart attack or a stroke and was brought home dead on his horse. Sixo maintains that he was killed ("Sixo had a knowing tale about everything. Including Mr. Garner's stroke, which he said was a shot in his ear put there by a jealous neighbor"—219), precisely for those traits that identified him as being special. No longer able to tolerate his nonconformity, one of his neighbors had simply shot him in a ritualized restoration of the status quo. Ironically, the shooting reduces Garner to the status of a slave in that his life becomes just as devalued. In suggesting that Sixo's explanation for Garner's death is the preferred one, Morrison consigns Sweet Home and its people to a land where reality is indeed large enough to contain myth and legend.

Conclusion

A study of Toni Morrison's use of folklore in her novels is a foray
into a texturally rich intertwining of folk, popular, and literary cultures. Through structure, characters, incidents, and events, Morrison
uses African-American folk culture to provide the ethos for her
fiction. Her kinship to a long line of black writers who have used
folk materials shows her expanding upon and transforming earlier
patterns of usage to forge a distinctive voice for herself; that voice at
times complements what has gone before and at other times health-
ily contradicts it. She consistently succeeds in questioning our assumptions, challenging the ways in which we view characters and
cultures, and reminding us of the inherent dangers in taking absolute positions on anything in life.

African-American folklore is an especially apt frame of reference
in which to consider Toni Morrison's novels because the lore and the
novels share a striking male-centered perspective, making Morrison's treatment of women particularly provocative. On the one
hand, characters such as Jadine and Sula defy traditional female
stereotypes by containing traits usually reserved for the badmen of
tradition, or those stereotypically identified with males; Morrison
has admitted that Sula does as men do in that she "behaves so
terribly."[1] Sula and Jadine exhibit a great degree of independence,
freedom of movement, and self-determination, traits which in African-American folklore are usually assigned to male figures. Even
when we apply trickster models to female characters in Morrison's
fiction, we do so with modifications upon masculine examples. On
the other hand, characters such as Ruth, Hagar, and Pecola are so

self-sacrificing and victimized that they seem to perpetuate, without any modification, the notion of the lesser value characteristic of females in the folk tradition. These contrasting but ultimately similar portrayals are especially striking in a period when most black women writers, and a few black males, are expanding what is possible for black female characters. And while Morrison frequently joins that expansion, she just as frequently creates female characters who are pathetic stepsisters to some of their historical literary sisters.

On the restrictive, traditional side, Morrison forces our attention to pause on characters such as Pecola and Hagar, who seem least able to assign value to themselves; on Nel, the conformist who bends imagination to community will; and on Geraldine, a more ruthless version of Nel, who mistakes middle-class norms for her own imaginative nest-building. As Susan Willis correctly points out, even those Morrison women who think they are in control are not. Of Geraldine, Willis writes: "In faking an orgasm, the woman negates her pleasure for the sake of her husband's satisfaction, thus defining herself as a tool of his sexual gratification."[2] Geraldine and the other women characters can easily be assigned value because they acquiesce in the assignment. They become objects, physical manifestations of someone else's notion of what girls/women should be. The most noticeable of these objects is Sweet, who is so objectified that she especially invites comparison to folkloristic portrayals.

As the prize in the contest between Milkman and the other men in *Song of Solomon*, Sweet approximates those females in trickster tales who do not define the rules of the contest, indeed are frequently absent from it, and who are used merely as the measure of a male's attainment of a victory. Since she is conceived as a giver of pleasure, no attention need be paid to Sweet as a flesh-and-blood woman (though admittedly when she asks Milkman who Solomon had left behind on his flight to Africa she utters one of the crucial questions of the novel). The assumption is that Milkman's wish is her command, that she would not possibly find him sexually unacceptable upon his unkempt, funky arrival at her house from a night of hunting. The men in the town have defined her as someone whose sexual favors it is their privilege (and right) to dispense.

Hannah Peace, another embodiment of the pleasure principle,

similarly evokes the roles assigned to females in African-American folk tradition. Like Sweet, she is a prize for the men of the community, even without the contest factor, and, like Sweet, she similarly seems to enjoy the pleasure she knows she is capable of giving. Her situation, though, is not unlike that of females who star in the fornication contests popularized in the toast tradition.[3] In such contests, women are defined biologically, and they consent, and sometimes actually take pride in, that definition. Braggadocio about their sexual prowess and their invitations to competition equal those of the males. In the competitive arena, their major asset is their vagina (not feminine charm or guile or any more expansive concept of femaleness), which can best an opponent or be subdued by one. The pleasure-giving Hannah presumably always bests her "opponents" because they keep coming back for more. Paradoxically, Hannah's seemingly harmless, adorable attributes simultaneously preclude her severance from traditional views of women who should please men, take care of them, and not cause any "real" problems for them (all the women know they have nothing to fear from Hannah because she is as much a victim of her body as are their husbands). She is as biologically determined as is Nella Larsen's Helga Crane; Hannah Peace's might be a more romantic act but it is no less escapable, no less negatively determining than Helga's Alabama experiences.[4]

It is especially noteworthy that patterns of female sacrifice in Morrison's novels parallel a consistent trend in the lore: females are of value only in direct proportion to their assistance in male objectives; more often than not, they suppress their desires, indeed sacrifice their lives and/or futures, to assist the males. That progression may in part reflect the adoption into African-American folklore from other oral traditions. For example, Jack tales are more frequently identified with Europeans and southern whites than with blacks. Yet in a version of one of the Jack tales that circulates in African-American communities, the female character, who is the devil's daughter, uses her extranatural powers to assist Jack in the completion of nearly impossible tasks imposed by her father.[5] Beatrice Devil, therefore, who is ostensibly a powerful woman, can only have that power filtered through the functions it serves for Jack. Like the females in trickster tales, she is the prize in a contest of masculine wills; by assisting Jack, she becomes his betrothed. Yet her power and her creative space in the tale get usurped by masculinity.

Jadine's talents are undercut by the negative response written into the text in evaluating her actions. Her efforts to help Son might be annoying, but they are finally more acceptable than her bid to be an independent, self-determining woman. Or we might say that the *tone* of her assistance is too "masculine," too much on a level of male/female equality than Son's fragile ego can take during their adventures in New York.

Ultimately, the question of who has value in Morrison's novels comes down to a seemingly easy answer: men. The answer only seems to be easy because the route to its arrival is circuitous. At a glance, for example, we might conclude that the Peace women rule in *Sula*. On closer examination, however, it becomes clear that masculinity is the driving force in the novel. BoyBoy shapes Eva's character; a white *man* turns Helene Wright to custard; Sula's independence is identified as masculine and undercut by Ajax, a "true" principle of masculinity. The women are set in motion, react, and shape their lives around the men in their lives or around traditionally masculine ideas. Indeed, the impetus to destruction of the Bottom is tantamount to war, the same male destructiveness that blasted Shadrack into his shell-shocked state.

The pattern holds especially in *Song of Solomon*. From Dr. Foster shaping Ruth's life, to the psychologically warping impact of Macon and Milkman, to the retaliatory activity of the Seven Days, the novel's world is one of masculine action and female reaction or submission. Pilate may be grand, but for all the romance of her being one of Morrison's esteemed ancestors, and in spite of her having a daughter and a granddaughter, she finally comes looking for Macon to complete the definition of herself as a family person.

At a glance, then, Morrison's works seem to continue the use and abuse of black women characters by making them victims in the traditional folkloristic patterns—generally devalued by males, to be seen and not heard, to submit to masculine will in reality if not in spirit. Is Milkman, for example, worth the victimization of Hagar, Ruth, Corinthians, Lena, and Pilate? If most of the women are to be sacrificed to community or to masculine growth, what does that suggest about a feminist perspective in Morrison's work? Is there any female character in Morrison's work who can fulfill herself and not be destroyed, or not be judged for doing so? Must all women be subsumed under some community standard, or ostracized if they do not adhere to such standards?

Another traditional view limiting Morrison's female characters is that so many of them are superficially considered to be witches and scapegoats. As Barbara Christian notes, "it is significant, too, the emphasis the author places on women as accessible scapegoat figures for communities, for any obviously conscious disregard of cultural mores on their part seems to represent not only a threat to the community but to the whole species as well—hence the preponderance of witches, pariahs, and insane women in the history of humanity."[6] From M'Dear to the insane Pecola to Sula to Pilate to Thérèse to Sethe, Morrison's female characters evoke uneasiness in their families and their communities. Such trepidations tie in to Lederer's "fear of women" and reinforce the belief that women are mysterious and dangerous. While such characterizations retain the inherent trait of defining women as "Other," the alternative side of the coin would suggest that such characterizations simultaneously show their power.

On this more expansive side, consider Morrison's creation of a character like Sethe Suggs. Sethe claims the power of self-determination, a right allotted in her world only to white men and a few death-defying black men. In her willful commission of violence, she explodes the myth of the acquiescent, long-suffering black matriarch who trusts her fate and that of those she loves to a benign if distant God. Nonconformist by all the standards of her day, she joins Sula in throwing community norms back into the faces of their upholders.

Even the quiet, sometimes frightened, Denver Suggs is also an expansive female character in the Morrison canon. Certainly in less dramatic ways than Sethe or Baby Suggs, she takes the lessons of the past and looks forward to the future. Unlike Pecola, who is driven insane by her surroundings, Denver buds forth with the potential for health, and that potential warrants viewing her in a different light. Almost none of the female characters who suffer assaults upon their minds and/or bodies in Morrison's novels survive those assaults. Sula and Hagar die, and Baby Suggs wills herself to death. The world ultimately is a Frau Welt for them; it does not live up to the promise of itself. But Denver survives the silence into which she is driven when she learns of Sethe's deed; she survives Beloved's assaults upon the house and her family; she survives being ostracized from the neighbors; and she survives her mother's temporary breakdown. In fact, witnessing what happens to Sethe during Beloved's takeover is the impetus for Denver's growth. The independence that she claims by leaving the porch to seek help from the neighbors, her renewing her acquaintance with Nelson Lord, and her newfound voice in strongly articulating her own view of the situation instead of accepting Paul D's, all portend possibility for her. And that possibility is more than Morrison leaves most of her female characters.

Appearing in Morrison's most recent novel, perhaps Denver and Sethe portend more female characters conceived with the expansive vision in mind, or perhaps it is natural that anyone who survives what these women have gone through must be considered bright signs for the future. At least there are no deaths, burnings, resignations, or howls of pain at the end of the novel (though admittedly Beloved's haunting disappearance is disturbing). And there seems to be more of a healthy future implied than in any of Morrison's previous novels. This healthy possibility, however, has to be balanced by a conspicuous fact: from all the drama of her life, it is Paul D who gives back to Sethe a sense of herself—not Baby Suggs, not Denver, not Beloved. On the landscape of Morrison's fictive imagination, women stand only with the assistance of men, but men grow over the deranged or dead bodies of women. Still, what is striking about these women is that they are unlike most of their historical literary sisters, and the oral cultures that aid in defining their characters is one of the reasons for their distinctiveness.

In her saturation of fiction with a folkloristic aura, and in the unusual twists she gives to her use of folklore, Toni Morrison stands in the forefront of contemporary black authors who are consciously creating new myths and new ways of perceiving what we mean by "folk." They are attracted to those realms beyond the realistic as they expand our conceptions of the novelistic form. Toni Cade Bambara, for example, in *The Salt Eaters* (1980), also incorporates African traditions into her fiction. There are many out-of-body experiences and sentient continuations beyond the demise of the body. Old Wife, Minnie Ransom's spirit guide for her healings, is a ghost; she and

Minnie talk to each other, go off dancing together, and discuss culture, politics, and romance. Minnie relies upon the healing forces of the universe in transforming her patients from illness to health. Bambara, like Morrison, recognizes no barriers between the temporal and supernatural realms, just as she shows no obvious division between past, present, and future.[7]

Paule Marshall has consciously tried to reconnect African-American and African traditions by exploring those in the Caribbean; her *Praisesong for the Widow* (1983) also incorporates a journey motif with a quest for ancestors through legends told about them and ceremonies performed for them. In the "Beg Pardon" ceremony in which the spirits of ancestors are evoked, there is recognition that spirits can traverse realms at will. Gloria Naylor in *Mama Day* (1988) and Alice Walker in *The Temple of My Familiar* (1989) join Morrison, Bambara, and Marshall in transcending temporality in their novels and in creating characters who have access to multiple planes of existence. Naylor's characters, a husband and wife, continue conversations with each other years after the husband's death, and Walker's characters fall in love with spirits of the deceased or are reincarnated through numerous generations and guises.

Other writers have drawn upon African-American history (American in its broadest connotations) in developing their novels, poetry, and short fiction. Like Toni Morrison's *Beloved*, Charles Johnson's *Oxherding Tale* (1982) is informed by the myths surrounding slavery (his earlier novel, *Faith and the Good Thing* (1974), has a character, "Swamp Woman," who might even rival Sula or Beloved). Ernest Gaines has consistently drawn upon the myths and folkways inherent in plantation life in his numerous novels and stories, and Julia Fields and Alice Walker in their short stories join Gaines in their concern with southern black folk culture. Leaving United States soil, as Morrison does in *Tar Baby*, Gayl Jones has consistently created new myths, especially in works like *Song for Anninho* (1982), which is essentially a mythical reading of Afro-Brazilian history.

Current trends suggest that most of these writers, Morrison among them, are fascinated by the possibilities inherent in African-American culture as a creative, vibrant phenomenon in and of itself. While writers like Jones and Gaines do depict conflicts between blacks and whites, the majority of the women focus instead on black societies and the richness of the oral traditions in them. They, like Zora Neale Hurston, believe that black people can indeed go about their lives without thinking about white people for at least twenty-four hours at a time. The twenty-four hours that Morrison and these other writers have chosen to reflect their folklore and culture may turn into a lifelong preoccupation.

Notes

Chapter 1

1. Toni Morrison, "Rootedness: The Ancestor as Foundation," in *Black Women Writers (1950–1980): A Critical Evaluation*, ed. Mari Evans (Garden City, N.Y.: Anchor Press/Doubleday, 1984), 341.
2. William Wells Brown, *Clotel; Or, The President's Daughter* (1853; rpt. New York: Collier, 1970), 108; also in the 1864 *Clotelle* (Boston: James Redpath), 57. Lawrence W. Levine, in *Black Culture and Black Consciousness: Afro-American Folk Thought from Slavery to Freedom* (New York: Oxford, 1977), identifies the rhyme as a "song" and traces it through variations from the 1880s to the Great Depression (249–50). The inequities Brown's slaves note were similarly noted by Frederick Douglass when he recounted his adventures as a slave in *Life and Times of Frederick Douglass* (Hartford, Conn.: Park Publishing Co., 1882):

    > We raise de wheat,
    > Dey gib us de corn:
    > We bake de bread,
    > Dey gib us de crust;
    > We sif de meal,
    > Dey gib us de huss;
    > We peel de meat,
    > Dey gib us de skin;
    > And dat's de way
    > Dey take us in;
    > We skim de pot,
    > Dey gib us de liquor,

And say dat's good enough for nigger.
Walk over! walk over!
Your butter and de fat;
Poor nigger, you can't get over dat!
                    Walk over— (181)

This inclusion indicates that literary and autobiographical sources drew upon African-American folk materials, which is noteworthy because the autobiographical genre became one of the most appealing for African-American writers.

3. See Douglass's *Narrative of the Life of Frederick Douglass* (1845; rpt. Cambridge, Mass.: Harvard Univ. Press, 1960), 101–3, and Bontemps's *God Sends Sunday* (New York: Harcourt, Brace and Co., 1931). Bontemps later collaborated with Countee Cullen to turn the novel into a play entitled *St. Louis Woman* (1946).

4. Gladys-Marie Fry, *Nightriders in Black Folk History* (Knoxville: Univ. of Tennessee Press, 1975), 45–73.

5. James Weldon Johnson, *God's Trombones* (New York: Viking, 1927), 13.

6. Jean Toomer, *Cane* (New York: Boni and Liveright, 1923), 2, 53, 63.

7. Richard Wright, *Uncle Tom's Children* (New York: Harper and Row, 1938).

8. Zora Neale Hurston, *Jonah's Gourd Vine* (1934; rpt., Philadelphia: Lippincott, 1971), 17.

9. Many scholars have dealt with the issue of folklore in/and literature. Among them are Richard M. Dorson and Daniel Hoffman in "Folklore in Literature: A Symposium," *Journal of American Folklore* 70 (1957): 1–24 (Dorson includes a listing of numerous articles treating folklore in literature); Alan Dundes, "The Study of Folklore in Literature and Culture: Identification and Interpretation," *Journal of American Folklore* 78 (Apr.–June 1965): 136–42 (one of the most influential articles); Donald M. Winkelman's "Three American Authors as Semi-Folk Artists," which appears in the same volume with Dundes (130–35), stresses how folklore can be used in literature for "style" (speech, folkways) or "structure." See also: Butler Waugh, "Structural Analysis in Literature and Folklore," *Western Folklore* 25 (1966): 153–64; William O. Hendricks, "Folklore and the Structural Analysis of Literary Texts," *Language and Style* 3 (Spring 1970): 83–121; and Carlos C. Drake, "Literary Criticism and Folklore," *Journal of Popular Culture* 5 (Fall 1971): 289–97.

10. Hennig Cohen, for example, posited that folklore in literary texts

could be "functionally . . . put to work in a number of ways—among them, to advance the plot, to characterize, to provide structure, and to defend, explain, and raise questions about the nature of society." See Cohen's "American Literature and American Folklore" in *Our Living Traditions: An Introduction to American Folklore*, ed. Tristram Potter Coffin (New York: Basic Books, 1968), 242.

11. See for example the series of articles published in *Southern Folklore Quarterly* 43 (1979). These include: Daniel R. Barnes, "Toward the Establishment of Principles for the Study of Folklore and Literature," 5–16; Neil R. Grobman, "A Schema for the Study of the Sources and Literary Simulations of Folkloric Phenomena," 17–37; Sandra K. D. Stahl, "Style in Oral and Written Narratives," 39–62; and David H. Stanley, "The Personal Narrative and the Personal Novel: Folklore as Frame and Structure for Literature," 107–20. Stahl has also published "Studying Folklore and American Literature," in *Handbook of American Folklore*, ed. Richard M. Dorson (Bloomington: Indiana Univ. Press, 1983), 422–33, an article that articulates especially well the problems inherent in such studies.

12. See Houston A. Baker, Jr., *Blues, Ideology, and Afro-American Literature: A Vernacular Theory* (Chicago: Univ. of Chicago Press, 1984), and Henry Louis Gates, Jr., *The Signifying Monkey* (New York: Oxford, 1988). See also Keith E. Byerman, *Fingering the Jagged Grain: Tradition and Form in Recent Black Fiction* (Athens: Univ. of Georgia Press, 1985). Byerman asserts that contemporary black writers "have shaped a technically sophisticated body of literature by combining the methods of modern fiction making with the materials of folk culture" (1), and he focuses on the "performative" (4) aspects of black folk culture, as well as a variety of folk forms and characters, to make his points.

13. For representative examples, see: Ann L. Rayson, "The Novels of Zora Neale Hurston," *Studies in Black Literature* 5 (Winter 1974): 1–10; Jerry W. Ward, Jr., "Folklore and the Study of Black Literature," *Mississippi Folklore Register* 6 (Fall 1972): 83–90; and William H. Wiggins, Jr., "Black Folktales in the Novels of John O. Killens," *The Black Scholar* 3 (Nov. 1971): 50–58.

14. Stephen Henderson, *Understanding the New Black Poetry: Black Speech and Black Music as Poetic References* (New York: William Morrow, 1973), 62–66.

15. In *Black Feminist Criticism: Perspectives on Black Women Writers* (New York: Pergamon, 1985), Barbara Christian also discusses Morrison's

penchant for inversion, especially in relation to "Truth" (52), particularly "the unnatural inversion of truth contained in the ideas of physical beauty and romantic love" (57), and "the natural order," particularly the seasons, as in *The Bluest Eye* (58).

Chapter 2

1. For a discussion of Morrison's incorporation of more historical items of folklore into *The Bluest Eye*, see my chapter entitled "Reconnecting Fragments: Afro-American Folk Tradition in *The Bluest Eye*" in *Critical Essays on Toni Morrison*, ed. Nellie Y. McKay (Boston: G. K. Hall, 1988), 68–76.
2. "Toni Morrison," in *Black Women Writers at Work*, ed. Claudia Tate (New York: Continuum, 1983), 125.
3. See Joey Lee Dillard, *Black Names* (The Hague: Mouton, 1976), and Murray Heller, ed., *Black Names in America: Origins and Usages* (Boston: G. K. Hall, 1975).
4. See Bernice Reagon, "We Are 'Girl,' 'Chile,' 'Lady,' That 'oman,' 'Hussy,' 'Heifer,' 'A Woman'; or, Naming That Imprisons and Naming That Sets You Free," paper presented at annual meeting of Modern Language Association, Washington, D.C., 27 Dec. 1984.
5. Similar rituals were used historically to insult darker-skinned children. See Mamie Garvin Fields and Karen Fields's discussion of this in *Lemon Swamp and Other Places: A Carolina Memoir* (New York: Free Press, 1983), 47, 214.
6. Zora Neale Hurston, "How Jack O'Lanterns Came to Be," in *Mules and Men* (1935; rpt., Bloomington: Indiana Univ. Press, 1978), 172–73; Langston Hughes and Arna Bontemps, eds.,*The Book of Negro Folklore* (New York: Dodd, Mead & Co., 1958), 164–66.
7. See, for example, Hurston's short stories "Spunk" and "Sweat" and the first section of *Their Eyes Were Watching God* (1937; rpt. Urbana: Univ. of Illinois Press, 1978).
8. In Langston Hughes and Arna Bontemps's Th*e Book of Negro Folklore*, Julia Peterkin discusses the importance of burial societies in African-American communities in the essay "The Bury League," 105–13. In her poem "southeast corner," Gwendolyn Brooks paints a Beauty School Madam being buried with her fortune ("the thickest, tallest monument," under which she rests in a "right red velvet lining" and "shot silk"), a glamorous extension of the

practice in black communities of being "laid out" well. See Brooks's
Blacks (Chicago: David Co., 1987), 23.

9. In *Black Women Novelists: The Development of a Tradition, 1892–1976*
    (Westport, Conn.: Greenwood Press, 1980), Barbara Christian refers
    to the seasons, the Dick and Jane primer, and Claudia's voice as the
    three "structural motifs . . . the building blocks of the book" (143).
    In her focus on theme and variation on a theme, the "jazz composi-
    tion" (144) and recurrent "dominant chords" (148) of the novel, she
    has suggested an additional structural motif for *Sula*—that of jazz
    composition.

10. Vladimir Propp, *Morphology of the Folktale* (Austin: Univ. of Texas
    Press, 1975), 36ff.

11. For a discussion of myth with classical origins in the novel, see
    Madonne M. Miner, "Lady No Longer Sings the Blues: Rape,
    Madness, and Silence in *The Bluest Eye*," in *Conjuring: Black Women,
    Fiction, and Literary Tradition*, ed. Marjorie Pryse and Hortense J.
    Spillers (Bloomington: Indiana Univ. Press, 1985), 176–91, and
    Karla F. C. Holloway and Stephanie A. Demetrakopoulos, *New
    Dimensions of Spirituality: A Biracial and Bicultural Reading of the
    Novels of Toni Morrison* (Westport, Conn.: Greenwood Press, 1987),
    31–36. For a discussion of more traditional fairy tale elements in the
    novel, see Bessie W. Jones and Audrey L. Vinson, *The World of Toni
    Morrison: Explorations in Literary Criticism* (Dubuque, Iowa:
    Kendall/Hunt, 1985), chap. 2, "Ironic Use of Fairy Tale Motifs in
    The Bluest Eye."

12. Wilfred D. Samuels and Clenora Hudson-Weems argue in *Toni
    Morrison* (Boston: Twayne, 1990) that the focus on eyes in the novel
    has Sartre's "The Look" as its basis (17–19).

13. Claudia and Frieda try to nullify Maureen's influence upon them
    by resorting to the negative effects of nicknaming that Reagon
    discusses: "when we found out that she had been born with six
    fingers on each hand and that there was a little bump where each
    extra one had been removed, we smiled. They were small tri-
    umphs, but we took what we could get—snickering behind her
    back and calling her Six-finger-dog-tooth-meringue pie. But we had
    to do it alone, for none of the other girls would cooperate with our
    hostility. They adored her" (48).

14. For an intriguing discussion of scapegoating in the novel, see
    Michael Awkward, " 'The Evil of Fulfillment': Scapegoating and
    Narration in *The Bluest Eye*," chap. 2 of his book, *Inspiriting Influ-*

ences: Tradition, Revision, and Afro-American Women's Novels (New York: Columbia Univ. Press, 1989).

Chapter 3

1. Noted in Tate, ed., Black *Women Writers at Work*, 122, and Jane Bakerman, "The Seams Can't Show: An Interview with Toni Morrison," *Black American Literature Forum* 12 (Summer 1978): 59.

2. Morrison emphasizes that she chose the "nightshade" and "black-berry" for their connotative as well as their literal values. "Both plants have darkness in them: 'black' and 'night.' One is unusual (nightshade) and has two darkness words: 'night' and 'shade.' The other (blackberry) is common. A familiar plant and an exotic one. A harmless one and a dangerous one. One produces a nourishing berry; one delivers toxic ones" ("Unspeakable Things Unspoken: The Afro-American Presence in American Literature," *Michigan Quarterly Review* 28 [Winter 1989]: 25). In her awareness of the plants, Morrison exhibits qualities of the folk healer. In structuring her novel around the positive and negative qualities of blackness drawn from natural imagery, she further enhances her ties to black folk traditions. She has also commented that she grew up in an environment where stories were told, where "black lore, black music, black language" were "prominent elements"; see Nellie Y. McKay, "An Interview with Toni Morrison," *Contemporary Literature* 24 (Winter 1983): 414–15.

3. For a discussion of passivity in fairy tales, see Kay Stone, "Things Walt Disney Never Told Us," in *Women and Folklore*, ed. Claire R. Farrer (Austin: Univ. of Texas Press, 1975), 42–50 and Marcia R. Lieberman, " 'Some Day My Prince Will Come': Female Accultura-tion Through the Fairy Tale," *College English* 34 (1972): 383–95. For a slightly different view, see Kay F. Stone, "The Misuses of Enchant-ment: Controversies on the Significance of Fairy Tales," in Rosan A. Jordan and Susan J. Kalčik, eds.,*Women's Folklore, Women's Culture*, (Philadelphia: Univ. of Pennsylvania Press, 1985), 125–45.

4. "Upon This Rock," one of the stories Dance has collected, illustrates the point well. Jesus tells a black man, a Jew, and an Italian to go out and collect stones during a day's walk. The black man, believ-ing that he is being timed, rushes back with a pebble. The Italian brings a wheelbarrow full of stones, and the Jew shoves a moun-tain. When Jesus turns the stones into bread, "the Black man had a biscuit. The Italian had a wheelbarrow *filled* with loaves of bread.

And the Jew had a *bakery*, of course." The next day, having been
given the same directions, the black man goes out and brings back
"a whole avalanche of mountains and boulders"; everyone must
wait until four A.M. for him to push them to the gathering site.
Upon his arrival, he discovers that the rules have changed from
morning to evening. "And finally the Lord said, 'Upon *these* rocks
I'll build my church.' And the Black man said, 'I be *damned* if you
will. You gon' make *bread* today!'" (Daryl Cumber Dance, *Shuckin'
and Jivin': Folklore from Contemporary Black Americans* [Bloomington:
Indiana Univ. Press, 1978], 9–10).

5. Hurston, *Mules and Men*, and *The Sanctified Church* (Berkeley: Turtle
Island, 1983).

6. See "Toni Morrison," in *Black Women Writers at Work*, ed. Tate, 130:
"There was no other place in the world she could have lived
without being harmed"; Sandi Russell, "It's OK to say OK,"
interview essay in *Critical Essays on Toni Morrison*, ed. McKay, 43–
47: "Although the community didn't like Sula and what she did,
they allowed her to 'be.' She couldn't have had these freedoms
elsewhere" (44); and McKay, "An Interview with Toni Morrison,"
413–29: Sula is "nevertheless protected there [in the Bottom] as she
would not be elsewhere" (426).

7. Robert Graves, *English and Scottish Ballads* (London: Heinemann,
1963), 5–7.

8. See Axel Olrik, "Epic Laws of Folk Narrative," in *The Study of
Folklore*, ed. Alan Dundes (Englewood Cliffs, N.J.: Prentice-Hall,
1965), 129–41.

9. Graves, *English and Scottish Ballads*, 89–91.

10. See Levine, *Black Culture and Black Consciousness*, 413–15.

11. As noted earlier, Barbara Christian makes a case for *The Bluest Eye*
also being based on African-American musical structures. See *Black
Women Novelists: The Development of a Tradition, 1892–1976*, 148–49.

12. Morrison has commented on her perception of black people's
willingness to accept difference: "Black people have a way of
allowing things to go on the way they're going. We're not too
terrified of death, not too terrified of being different, not too upset
about divisions among things, people. Our interests have always
been, it seems to me, on how un-alike things are rather than how
alike things are." Tate, ed., *Black Women Writers at Work*, 123.

13. In the transformation to "ba-ad" woman, Sula's presumed pecu-
liarities approximate those of some of the male heroes of African-
American tradition. Consider one description of badman Stagolee:
"Stagolee was so bad that the flies wouldn't even fly around his

head in the summertime, and snow wouldn't fall on his house in the winter," Julius Lester, *Black Folktales* (New York: Baron, 1969), 113. Sula started on the road to "ba-adness" when she sliced off the tip of her finger to prevent the white boys from attacking her and Nel (54–55).

14. Philip M. Royster discusses how the Bottom uses Sula and Shadrack as scapegoats in "A Priest and a Witch against The Spiders and The Snakes: Scapegoating in Toni Morrison's *Sula*," *Umoja* 2 (Fall 1978): 149–68.

15. Holloway and Demetrakopoulos, *New Dimensions of Spirituality*, 58–59.

16. Barbara Christian has discussed the importance of naming in the novel, connecting it in Eva's case to the African concept of Nommo. See *Black Women Novelists*, as well as Jones and Vinson, *The World of Toni Morrison: Explorations in Literary Criticism*, 13–15, and Holloway and Demetrakopoulos, *New Dimensions of Spirituality*, 21–22, 41, 69, 75–76.

17. Darwin T. Turner, "Theme, Characterization, and Style in the Works of Toni Morrison," in *Black Women Writers (1950–1980): A Critical Evaluation*, ed. Evans, 361–69.

18. See Paule Marshall's *The Chosen Place, The Timeless People* (New York: Harcourt Brace & World, 1969) and Hurston's *Mules and Men*.

19. For more information on memorates and legend formation, see Sandra K. D. Stahl, "Personal Experience Stories," in *Handbook of American Folklore*, ed. Dorson, 268–76.

20. Wayland D. Hand, ed., *The Frank C. Brown Collection of North Carolina Folklore*, vols. 6 and 7 (Durham: Duke Univ. Press, 1961, 1964); see sections on "portents."

21. The narrator refers to Sula's birthmark as a "stemmed rose" (52, 144) and "like a stem and rose" (74). Shadrack, who does not share in the community disdain for Sula, sees the birthmark as a "tadpole" (157), a friendlier image than any of the other characters visualize. Karla Holloway views the varying images of Sula's birthmark as "physical manifestations" of the "African archetypes" of fire, water, and ground (*New Dimensions of Spirituality*, 68, 69).

22. See Dundes, "The Study of Folklore in Literature and Culture: Identification and Interpretation," 136–42, and Cohen, "American Literature and American Folklore," 238–47.

23. See, for example, Ernest Gaines's "A Long Day in November" in *Bloodline* (New York: Dial, 1968).

24. See Richard M. Dorson, *American Negro Folktales* (Greenwich,

Conn.: Fawcett, 1967), 75–76, and Langston Hughes and Arna
Bontemps, *The Book of Negro Folklore*, 6–8.

25. For a selection of Aunt Dicy tales, see J. Mason Brewer, *American
    Negro Folklore* (Chicago: Quadrangle Books, 1968), 69–74. These are
    somewhat diminished from pure trickster tales, but they nonethe-
    less show a woman getting the better of her adversaries. And we
    need not necessarily look for feminine features of the trickster in
    discussing Sula, for Morrison, and several critics, have commented
    on how masculine Sula is in the courses of action she chooses; see
    the interview with Morrison in Jones and Vinson, *The World of Toni
    Morrison*.

26. See, for example, "Who Ate Up the Butter?" in Richard M. Dorson's
    Negro Folktales in Michigan (Cambridge: Harvard Univ. Press, 1956),
    33–35, and "Playing Godfather," in Hughes and Bontemps's *The
    Book of Negro Folklore*, 6–8.

27. See Wolfgang Lederer, *The Fear of Women* (New York: Grune &
    Stratton, 1968) and Hurston, *Tell My Horse* (1938; rpt. Berkeley:
    Turtle Island, 1983), 143–51.

28. See Walter Blair, ed., *Selected Shorter Writings of Mark Twain* (Boston:
    Houghton Mifflin, 1962), 306–88.

29. This spirit of experimentation brings to mind the folktale in which
    Brer Rabbit introduces the alligator family to fire simply for the
    sake of observing their reaction. He lures them out of the water to a
    dry field of grass and sets it on fire ("Why Br' Gator's Hide Is So
    Horny," Hughes and Bontemps, eds., *The Book of Negro Folklore*, 23–
    30), thereby causing their silvery white hides to be burned to a
    crinkly brown (and explaining why they currently look the way
    they do). Compare this to Sula's penchant for making others
    uncomfortable solely for the sake of registering their discomfort:
    "In the midst of a pleasant conversation with someone she might
    say, 'Why do you chew with your mouth open?' not because the
    answer interested her but because she wanted to see the person's
    face change rapidly" (119).

Chapter 4

1. Baron FitzRoy Richard Somerset Raglan, *The Hero: A Study in
    Tradition, Myth, and Drama* (1956; rpt. Westport, Conn.: Greenwood
    Press, 1975); Joseph Campbell, *The Hero with a Thousand Faces*
    (London: Abacus, 1975).

2. Some of these articles include Jacqueline de Weever, "Toni
    Morrison's Use of Fairy Tale, Folk Tale, and Myth in *The* [*sic*] *Song
    of Solomon*," *Southern Folklore Quarterly* 44 (1980): 131–44; A. Leslie
    Harris, "Myth as Structure in Toni Morrison's *Song of Solomon*,"
    MELUS 7 (1980): 69–76; Wilfred D. Samuels, "Liminality and the
    Search for Self in Toni Morrison's *Song of Solomon*," *Minority Voices*
    5 (1981): 59–68 (expanded in Samuels and Hudson-Weems, *Toni
    Morrison*, 53–78); Cynthia A. Davis, "Self, Society, and Myth in Toni
    Morrison's Fiction," *Contemporary Literature* 23 (1982): 323–42;
    Dorothy H. Lee, "*Song of Solomon:* To Ride the Air," *Black American
    Literature Forum* 16 (Summer 1982): 64–70; and Jones and Vinson,
    The World of Toni Morrison. Although Gerry Brenner, in "*Song of
    Solomon:* Rejecting Rank's Monomyth and Feminism," in *Critical
    Essays on Toni Morrison*, ed. McKay, 114–25, notes Morrison's
    rejection of the superimposition of "other kinds of structures" on
    her works, he nonetheless illustrates briefly how Otto Rank's
    monomyth applies to *Song of Solomon*; however, he asserts that
    Morrison "undercuts its conventional celebration of the role of the
    hero in our culture" (117). He also points out the shortcomings in
    the work of some of the other scholars who have discussed myth in
    connection with the novel and spends the bulk of his discussion
    arguing that the "subtext" for Milkman's journey "is satiric" (118).
3. For an example of an article that tries to resolve this problem by
    discussing Morrison's first three novels as larger than the black
    community, but solidly grounded in it and its aesthetic, see Norris
    Clark, "Flying Black: Toni Morrison's *The Bluest Eye, Sula* and *Song
    of Solomon*," *Minority Voices* 4 (1980): 51–63.
4. Thomas LeClair, "'The Language Must Not Sweat': A Conversation
    with Toni Morrison," *The New Republic* 184 (21 Mar. 1981): 26–27.
5. Perhaps a case could be made for Pilate being religious—she keeps
    a faith, but one created out of the mythmaking circumstances of her
    personal history.
6. See Joseph T. Skerrett, Jr., "Recitation to the *Griot*: Storytelling and
    Learning in Toni Morrison's *Song of Solomon*," in *Conjuring: Black
    Women, Fiction, and Literary Tradition*, ed. Pryse and Spillers, 192–
    202. See also Valerie Smith's "Toni Morrison's Narratives of
    Community," in her *Self-Discovery and Authority in Afro-American
    Narrative* (Cambridge: Harvard Univ. Press, 1987), 122–53.
7. John W. Roberts, *From Trickster to Badman: The Black Folk Hero in
    Slavery and Freedom* (Philadelphia: Univ. of Pennsylvania Press,
    1989), 1.

8. Questions as to whether Milkman was born "with a caul" (10) to account for his seeming early "mysterious" nature do not lead to any tangible later result and thus do not select him in any particular way.

9. In *Morphology of the Folktale,* Propp asserts that seeker heroes on various journeys are assisted by helpers who may show them the way to a particular objective, provide them with a talisman that will help them in their quest, or travel along with them for a period of time (39–51).

10. Keith E. Byerman has also pointed out the ambiguity in Milkman's name and how it gets clarified in direct proportion to his finding a purpose in life. See *Fingering the Jagged Grain: Tradition and Form in Recent Black Fiction,* 207.

11. Philip M. Royster argues that Milkman is a scapegoat in the circumstances surrounding his birth, which take on legendary overtones as well. Such an approach provides an additional direction for folkloristic commentary in the novel. See "Milkman's Flying: The Scapegoat Transcended in Toni Morrison's *Song of Solomon,*" *CLA Journal* 24 (June 1982): 421.

12. See Tate, ed., *Black Women Writers at Work,* 128. This idea of the black woman inventing herself is not new for Morrison. As early as 1971, she commented that the pressures of romantic relationships, children, and jobs let the black woman know that there was no place and no one to whom she could pass her burdens: "And she had nothing to fall back on: not maleness, not whiteness, not ladyhood, not anything. And out of the profound desolation of her reality she may very well have invented herself"; Morrison, "What the Black Woman Thinks About Women's Lib," *New York Times Magazine* (22 Aug. 1971): 63. This idea is echoed almost verbatim in *Sula* (52).

13. Ruth also talks with her dead father, but he does not appear to her, as Pilate's father appears to her. Morrison has also commented on the special, almost extranatural relationship she has with her own father, who died before she started work on *Song of Solomon.* See Jean Strouse, "Toni Morrison's Black Magic," *Newsweek* (30 Mar. 1981): 57.

14. For a discussion of Pilate's witch-like, extranatural, and supernatural powers, see Jones and Vinson, *The World of Toni Morrison,* chap. 5, "Pilate Dead: Conjuress," and chap. 6, "Pilate Dead: A Symbol of the Creative Imagination."

15. In contrast to this view, Jane S. Bakerman asserts that Pilate's life is

a "failure" ("Failures of Love: Female Initiation in the Novels of
Toni Morrison," *American Literature* 52 [1981]: 556), and Gerry
Brenner notes that "her mission is exemplary, because it is nothing
less than to live her life in manifest repudiation of the grasping
ambitiousness and obsessive desires of those around her who end
up as grotesques, fanatics, neurotics, or fantasists" ("*Song of
Solomon:* Rejecting Rank's Monomyth and Feminism," 123). Both
positions fail to see the complexity of the African-American world
view animating Pilate's portrayal.

16. For a discussion of one such transition from devil to disciple, see
William Ferris's film, *Two Black Churches* (New Haven: Yale Univ.
Design Studio, 1975); the minister in the New Haven church
recounts what his life was like before he was called to preach and
explains how he will not go back to that manner of ungodliness.
Perhaps the most famous of these instances is the transformation of
Malcolm X, which he recounts in *The Autobiography of Malcolm X*
(1965); I am grateful to Mary Hoover of San Francisco State Univ.
for suggesting this comparison.

17. A striking exception to this general trend of charting the course
north is John Walden in Charles W. Chesnutt's *The House Behind the
Cedars* (1900). John migrates from North Carolina to South Carolina
to pass for white and pursue a career as a lawyer.

18. Dorothy H. Lee, "*Song of Solomon:* To Ride the Air," 69.

19. Jane Campbell views this devolutionary process in Milkman's
journey as a return to the pastoral, where he can he prepared to
show kinship to nature and appreciate the "lessons of a rural
setting"; *Mythic Black Fiction: The Transformation of History* (Knoxville: Univ. of Tennessee Press, 1986), 142. Campbell also explores
the heroic/mythic nature of Milkman's quest "for selfhood" and
how it awakens him to his "heritage: ancestor worship, the supernatural, and African religion and folklore" (137).

20. As Genevieve Fabre correctly points out, "the tests and trials
become necessary rites of passage. They further purify him and
initiate him back into the tribe" ("Genealogical Archaeology or the
Quest for Legacy in Toni Morrison's *Song of Solomon,*" in *Critical
Essays on Toni Morrison,* ed. McKay, 112–13). Allowing Milkman to
pull out the bobcat's heart, and later, pointing him to Sweet, are the
obvious signs of his incorporation into the tribe.

21. Dorson, *American Negro Folktales,* "Coon in the Box," 126–29, and
Hurston, *Mules and Men,* 87–88.

22. Any number of scholars have discussed naming in the novel,

including Genevieve Fabre in "Genealogical Archaeology or the
Quest for Legacy in Toni Morrison's *Song of Solomon*," 108–10;
Jacqueline de Weever in "Toni Morrison's Use of Fairy Tale, Folk
Tale and Myth in *The* [sic] *Song of Solomon*"; Dorothy H. Lee in
"*Song of Solomon*: To Ride the Air" (Lee also includes commentary
on biblical names); Cynthia A. Davis, "Self, Society, and Myth in
Toni Morrison's Fiction"; and Ruth Rosenberg, "'And the Children
May Know Their Names': Toni Morrison's *Song of Solomon*,"
Literary Onomastics Studies 8 (1981): 195–219. Although I disagree
with Rosenberg's assessment of the value of nicknames in the novel
(204–5), her study is nonetheless engaging.

23. For a discussion of Morrison's use of the folktale of the flying
Africans, see Susan L. Blake, "Folklore and Community in *Song of
Solomon*," *MELUS* 7 (1980): 77–82, and Dorothy H. Lee, "*Song of
Solomon*: To Ride the Air," 64–70. Lee also traces patterns of the
monomyth identified by Joseph Campbell and others in her
discussion of the novel, but she weaves in African-American
connections as well. For versions of the tale of the flying Africans,
see Georgia Writers Project, *Drums and Shadows* (1940; rpt.
Westport, Conn.: Greenwood Press, 1973); Julius Lester, *Black
Folktales*, 147–52; and Virginia Hamilton, *The People Could Fly:
American Black Folktales* (New York: Knopf, 1985), 166–73. Karla
Holloway notes that the flying motif in the black folk spiritual
tradition also informs the novel; *New Dimensions of Spirituality*,
101–2.

24. Ralph Story provides an intriguing and provocative discussion of
the historical and political background informing the creation of
Guitar and the Seven Days in "An Excursion into the Black World:
The 'Seven Days' in Toni Morrison's *Song of Solomon*," *Black
American Literature Forum* 23 (Spring 1989): 149–58.

25. For a striking contrast to my emphasis on the positive value of the
folk culture in the novel, see James W. Coleman, "Beyond the
Reach of Love and Caring: Black Life in Toni Morrison's *Song of
Solomon*," *Obsidian II* 1 (Winter 1986): 151–61. Coleman argues that
"critics are inaccurate when they talk about the positive, restorative
effect of the Black folkloric tradition in the novel" (160) because,
while it might work for Pilate and Milkman, "the situation for the
Black community is just as dismal as it was before Milkman left
Michigan" (160–61).

26. For a discussion of how Morrison uses fairy tales in the novel, see
Jacqueline de Weever, "Toni Morrison's Use of Fairy Tale, Folk Tale

and Myth in *The* [sic] *Song of Solomon.* de Weever refers to Corinthians as "a black princess" who has constructed an "artificial life" (140) before Porter stirs her from the passive state so endemic to fairy tale heroines.

27. See Propp, *Morphology of the Folktale*, 36.

28. The two women at Solomon's store should be added to this number because it is their intervention in the fight that prevents Milkman from being "sliced to ribbons," as the folk would say; "and he probably would have had his throat cut if two women hadn't come running in screaming, 'Saul! Saul!'" (268).

29. Grace Ann Hovet and Barbara Lounsberry argue that, "though Morrison creates some sympathy for the deserted woman, she refuses to depict Hagar as the conventional 'victim' because Hagar herself initiated her tailspin by becoming overly possessive"; see "Flying as Symbol and Legend in Toni Morrison's *The Bluest Eye, Sula,* and *Song of Solomon*," *CLA Journal* 27 (Dec. 1983): 135. While Hagar is certainly attracted to Milkman and is active rather than passive, that does not absolve Milkman of responsibility for accepting her initiated activities and for treating her as he does.

30. For a discussion of "the chorus as ritual dance, song, and commentary" in the novel, see Kathleen O'Shaughnessy, "'Life life life life': The Community as Chorus in *Song of Solomon*," in *Critical Essays on Toni Morrison*, ed. McKay, 125–33.

Chapter 5

1. For a discussion of animal and human tricksters in African-American oral culture, see Levine, *Black Culture and Black Consciousness*, chap. 2. I have called attention to the word "hero" to indicate the varying qualifications for that status, as Roberts concludes in *From Trickster to Badman*.

2. In "The 'John and Old Master' Stories and the World of Slavery: A Study in Folktales and History," *Phylon* 35 (1974), 418–29, Dickson D. Bruce, Jr., pursues a similar argument for how this fluctuating phenomenon works with human tricksters.

3. Hughes and Bontemps, eds., *The Book of Negro Folklore*, 1–2. The version of the tale that Richard M. Dorson collected in *American Negro Folktales*, 75–76, ends with the same punchline, but the impetus for the construction of the tar baby is Brer Rabbit's stealing of milk from Brer Fox.

4. Joel Chandler Harris, *Uncle Remus: His Songs and His Sayings* (1880; rpt., New York: Penguin, 1982).

5. For a discussion of the "stick-fast" motif, which refers to the five points of contact, see especially Aurelio Espinosa, "Notes on the Origin and History of the Tar-Baby Story," *Journal of American Folklore*, 43 (1930): 129–209. Although Espinosa's bias is clearly to locate a non-African country of origin for the tale (he claims India), he nonetheless recognizes the African contributions to its development.

6. Uncle Remus consistently refers to the little white boy as "honey," a reference we usually assume is used only with females. This characteristic of mixing pronouns and gender, therefore, might also be an idiosyncrasy of Uncle Remus. However, the point about the tar baby's gender is nonetheless well taken. For another version of the tar baby story with a female as the tar baby, also from the sea islands, see A. M. H. Christensen, *Afro-American Folk Lore* (1892; rpt., New York: Negro Universities Press, 1969), 62–72.

7. I should point out that Morrison is explicit in emphasizing that she did not read "a modern or westernized version of the story." She stresses that she "remembered" "the *told* story" (which connects her explicitly with the African-American folk tradition) and then formulated questions about it that she wanted to guide her creation. See her "Memory, Creation, and Writing," *Thought* 59 (Dec. 1984): 389–90.

8. A version of the tale is collected in Harris's *Uncle Remus: His Songs and His Sayings*; see "Mr. Rabbit Grossly Deceives Mr. Fox," 66–70. See also Dorson, *American Negro Folktales*, "Mr. Rabbit and Mr. Frog Make Mr. Fox and Mr. Bear Their Riding-Horses," 87–89.

9. Remember that Brer Rabbit's tricks are never permanent, that his status can change quickly; he usually toys with the other animals for the sake of diversion, for the sake of an ego that assures him that he *can* play with other animals' lives and get away with it.

10. By contrast, James Coleman finds the issues unresolved and the ending of the novel sufficiently unsatisfactory to judge the book a "failure" because Morrison has not clearly shown how folk values can be sustained in a materialistic, twentieth-century world. See "The Quest for Wholeness in Toni Morrison's *Tar Baby*," *Black American Literature Forum* 20 (Spring–Summer 1986): 71, 72.

11. Craig H. Werner, in another reading of the tar baby story in the novel, treats the multiple implications and applications of its mythic connotations; see "The Briar Patch as Modernist Myth:

Morrison, Barthes and Tar Baby As-Is," in *Critical Essays on Toni Morrison*, ed. McKay, 150–67.

12. See, for example, Pearl K. Bell, "Self-Seekers," *Commentary* 72 (Aug. 1981): 56–60; Holloway and Demetrakopoulos, *New Dimensions of Spirituality*, 117–29; and Eleanor W. Traylor, "The Fabulous World of Toni Morrison: *Tar Baby*," in *Critical Essays on Toni Morrison*, ed. McKay, 135–50. Traylor also offers a reading of the use of the tar baby folktale in the novel.

13. As Samuels and Hudson-Weems point out, Sydney and Ondine have in fact "paradoxically" orphaned Jadine even further by pushing her toward middle-classness; they have put her *"outdoors,"* à la Cholly Breedlove, and "weaned" her away "from her black heritage"; see *Toni Morrison*, 83. Coleman initially developed this idea in "The Quest for Wholeness in Toni Morrison's *Tar Baby*": Ondine sent Jadine to white schools, treated her like a "star," and "did not inculcate, by example, Black folk principles, ideas, and feelings in her niece. . . . she has not kept Jadine in contact with her Black folk heritage" (68).

14. Roberts, *From Trickster to Badman*, 171.

15. Sydney may identify with the middle-class "Philadelphia Negro" (he has moved to Philadelphia from Baltimore), but Jadine will finally place no special value on that. She views her aunt and uncle merely as servants—useful, but servants nonetheless, with connotations of lacking sophistication—and separates herself from them accordingly.

16. The specific tale referred to here is recounted in Hurston's *Mules and Men*, 174, in which God grants the devil the east coast of Florida when He shouts "Christmas Gift" on Christmas morning. The tale serves to explain why that section of Florida is so stormy and mosquito-ridden; it belongs to the devil.

17. Consider the tale in which the devil takes in extra Christians because heaven is overcrowded or because they have become bothersome enough for God to want to be rid of them (Dance, "Fund Raiser," *Shuckin' and Jivin'*, 15); the one where the word "unh hunh" is invented (Hurston, "How the Devil Coined a Word," *Mules and Men*, 169–70); or the one where the man newly arrived in heaven goes to a party in hell and decides to stay there— he just returns to ask Saint Peter for his clothes (Dance, "I Don't Want to Staaay," *Shuckin' and Jivin'*, 14–15).

18. See, for example, Byerman, *Fingering the Jagged Grain*, 208, and Lauren Lepow, "An Edenic Myth in Toni Morrison's *Tar Baby*,"

Contemporary Literature, 28 (1987): 363–77. Morrison herself has referred to the island as "a kind of Eden"; see McKay, "An Interview with Toni Morrison," 417.

19. See Philip Freund, *Myths of Creation* (New York: Washington Square Press, 1965), and Obiakoizu A. Iloanusi, *Myths of the Creation of Man and the Origin of Death in Africa* (Bern: Peter Lang, 1984).

20. Morrison has commented that the nonhuman beings in the novel act as a kind of "chorus" for the events. See her "Rootedness: The Ancestor as Foundation," 341.

21. Byerman, *Fingering the Jagged Grain*, 215.

22. This pattern is true from *King Lear*, where the raging storm reflects the disorder of the king's mind and his emerging insanity, to works in the twentieth century such as Toomer's *Cane*, where howling dogs and cackling hens herald the impending socially taboo fight between black Tom Burwell and white Bob Stone, which leads to Bob Stone's death; see "Blood-Burning Moon."

Chapter 6

1. The volume depends upon stereotypical conceptions of women, but it is nonetheless an interesting historical recapitulation of traditional perceptions of femaleness; Lederer, *The Fear of Women*.

2. Daryl C. Dance, *Shuckin' and Jivin'*, 56–57.

3. Gloria Naylor and Toni Morrison, "A Conversation," *Southern Review* 21 (July 1985): 593. While this comment could apply to the writing practice Morrison gained in her previous novels in preparation for writing the difficult tale of a mother killing her child, it could also apply to touching briefly on the unorthodox ideas that would inform the substance of *Beloved*. See pp. 583–84 of the above interview for Morrison's discussion of the two incidents that shaped the idea for *Beloved*: that of Margaret Garner, the slave woman who preferred death rather than slavery for her children, and that of an eighteen-year-old dead girl photographed in Harlem by James Van der Zee; the girl had sacrificed her own life in order to allow the jealous lover who had shot her sufficient time to escape the scene of the crime.

4. See "Daid Aaron," in Hughes and Bontemps, eds., *The Book of Negro Folklore*, 175–78.

5. Strouse, "Toni Morrison's Black Magic," 54.

6. Toomer, *Cane*, 16.

7. Indeed, some of the comments that Charles Scruggs makes about desire in *Song of Solomon* could also apply to *Beloved*. See "The Nature of Desire in Toni Morrison's *Song of Solomon*," *Arizona Quarterly* 38 (Winter 1982): 311–35.

8. While Terry Otten also recognizes Beloved's demonic nature and the fact that she is "an evil thing," he asserts that she may be "a Christ figure come to save," "the 'beloved' one come to reclaim Sethe and from whom Sethe seeks forgiveness." See Otten, *The Crime of Innocence in the Fiction of Toni Morrison* (Columbia: Univ. of Missouri Press, 1989), 84, 85. In *Toni Morrison*, Samuels and Hudson-Weems assert that Paul D is a Christ figure (134). Instead of this designation, with its attendant connotation of absolute goodness, perhaps it would be more productive to view Paul D in the ambivalent mode of some of Morrison's earlier heroes, such as Milkman and Son.

9. For a discussion of the multiple voices and characters Beloved represents in the novel, see Deborah Horvitz, "Nameless Ghosts: Possession and Dispossession in *Beloved*," *Studies in American Fiction* 17 (Autumn 1989): 157–67. On the other hand, Elizabeth B. House, in "Toni Morrison's Ghost: The Beloved Who Is Not Beloved," *Studies in American Fiction* 18 (Spring 1990): 17–26, argues that Beloved is not a ghost but merely a runaway who has suffered the blights of slavery. These in turn intersect coincidentally with Sethe's relationship to her deceased daughter.

10. Otten comments that "in attacking [Bodwin], Sethe achieves an exorcism; in saving Beloved by offering herself, she at last frees herself from the demonic presence that will not release her from the past. Once Sethe acts to save Beloved, retestifying to her love, the ghost disappears"; *The Crime of Innocence*, 94.

11. See *The Frank C. Brown Collection of North Carolina Folklore*, vol. 7, ed. Hand, 144, 145, 147. Dog ghosts are also painted in the lore as being some of the most benign spirits humans can encounter. See J. Mason Brewer, *Dog Ghosts and Other Texas Negro Folk Tales* (Austin: Univ. of Texas Press, 1958).

12. See Hughes and Bontemps, "De Ways of de Wimmens," in *The Book of Negro Folklore*, 130–35, and Hurston, "Why Women Always Take Advantage of Men," in *Mules and Men*, 33–38.

13. See Hughes and Bontemps, eds., *The Book of Negro Folklore*.

14. See Stanley, "The Personal Narrative and the Personal Novel: Folklore as Frame and Structure for Literature," 116–17.

15. Morrison, "Memory, Creation, and Writing," 388–89.

16. Earlier in her career, Morrison commented that she worked to achieve that effect in her work: "To make the story appear oral, meandering, effortless, spoken . . . is what's important"; see her "Rootedness: The Ancestor as Foundation," 341.

17. Mel Watkins, "Talk with Toni Morrison," *New York Times Book Review* (11 Sept. 1977), 48.

18. LeClair, "'The Language Must Not Sweat': A Conversation with Toni Morrison," 27.

19. Samuels and Hudson-Weems also refer to Baby Suggs as a "ritual priestess," which also brings to mind secular rather than Christian connotations; *Toni Morrison*, 117.

20. For a discussion of the importance of such rites, see Arnold van Gennep, *The Rites of Passage* (1908; rpt., Chicago: Univ. of Chicago Press, 1960).

21. Of course it could be argued that Baby Suggs retains a somewhat legendary, positive effect upon Denver, who uses memories of her as a touchstone of sanity when she contemplates the circumstances at 124 Bluestone Road.

22. "Master's Gone to Philly-Me-York," in Dorson, *American Negro Folktales*, 151–52, and Hurston, *Mules and Men*, 88–89. Paul Laurence Dunbar, "The Party," in *The Collected Poems of Paul Laurence Dunbar* (New York: Dodd, Mead, 1967), 134–38.

23. Morrison has defended this tendency by commenting: "Sometimes I have been accused—or complimented, I'm not sure—of writing about people who are bigger than life. I was always befuddled by that observation, and I still am a little bit. But I felt that I was writing about people who were as big as life, not bigger than. Life is very big. There are people who try to make it small, safe, unexamined. If some of my characters are as big as the life they have, they may seem enormous exaggerations, but [only to] a reader whose sense of life is more diminished than mine"; in Amanda Smith's interview, "Toni Morrison," *Publishers Weekly* (21 Aug. 1987): 51.

24. Terry Otten adopts Hannah Arendt's term in calling the Garners "nice Nazis": "The Garners were kindhearted people but also participants in the system—nice Nazis, but Nazis nonetheless. By their accommodation of slavery, they made possible the prototypal evil of schoolteacher"; *The Crime of Innocence*, 86.

Conclusion

1. See the interview with Toni Morrison in Jones and Vinson, *The World of Toni Morrison*, 148. This is the first of many paradoxes Morrison creates in which women who denounce nurturing for self-determination have their newfound freedom stereotypically defined as "male," so that their very process of liberation creates another "bind" for them.
2. Susan Willis, *Specifying: Black Women Writing the American Experience* (Madison: Univ. of Wisconsin Press, 1987), 88.
3. See, for example, Bruce Jackson, *Get Your Ass in the Water and Swim Like Me: Narrative Poetry from Black Oral Tradition* (Cambridge: Harvard Univ. Press, 1974), especially 145–60, and Dennis Wepman, et al., *The Life: The Lore and Folk Poetry of the Black Hustler* (Philadelphia: Univ. of Pennsylvania Press, 1976).
4. In discussing the women in *Sula*, Barbara Christian writes: "This community absorbs many styles—Helene's ladylike and hypocritical demeanor, Hannah's elegant sensuality, even Eva's arrogant murder of her son—as long as they remain within its definition of woman as wife, mother, or man lover." See *Black Women Novelists: The Development of a Tradition, 1892–1976*, 161.
5. See Hurston, *Mules and Men*, 51–58. The concluding comment is a line about how *Jack* "beat de Devil."
6. Christian, *Black Women Novelists*, 168.
7. It is worth noting that Morrison was Bambara's editor for *The Salt Eaters* during her years at Random House.

Works Cited or Consulted

Books

Abrahams, Roger D. *Deep Down in the Jungle: Negro Narrative Folklore from the Streets of Philadelphia.* Chicago: Aldine, 1970.

Awkward, Michael. *Inspiriting Influences: Tradition, Revision, and Afro-American Women's Novels.* New York: Columbia Univ. Press, 1989.

Baker, Houston A., Jr. *Blues, Ideology, and Afro-American Literature: A Vernacular Theory.* Chicago: Univ. of Chicago Press, 1984.

Bell, Bernard W. *The Afro-American Novel and Its Tradition.* Amherst: Univ. of Massachusetts Press, 1987.

Blair, Walter, ed. *Selected Shorter Writings of Mark Twain.* Boston: Houghton Mifflin, 1962.

Brewer, J. Mason. *American Negro Folklore.* Chicago: Quadrangle Books, 1968.

———. *Dog Ghosts and Other Texas Negro Folk Tales.* Austin: Univ. of Texas Press, 1958.

Brooks, Gwendolyn. *Blacks.* Chicago: David Co., 1987.

Brown, William Wells. *Clotel; Or, The President's Daughter.* 1853. Rpt. New York, 1969.

Byerman, Keith E. *Fingering the Jagged Grain: Tradition and Form in Recent Black Fiction.* Athens: Univ. of Georgia Press, 1985.

Campbell, Jane. *Mythic Black Fiction: The Transformation of History.* Knoxville: Univ. of Tennessee Press, 1986.

Campbell, Joseph. *The Hero with a Thousand Faces.* London: Abacus, 1975.

Chesnutt, Charles Waddell. *The Conjure Woman.* 1899. Rpt. Ann Arbor: Univ. of Michigan Press, 1969.

Christensen, A. M. H. *Afro-American Folk Lore.* 1892. Rpt. New York: Negro Universities Press, 1969.

Christian, Barbara. *Black Feminist Criticism: Perspectives on Black Women Writers*. New York: Pergamon, 1985.

———. *Black Women Novelists: The Development of a Tradition, 1892–1976*. Westport, Conn.: Greenwood Press, 1980.

Crowley, Daniel J. *African Folklore in the New World*. Austin: Univ. of Texas Press, 1977.

Dance, Daryl Cumber. *Shuckin' and Jivin': Folklore from Contemporary Black Americans*. Bloomington: Indiana Univ. Press, 1978.

Dillard, Joey Lee. *Black Names*. The Hague: Mouton, 1976.

Dixon, Melvin. *Ride Out the Wilderness: Geography and Identity in Afro-American Literature*. Urbana: Univ. of Illinois Press, 1987.

Dorson, Richard M. *American Negro Folktales*. Greenwich, Conn.: Fawcett, 1967.

———. *Negro Folktales in Michigan*. Cambridge: Harvard Univ. Press, 1956.

Dorson, Richard M., ed. *Handbook of American Folklore*. Bloomington: Indiana Univ. Press, 1983.

Douglass, Frederick. *Life and Times of Frederick Douglass*. Hartford, Conn.: Park Publishing Co., 1882.

———. *Narrative of the Life of Frederick Douglass: An American Slave*. 1845. Rpt. Cambridge, Mass.: Harvard Univ. Press, 1960.

Dunbar, Paul Laurence. *The Collected Poems of Paul Laurence Dunbar*. New York: Dodd, Mead, 1967.

Dundes, Alan. *Mother Wit from the Laughing Barrel: Readings in the Interpretation of Afro-American Folklore*. Englewood Cliffs, N.J.: Prentice-Hall, 1973.

———. *The Study of Folklore*. Englewood Cliffs, N.J.: Prentice-Hall, 1973.

Eliot, T. S. *The Waste Land*, in *The Complete Poems and Plays*. New York: Harcourt Brace, 1952, 37–55.

Evans, Mari, ed. *Black Women Writers (1950–1980): A Critical Evaluation*. Garden City, N.Y.: Anchor Press/Doubleday, 1984.

Farrer, Claire R., ed. *Women and Folklore*. Austin: Univ. of Texas Press, 1975.

Fields, Mamie Garvin, with Karen Fields. *Lemon Swamp and Other Places: A Carolina Memoir*. New York: Free Press, 1983.

Freund, Philip. *Myths of Creation*. New York: Washington Square Press, 1965.

Fry, Gladys-Marie. *Nightriders in Black Folk History*. Knoxville: Univ. of Tennessee Press, 1975.

Gaines, Ernest. *Bloodline*. New York: Dial, 1968.

Gates, Henry Louis, Jr. *Black Literature and Literary Theory.* New York: Metheun, 1984.

——. *The Signifying Monkey.* New York: Oxford, 1988.

Gennep, Arnold van. *The Rites of Passage.* 1908. Rpt. Chicago: Univ. of Chicago Press, 1960.

Georgia Writers Project. *Drums and Shadows.* 1940. Rpt. Westport, Conn.: Greenwood Press, 1973.

Graves, Robert. *English and Scottish Ballads.* London: Heinemann, 1963.

Hamilton, Virginia. *The People Could Fly: American Black Folktales.* New York: Knopf, 1985.

Hand, Wayland D., ed. *The Frank C. Brown Collection of North Carolina Folklore.* Vols. 6 and 7. Durham: Duke Univ. Press, 1961, 1964.

Harris, Joel Chandler. *Uncle Remus: His Songs and His Sayings.* 1880. Rpt. New York: Penguin, 1982.

Harris, Middleton, compiler, and Toni Morrison, ed. *The Black Book.* New York: Random House, 1974.

Harris, Trudier. *Exorcising Blackness: Historical and Literary Lynching and Burning Rituals.* Bloomington: Indiana Univ. Press, 1984, 148–62.

——. *From Mammies to Militants: Domestics in Black American Literature.* Philadelphia: Temple Univ. Press, 1982, 59–69.

Heller, Murray, ed. *Black Names in America: Origins and Usages.* Boston: G. K. Hall, 1975.

Henderson, Stephen. *Understanding the New Black Poetry: Black Speech and Black Music as Poetic References.* New York: William Morrow, 1973.

Hogue, W. Lawrence. *Discourse and the Other: The Production of the Afro-American Text.* Durham: Duke Univ. Press, 1986.

Holloway, Karla F. C., and Stephanie A. Demetrakopoulos. *New Dimensions of Spirituality: A Biracial and Bicultural Reading of the Novels of Toni Morrison.* Westport, Conn.: Greenwood Press, 1987.

Hughes, Langston. *Not Without Laughter.* New York and London: Knopf, 1930.

——. *Tambourines to Glory.* New York: John Day, 1958.

——. *The Weary Blues.* New York: Knopf, 1926.

Hughes, Langston, and Arna Bontemps, eds. *The Book of Negro Folklore.* New York: Dodd, Mead & Co., 1958.

Hurston, Zora Neale. *Jonah's Gourd Vine.* 1934. Rpt. Philadelphia: Lippincott, 1971.

——. *Mules and Men.* 1935. Rpt. Bloomington: Indiana Univ. Press, 1978.

——. *The Sanctified Church.* Berkeley: Turtle Island, 1983.

————. *Tell My Horse*. 1938. Rpt. Berkeley: Turtle Island, 1983.

————. *Their Eyes Were Watching God*. 1937. Rpt. Urbana: Univ. of Illinois Press, 1978.

Iloanusi, Obiakoizu A. *Myths of the Creation of Man and the Origin of Death in Africa*. Bern: Peter Lang, 1984.

Jackson, Bruce. *Get Your Ass in the Water and Swim Like Me: Narrative Poetry from Black Oral Tradition*. Cambridge: Harvard Univ. Press, 1974.

Johnson, James Weldon. *God's Trombones: Seven Negro Sermons in Verse*. New York: Viking, 1927.

Jones, Bessie W., and Audrey L. Vinson. *The World of Toni Morrison: Explorations in Literary Criticism*. Dubuque, Iowa: Kendall/Hunt, 1985.

Jordan, Rosan A., and Susan J. Kalčik, eds. *Women's Folklore, Women's Culture*. Philadelphia: Univ. of Pennsylvania Press, 1985.

Lederer, Wolfgang. *The Fear of Women*. New York: Grune & Stratton, 1968.

Lester, Julius. *Black Folktales*. New York: Baron, 1969.

Levine, Lawrence W. *Black Culture and Black Consciousness: Afro-American Folk Thought from Slavery to Freedom*. New York: Oxford Univ. Press, 1977.

Marshall, Paule. *The Chosen Place, The Timeless People*. New York: Harcourt Brace & World, 1969.

————. *Praisesong for the Widow*. New York: Putnam, 1983.

McKay, Nellie Y., ed. *Critical Essays on Toni Morrison*. Boston: G. K. Hall & Co., 1988.

Morrison, Toni. *Beloved*. New York: Knopf, 1987.

————. *The Bluest Eye*. New York: Holt, Rinehart, and Winston, 1970.

————. *Song of Solomon*. New York: Knopf, 1977.

————. *Sula*. New York: Knopf, 1974.

————. *Tar Baby*. New York: Knopf, 1981.

Otten, Terry. *The Crime of Innocence in the Fiction of Toni Morrison*. Columbia: Univ. of Missouri Press, 1989.

Propp, Vladimir. *Morphology of the Folktale*. Austin: Univ. of Texas Press, 1975.

Pryse, Marjorie, and Hortense J. Spillers, eds. *Conjuring: Black Women, Fiction, and Literary Tradition*. Bloomington: Indiana Univ. Press, 1985.

Puckett, Newbell Niles. *Folk Beliefs of the Southern Negro*. Chapel Hill: Univ. of North Carolina Press, 1926.

Raglan, FitzRoy Richard Somerset, Baron. *The Hero: A Study in Tradition*,

Myth, and Drama. 1956. Rpt. Westport, Conn.: Greenwood Press, 1975.

Roberts, John W. *From Trickster to Badman: The Black Folk Hero in Slavery and Freedom.* Philadelphia: Univ. of Pennsylvania Press, 1989.

Samuels, Wilfred D., and Clenora Hudson-Weems. *Toni Morrison.* Boston: Twayne Publishers, 1990.

Shine, Ted. *Contribution.* In *Black Drama: An Anthology,* ed. William Brasmer and Dominick Consolo. Columbus, Ohio: Charles E. Merrill, 1970.

Smith, Valerie. *Self-Discovery and Authority in Afro-American Literature.* Cambridge: Harvard Univ. Press, 1987.

Tate, Claudia, ed. *Black Women Writers at Work.* New York: Continuum, 1983.

Thomas, Joyce Carol. *Marked By Fire.* New York: Avon, 1982.

Toomer, Jean. *Cane.* New York: Boni and Liveright, 1923.

Wade-Gayles, Gloria. *No Crystal Stair: Visions of Race and Sex in Black Women's Fiction.* New York: Pilgrim, 1984.

Ward, Douglas Turner. *Happy Ending and Day of Absence.* New York: Third Press, 1966.

Wepman, Dennis, and Ronald B. Newman and Murray B. Binderman. *The Life: The Lore and Folk Poetry of the Black Hustler.* Philadelphia: Univ. of Pennsylvania Press, 1976.

Willis, Susan. *Specifying: Black Women Writing the American Experience.* Madison: Univ. of Wisconsin Press, 1987.

Wright, Richard. *Uncle Tom's Children.* New York: Harper and Row, 1938.

————. *The Outsider.* New York: Harper and Brothers, 1953.

Articles and Parts of Books

Baker, Houston A., Jr. "Black Folklore and Black American Literature." In his *Long Black Song: Essays in Black American Literature and Culture.* Charlottesville: Univ. of Virginia Press, 1972. 18–41.

Bakerman, Jane S. "Failures of Love: Female Initiation in the Novels of Toni Morrison." *American Literature* 52 (1981): 541–63.

Barnes, Daniel R. "Toward the Establishment of Principles for the Study of Folklore and Literature." *Southern Folklore Quarterly* 43 (1979): 5–16.

Bauman, Richard. "Ed Bell, Texas Storyteller: The Framing and Reframing of Life Experience." *Journal of Folklore Research* 24 (Sept.–Dec. 1987): 197–221.

Bell, Pearl K. "Self-Seekers." *Commentary* 72 (Aug. 1981): 56–60.

Bennett, Gillian. "Narrative as Expository Discourse." *Journal of American Folklore* 99 (1986): 415–34.

Blake, Susan L. "Folklore and Community in *Song of Solomon*." *MELUS* 7 (1980): 77–82.

Bruce, Dickson D., Jr. "The 'John and Old Master' Stories and the World of Slavery: A Study in Folktales and History." *Phylon* 35 (1974): 418–29.

Clark, Norris. "Flying Black: Toni Morrison's *The Bluest Eye, Sula* and *Song of Solomon*." *Minority Voices* 4 (1980): 51–63.

Cohen, Hennig. "American Literature and American Folklore." In *Our Living Traditions: An Introduction to American Folklore*, ed. Tristram Potter Coffin. New York: Basic Books, 1968. 238–47.

Coleman, James W. "Beyond the Reach of Love and Caring: Black Life in Toni Morrison's *Song of Solomon*." *Obsidian II* 1 (Winter 1986): 151–61.

———. "The Quest for Wholeness in Toni Morrison's *Tar Baby*." *Black American Literature Forum* 20 (Spring–Summer 1986): 63–73.

Cooper, Barbara E. "Milkman's Search for Family in Toni Morrison's *Song of Solomon*." *CLA Journal* 33 (Dec. 1989): 145–56.

Davis, Cynthia A. "Self, Society, and Myth in Toni Morrison's Fiction." *Contemporary Literature* 23 (1982): 323–42.

de Weever, Jacqueline. "Toni Morrison's Use of Fairy Tale, Folk Tale, and Myth in *The* [sic] *Song of Solomon*." *Southern Folklore Quarterly* 44 (1980): 131–44.

Dorson, Richard M., and Daniel Hoffman. "Folklore in Literature: A Symposium." *Journal of American Folklore* 70 (1957): 1–24.

Dowling, Colette. "The Song of Toni Morrison." *New York Times Magazine*, 20 May 1979: 40–42, 48, 52, 54, 56, 58.

Drake, Carlos C. "Literary Criticism and Folklore." *Journal of Popular Culture* 5 (Fall 1971): 289–97.

Dundes, Alan. "The Study of Folklore in Literature and Culture: Identification and Interpretation." *Journal of American Folklore* 78 (Apr.–June 1965): 136–42.

Espinosa, Aurelio. "Notes on the Origin and History of the Tar-Baby Story." *Journal of American Folklore* 43 (1930): 129–209.

"Folklore in Literature: A Symposium." *Journal of American Folklore* 70 (1957): 1–24.

Georges, Robert A. "Timeliness and Appropriateness in Personal Experience Narrating." *Western Folklore* 46 (Apr. 1987): 115–20.

Grobman, Neil R. "A Schema for the Study of the Sources and Literary

Simulations of Folkloric Phenomena." *Southern Folklore Quarterly* 43 (1979): 17–37.

Harris, A. Leslie. "Myth as Structure in Toni Morrison's *Song of Solomon.*" *MELUS* 7 (1980): 69–76.

Hendricks, William O. "Folklore and the Structural Analysis of Literary Texts." *Language and Style* 3 (Spring 1970): 83–121.

Horvitz, Deborah. "Nameless Ghosts: Possession and Dispossession in *Beloved.*" *Studies in American Fiction* 17 (Autumn 1989): 157–67.

House, Elizabeth B. "Toni Morrison's Ghost: The Beloved Who Is Not Beloved." *Studies in American Fiction* 18 (Spring 1990): 17–26.

Hovet, Grace Ann, and Barbara Lounsberry. "Flying as Symbol and Legend in Toni Morrison's *The Bluest Eye, Sula,* and *Song of Solomon.*" *CLA Journal* 27 (Dec. 1983): 119–40.

Lee, Dorothy H. "*Song of Solomon*: To Ride the Air." *Black American Literature Forum* 16 (Summer 1982): 64–70.

Lee, Valerie Gray. "The Use of Folktalk in Novels By Black Women Writers." *CLA Journal* 23 (Mar. 1980): 266–72.

Lepow, Lauren. "An Edenic Myth in Toni Morrison's *Tar Baby.*" *Contemporary Literature* 28 (1987): 363–77.

Lieberman, Marcia R. " 'Some Day My Prince Will Come': Female Acculturation Through the Fairy Tale." *College English* 34 (1972): 383–95.

Miner, Madonne M. "Lady No Longer Sings the Blues: Rape, Madness, and Silence in *The Bluest Eye.*" In *Conjuring: Black Women, Fiction, and Literary Tradition*, ed. Pryse and Spillers. 176–91.

Montgomery, Maxine Lavon. "A Pilgrimage to the Origins: The Apocalypse as Structure and Theme in Toni Morrison's *Sula.*" *Black American Literature Forum* 23 (Spring 1989): 127–37.

Morrison, Toni. "Memory, Creation, and Writing." *Thought* 59 (Dec. 1984): 385–90.

———. "Rootedness: The Ancestor as Foundation." In *Black Women Writers (1950–1980): A Critical Evaluation*, ed. Evans. 339–45.

———. "Unspeakable Things Unspoken: The Afro-American Presence in American Literature." *Michigan Quarterly Review* 28 (Winter 1989): 1–34.

———. "What the Black Woman Thinks About Women's Lib." *New York Times Magazine* (22 Aug. 1971): 14–15, 63–64, 66.

———. "Writers Together." *The Nation* (24 Oct. 1981): 396–97, 412.

Naylor, Gloria, and Toni Morrison. "A Conversation." *Southern Review* 21 (July 1985): 567–93.

Olrik, Axel. "Epic Laws of Folk Narrative." In *The Study of Folklore*, ed. Dundes. 129–41.

Rayson, Ann L. "The Novels of Zora Neale Hurston." *Studies in Black Literature* 5 (Winter 1974): 1–10.

Reagon, Bernice. "We Are 'Girl,' 'Chile,' 'Lady,' That 'oman,' 'Hussy,' 'Heifer,' 'A Woman': or, Naming That Imprisons and Naming That Sets You Free." Paper presented at annual meeting of Modern Language Association, Washington, D.C., 27 Dec. 1984.

Roberts, John W. "The Individual and the Community in Two Short Stories By Ernest J. Gaines." *Black American Literature Forum* 18 (Fall 1984): 110–13.

Robinson, John A. "Personal Narratives Reconsidered." *Journal of American Folklore* 94 (1981): 58–85.

Rosenberg, Ruth. "'And the Children May Know Their Names': Toni Morrison's *Song of Solomon*." *Literary Onomastics Studies* 8 (1981): 195–219.

Royster, Philip M. "Milkman's Flying: The Scapegoat Transcended in Toni Morrison's *Song of Solomon*." *CLA Journal* 24 (June 1982): 419–40.

———. "A Priest and a Witch against The Spiders and The Snakes: Scapegoating in Toni Morrison's *Sula*." *Umoja* 2 (Fall 1978): 149–68.

Samuels, Wilfred D. "Liminality and the Search for Self in Toni Morrison's *Song of Solomon*." *Minority Voices* 5 (1981): 59–68.

Scruggs, Charles. "The Nature of Desire in Toni Morrison's *Song of Solomon*." *Arizona Quarterly* 38 (Winter 1982): 311–35.

Skerrett, Joseph T., Jr. "Recitation to the *Griot*: Storytelling and Learning in Toni Morrison's *Song of Solomon*." In *Conjuring: Black Women, Fiction, and Literary Tradition*, ed. Pryse and Spillers. 192–202.

Spillers, Hortense J. "A Hateful Passion, A Lost Love." *Feminist Studies* 9 (Summer 1983): 293–323.

Stahl, Sandra K. D. "Personal Experience Stories." In *Handbook of American Folklore*, ed. Dorson. 268–76.

———. "Studying Folklore and American Literature." In *Handbook of American Folklore*, ed. Dorson. 422–33.

———. "Style in Oral and Written Narratives." *Southern Folklore Quarterly* 43 (1979): 39–62.

Stanley, David H. "The Personal Narrative and the Personal Novel: Folklore as Frame and Structure for Literature." *Southern Folklore Quarterly* 43 (1979): 107–20.

Stein, Karen. "Toni Morrison's *Sula*: A Black Woman's Epic." *Black American Literature Forum* 18 (Winter 1984): 146–50.

Story, Ralph. "An Excursion into the Black World: The 'Seven Days' in Toni Morrison's *Song of Solomon*." *Black American Literature Forum* 23 (Spring 1989): 149–58.

Strouse, Jean. "Toni Morrison's Black Magic." *Newsweek* (30 Mar. 1981): 52–57.

Ward, Jerry, Jr. "Folklore and the Study of Black Literature." *Mississippi Folklore Register* 6 (Fall 1972): 83–90.

Waugh, Butler. "Structural Analysis in Literature and Folklore." *Western Folklore* 25 (1966): 153–64.

Wiggins, William H., Jr. "Black Folktales in the Novels of John O. Killens." *The Black Scholar* 3 (Nov. 1971): 50–58.

Winkelman, Donald M. "Three American Authors as Semi-Folk Artists." *Journal of American Folklore* 78 (Apr.–June 1965): 130–35.

Interviews

Bakerman, Jane. "The Seams Can't Show: An Interview with Toni Morrison." *Black American Literature Forum* 12 (Summer 1978): 56–60.

LeClair, Thomas. "'The Language Must Not Sweat': A Conversation with Toni Morrison." *The New Republic* 184 (21 Mar. 1981): 25–29.

McKay, Nellie Y. "An Interview with Toni Morrison." *Contemporary Literature* 24 (Winter 1983): 413–29.

Smith, Amanda. "Toni Morrison." *Publishers Weekly* (21 Aug. 1987): 50–51.

Stepto, Robert B. "'Intimate Things in Place': A Conversation with Toni Morrison." In *Chant of Saints: A Gathering of Afro-American Literature, Art, and Scholarship*, ed. Michael S. Harper and Stepto. Urbana: Univ. of Illinois Press, 1979. 213–29.

"Toni Morrison." In *Black Women Writers at Work*, ed. Tate. 117–31.

Washington, Elsie B. "Toni Morrison Now." *Essence*, Oct. 1987: 58, 136–37.

Watkins, Mel. "Talk with Toni Morrison." *New York Times Book Review* (11 Sept. 1977): 48, 50.

Thesis

Boydstun, Laurence C. "The Classification and Analysis of the Spanish-American Versions of the Tar-Baby Story." Stanford Univ., 1947.

Reviews (of *Beloved*)

Atwood, Margaret. "Haunted by Nightmares." *The New York Times Book Review* (13 Sept. 1987): 1, 49–50.

Brown, Rosellen. "The Pleasure of Enchantment." *The Nation* (17 Oct. 1987): 418–21.

Crouch, Stanley. "Aunt Medea." *The New Republic* (19 Oct. 1987): 38–43.

Harris, Trudier. "Of Demons and Mother Love: Toni Morrison's *Beloved.*" *Callaloo* 35 (Spring 1988): 387–89.

Reed, Dennis. "*Beloved.*" *CLA Journal* 31 (Dec. 1987): 256–58.

Snitow, Ann. "Death Duties: Toni Morrison Looks Back in Sorrow." *Voice Literary Supplement* (Sept. 1987): 25–26.

Index

Fiction and Folklore was designed by Dariel Mayer and composed at the University of Tennessee on the Apple Macintosh. Linotronic pages were generated by AMPM, Inc. The book is set in Palatino and printed on 60-lb. Glatfelter Natural, B-16. Manufactured in the United States of America by Thomson-Shore, Inc.